Military Technology of the First World War

Development, Use and Consequences

Wolfgang Fleischer

(translated by Geoffrey Brooks)

Pen & Sword
MILITARY

Originally published as *Militärtechnik des Ersten Weltkriegs – Entwicklung, Einsatz, Konsequenzen*
Copyright © 2014, Motorbuch Verlag, Stuttgart

First published in Great Britain in 2017 by
Pen & Sword Military
an imprint of
Pen & Sword Books Ltd
47 Church Street
Barnsley
South Yorkshire
S70 2AS

Copyright © Wolfgang Fleischer 2017

ISBN 978 1 47385 419 2

Typeset in Ehrhardt by
Mac Style Ltd, Bridlington, East Yorkshire
Printed and bound in India by Replika Press Pvt Ltd.

Pen & Sword Books Ltd incorporates the imprints of Pen & Sword Archaeology, Atlas, Aviation, Battleground, Discovery, Family History, History, Maritime, Military, Naval, Politics, Railways, Select, Transport, True Crime, Fiction, Frontline Books, Leo Cooper, Praetorian Press, Seaforth Publishing and Wharncliffe.

For a complete list of Pen & Sword titles please contact
PEN & SWORD BOOKS LIMITED
47 Church Street, Barnsley, South Yorkshire, S70 2AS, England
E-mail: enquiries@pen-and-sword.co.uk
Website: www.pen-and-sword.co.uk

Photograph credits: Carls (1), Eiermann (11), Fleischer (252), Hensel (7), Heuschkel (1), Liebscher (2), Thiede via Max Planck Gesellschaft (3), Schulz (6), Wulff (1).

CONTENTS

Introduction

COMMAND IN CRISIS

Massed armies, technologies of annihilation, and trench warfare

During the course of the First World War, hostilities embraced nearly all continents and oceans because of the global extent of the system of alliances in force as at 1914. The fighting on land was concentrated principally in Europe, the main fronts being in the East and West. Subsidiary fronts with changing theatres developed in the South and South-East of the continent, in the Near and Middle East and in Africa.

Already at the turn of the 19th century, the major Powers Germany, France, Great Britain and Czarist Russia had military forces numbered in the millions for the event of war. The great advances in science and technology were being constantly adapted by the military to improve their equipment and armament, but also sought were new methods to confront enemy forces effectively. Accordingly after the outbreak of war in August 1914 the old adage was confirmed: war remained a catalyst for scientific-technological development. Also on this occasion.

The word "development" is used above deliberately, and not the concept "progress", for the latter took no account of the long-term negative outcome of research projects where the priority was profiled increasingly as one of supply by private concerns to the military. In this context ethics hardly counted any longer. Understandably, it was the point of view of the military leaders that even in peacetime, under the slogan "Producing Security", it was their duty to issue contracts and instigate the invention of ever better machines of annihilation. Amongst the consequences of this policy in the First World War was a hitherto unknown level of killing and reduction of humane principles. That also applied of course to the use of natural resources where to the present day the effect on the environment has not been assessed conclusively.

New Dimensions of Warfare

In no military conflict of the past had technical knowledge and abilities been so decisive as in this war. They brought about many changes to the typical weaponry and equipment already in service in the armies. Artillery range and shell effects were increased substantially. To the arsenal of classical weapons, science brought new weapons for close combat; mine-throwers, mortars and technically advanced pioneer equipment. The war required the use of chemicals and new personnel carriers: initially battlefield gases and armoured vehicles. Technology made it possible to create new theatres of war in which to spread the conflict: airships and aircraft roamed the skies, submarines the underwater world. Radio and telephone technologies enabled military operations to be directed by the battlefield commanders.

The new basic experiences of this war included massed attacks and advanced weaponry. The use of the latter in the opening phase of the war caused major problems. The expenditure of ammunition reached levels never thought possible until then. Additional problems were generated by the belief that the war would be short, so that no economic preparations had been made for a protracted one. This meant that the economic, mental and moral energies of all German society had to be mobilized in order to keep the war going: the population was now involved to a far greater

Shells arrayed at a British ammunition factory. Shown here are AP munitions for 152.4 mm (6-inch) and 234 mm (9.2-inch) howitzers. In a single week at the end of June 1916 on the Somme, British forces fired four million shells of all calibres.

A German machine-gun position in a half-protected dug-out. Field fortifications made it easier for weaker forces to keep a superior enemy at bay. In the first year of the war the Germans used the term "*Tiefengliederung*" (staggered arrangement in depth) where two trenches were developed one behind the other.

extent in the war effort than had ever been the case in previous conflicts.

The extent to which science and technology would influence military strategy and tactics had not been recognized before the First World War. For example, the Prussian War Minister, General Erich von Falkenhayn relieved Colonel-General Helmut von Moltke of his post as Chief of the General Staff because Falkenhayn was of the opinion that trench warfare should not be planned for

German heavy MG 08 in firing position. Together with artillery fire power, it was the devastating effect of this fully-automatic weapon which deprived the war of mobility in 1914 and by the turn of the year brought about trench warfare.

beyond the spring of 1915. That it represented something more than a temporary withdrawal of the troops into "battlefield winter quarters" was only gradually being realised by his contemporaries.

The inter-relationship of military technology and tactics shaped the man. The changes found necessary to be made in 1914/15 – which amounted to nothing less than a revolution in fighting procedures – were contrary to the pre-war training and experience of military officers at all levels. The learning process now being introduced in all branches of the military forces was very contradictory and noteworthy above all for its high casualty rate in men and materials.

The primary aim of the offensive in the West was to break through the enemy defences. The basic problem for the attacker was to reduce the enemy's firepower. This created the competition for superiority in numbers in men and weaponry on the battlefield. The clearest expression of it here were the increases in length and intensity of softening-up by artillery, and trench building by the pioneers. Both made enormous demands on the transport capabilities of the supply troops. Surprise manouevres were thus virtually impossible to achieve. Weeks of artillery bombardment failed to destroy the enemy's trench systems nor his carefully entrenched weapons.

This begs the question regarding the efficiency of the weapons deployed, a study which occupied Dr.B.H.Jahn in the 1930s. In his article published in the July 1936 issue of *Wehrtechnische Monatsheft* he made the point that in the tribal feuds of the indigenous peoples, only a few arrows or spears were found on every wounded or dead warrior, yet for every shell or round fired in the First World War, one could have erected a small hill over the grave of every wounded or fallen soldier. Jahn was relying on statistics from the United States in which the cost of the war was estimated at 700 billion gold marks of which the money value of all ammunition expended was put at 125 billion gold marks. The fallen were put at 10 million, the wounded at 17 million.[1] This meant that ammunition to the value of 4300 gold marks was used to make each of these casualties unfit for the front by wounding or killing them. This corresponded on average to between 50 and 100 artillery shells and 20,000 rifle rounds.

The Quest for the War of Mobility

Looked at from this viewpoint, the search was now on for more refined methods of operation: for the artillery, or for new technically advanced vehicles such as tanks and bombers: all in all a striving for more effective ways to destroy and kill. It was hoped that these new methods would restore mobility to warfare.

The new military technology brought about lasting change in the conduct of warfare and the composition of the fighting forces. The importance of infantry was reduced, that of the other branches of service increased. The table below provides the example for the German side.

Weapons and the new vehicles of technology could not change the course of the war alone: this was done by the people who developed them, who met the material requirements for their mass production and brought to bear their qualitative attributes on the battlefield. Ultimately these were the decisive factors behind victory for the Entente in the First World War.

The historical debate on this war therefore cannot be limited to the technical innovations and their influence on strategy and tactics. The First World War proved again that the

Help us win! Subscribe to War Loans. War loan poster designed by Prof.F.Erler of Munich. In the German Kaiserreich war loans were a means to help finance the war through long term borrowings from within the population.

Composition of the German Fighting Forces in the First World War

Branch	May 1915	June 1916	Oct 1916	Apr 1918	Jul 1918	Oct 1918
Infantry	71.8%	66.7%	60.4%	56.98%	54.6%	50.4%
Cavalry	4.8%	4.2%	3.7%	3.4%	3.6%	4.0%
Artillery	18.1%	22.3%	27.7%	30.7%	32.4%	35.7%
Pioneers	4.9%	5.6%	6.4%	6.6%	6.7%	6.9%
Army Air Force	0.4%	1.2%	1.8%	2.4%	2.7%	3.0%
Total	100%	100%	100%	100%	100%	100%

The armoured fighting vehicle, known to the British as a tank, was only intended initially to enable their infantry to overwhelm machine-gun nests.

Medium mine-thrower under tow by its crew. Developed originally as a siege warfare mortar for the pioneers, it gained major importance in trench warfare in the First World War.

In the course of the war all armies introduced towing machines for their artillery since the weights were too great for horses. In the photo is a German 60 hp Bräuer motorised tractor limbered to a Rheinmetall 8.8-cm flak gun L/45.

Together with losses to artillery caused by enemy action, an unexpectedly high number of guns were damaged or destroyed by shells detonating inside the barrel. There were many causes for this, amongst others defective ammunition and fuzes. In the picture is a German 15-cm heavy field howitzer 02 with a burst barrel. During a three month period in 1916, 5.Army alone lost 13 of its 125 guns of this type to premature detonation.

resolution of military conflicts does not rest alone on wiping out the enemy's military potential. Also decisive for the outcome of the war was the effect on morale of attacks against civilian populations – including criminal terror attacks from the air – and the destruction of industrial installations.

Another aspect merits special attention: most of the themes presented in this book – at least at the outset – bear a direct relationship to pioneers and siege warfare, since the pre-requirement for the construction (and destruction) of fortifications was mathematical precision and technical knowledge. As the result of the increasing influence of science and technology, siege warfare developed in the 19th century into a branch of the military profession, described nowadays as "high technology". Therefore fortress building, a military art since times immemorial, was to a certain extent the midwife to the techniques of protection and destruction which characterised the First World War.

It is not possible within the framework of this book to investigate the complexities of that war. The author and publishers have selected scientific-technological developments as episodes in an economic but primarily military context and hope thereby to contribute to the ongoing debate on a war of annihilation which lasted four years, and had its roots going back 100 years.

Note

1. More recent research puts the number of fallen in the First World War at 7.9 million, and the wounded at 19.4 million.

Fighter aircraft R.A.F. F.E.8 of the Royal Aircraft Factory. Machines of this type arrived at the front as from August 1916. 295 models were delivered and used by British fighter pilots until mid-1917. Especially due to technological advances – to which the air forces owed their existence – replacement cycles were reduced drastically.

The signals units, comparable to the threads and fibres of a nerve system, made a significant contribution at command levels. The most efficient methods of communications remained the telephone and telex. At left is a commemorative photo of the Somme telephone unit with field cables, telephones and equipment from the year 1917.

A telephone exchange with field drop-type switchboard for twenty lines. Photo from 1918.

Photo taken in 1915 showing captured trench with the shredded body of a British soldier, one of 7.9 miliion men who lost their lives in the First World War. The wounded numbered 19.4 million, amongst them many blinded and amputees, and not counting those left with permanent mental trauma.

Whether in Flanders, on the Somme or in the Argonnen woods – after week-long artillery bombardent any battlefield became a landscape laid waste into unrecognizability.

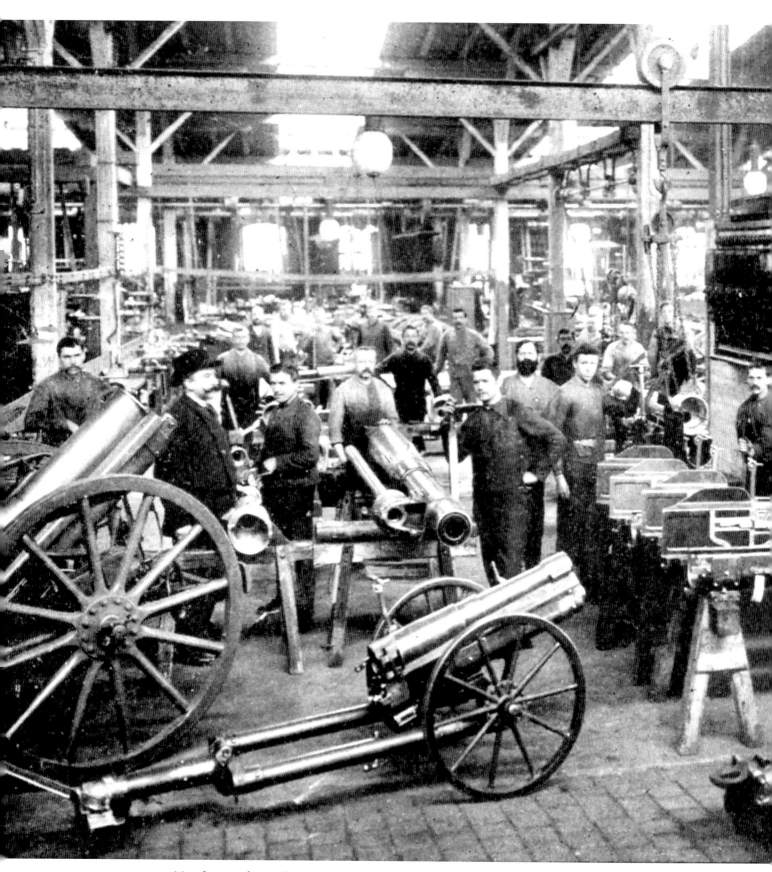

Manufacture of gun chassis at the Eisenach vehicle factory. In the centre of the photograph is a Rheinmetall 7.5-cm mountain gun. Before the First World War guns of this kind were prepared mainly for export. In 1914 the Army administration took charge of what was left.

Chapter One

THE ADMINISTRATION OF SCARCITY
The War Economy

After the political and military collapse of the German Kaiserreich in the autumn of 1918, the search began for the causes of the defeat. The answers were as varied as personal motives or political orientation.

Everybody was agreed on one thing: the reason was not the mobilization of the German Army in August 1914. It had gone ahead in exemplary fashion and was one of the important preconditions for a decisive result on the battlefield in the shortest time. But the Schlieffen Plan came to grief at the Marne.

Was the Plan based on a false premise? The experiences gathered by the German General Staff since the Franco-German War of 1870/71 had been decisive for the Plan. That the Russo-Turkish War of 1877/78, and the Russo-Japanese War of 1904/05 did not correspond to the current picture of warfare was known and had been evaluated, but not understood. The length in time of the two wars, the high expenditure in ammunition and the periods which the belligerents had spent in trenches had been recognised but the causes attributed to the contemporary theatres of war, and the circumstances were held not to be applicable to those prevailing in Central and Western Europe.

Retired Lt-General Max Schwarte wrote in 1920: "The reasons for the undoubted underestimation by the Army pre-war of the new technologies probably resulted from the events of the earlier wars, the conclusions drawn and the failure to apply them having regard to the corresponding major progress of the time. Above all they were to be found in the inadequate appreciation within the decisive State offices, particularly the Army, as to the nature of the emergent technologies and the faulty assessment of the same."

The Belief in a Quick Victory

Optimism that Germany would emerge victorious from a quick war such as in 1871 was an impediment to the mobilization of industry in total ignorance of the demands of a modern war. However this would have been difficult in any case.

Industrial mobilization might have caused further irritation abroad and burdened the Exchequer additionally with the financing of stockpiles of imported raw materials for the war effort. Industry was still in private hands and every intervention by the State, such as raising new taxes or customs duties, interfered with its smooth running. These interventions into the financial and economic life of the nation could not have been avoided and would probably have encountered parliamentary opposition. For these reasons, industrial mobilization was never considered pre-war.

Accordingly there were no strategic reserves, no stockpiles of vital raw materials for the war effort and no contingency plan for the "Walk to Paris" lasting beyond the year's end.

After the collapse on the Marne, State intervention into industry quickly became reality: enforced control of raw materials, a change in the coinage regulations and the extension of the set terms in the laws relating to bills of exchange and cheques were all a consequence of the industrial mobilization embarked upon in Germany initially only with reluctance.

On economic grounds, a long war had already been ruled out in Germany, dependent

The new lathe shop for shells at the Rheinische Maschinen-und Metallwarenfabrik in Düsseldorf. It was one of the leaders in the field of German armaments and therefore received preferential treatment in the distribution of important raw materials for the war effort.

In order to make up for the lack of raw materials, during the First World War Germany experienced a real mania for collecting. Included were household metal objects, church bells, woollen waste and rags, kitchen waste (as cattle fodder), acorns, beechnuts, chestnuts and lichens, fruit kernels for manufacture of oils and edible oils, and waste paper.

on imports of raw materials, but also in Britain, France and the other industrial nations: nobody was thinking of a long war. In the third quarterly issue of *Vierteljahreshefte für Truppenführung und Heereskunde*, Year 1913, Arthur Dix wrote an article on "The Political-Economic Provision for War": "The most capable Army and the most circumspect Army Command will be required to make the fullest political capital out of all battlefield successes in order to prevent the political economy falling swiftly into ruin, especially in the case of a longer lasting war on several fronts."

He went on to say that as a result of restrictions on commerce and the loss of access to world markets, unemployment and famine would lead to "politico-economic and social calamities" and to social unrest at the rear of the fighting army. His suggested solution was neither new nor original: "The more successfully the offensive spirit is alive in the Army, the less will the economic disruption be felt."

In the summer and autumn of 1914 the material means for a quick victory were absent. Only the groups mobilized according to plan were up to strength in weapons, artillery, vehicles and equipment. Reserve corps had no heavy artillery and the stand-by divisions were short 50% of guns and MGs available for deployment while a section of the Landwehr veterans had to make do without them altogether.

The reserves of equipment stored at the depots were now intended for the replacement of losses. They had been meant for the setting up of four new Army corps, but proved insufficient. The 1911 authorised Army estimates for ammunition had been diverted to other areas of Army armaments and the substantial requirement for artillery ammunition could not be met. An example here: there were 3,367,000 rounds available for the 7.7-cm light field gun 96 n/A. This may appear an impressive stock, but it boiled down to between 457 and 987 rounds per gun which would not last a week at the front since the average expenditure quickly reached 300 to 350 rounds daily. Before the end of August 1914 the Superintendent of Ammunition in

The production of barrels for heavy artillery in a State weapons factory. In September 1914 twenty heavy guns were manufactured; three years later in September 1917 industry turned out four hundred.

The principal producers of infantry weapons were the State firearms factories at Danzig, Erfurt and Spandau. Because of insufficient capacity, the work was farmed out to numerous private concerns. In 1916 alone, 2,576,448 rifles and carbines were manufactured.

the field raised the alarm; the requirements at the front were growing and the depots were being emptied; recourse was now being had to munitions stored in the fortresses. Moreover, not all the armies could be supplied uniformly, particularly those fighting at the Marne had priority. Additionally, ever more requisitions were being submitted for the new weapons such as heavy mortars which had proved their special worth in the trenches. The supply of these mines in 1915 was around one million. A similar situation existed with close-combat weapons; egg- and stick-grenades, and mortar bombs, of which 36 million reached the front during 1916. Next came the increase in the production of guns, from 14 monthly before the outbreak of war to 100 monthly in December 1914. In 1917, 2,000 field and 400 heavy guns were being delivered monthly, and these originated from 580 manufacturers. The War Labour Programme developed in peacetime proved totally inadequate. According to this plan, only eight firms were to turn out the ammunition and not once had they managed to get close to the estimates. The "Industrial Mobilization" therefore turned out to be a washout.

Production Bottlenecks and Shortages of Raw Materials at the Very Outbreak of War

Bottlenecks of raw materials and half-finished products began to develop after a few weeks. This included copper, indispensable for the manufacture of shell casings and cartridges for the artillery, but which was also urgently needed for telephone cables of the nascent signals branch. It was soon decided to reduce the copper component of the alloy from 72 per cent to 67 per cent. Rheinmetall designed a steel casing which performed well but was insufficiently sparing of copper, and finally substitute casings of steel and later iron were mass produced.

Other raw material shortages were natural rubber for vehicle tyres, cotton for the manufacture of nitro-cellulose propellant and saltpetre imported in large quantities from Chile. The requisitioning of all stocks of saltpetre – essential in the manufacture of

explosives and fertilizers – and the capture of large quantities in warehouses at Antwerp, were only a drop in the ocean. One cannot help mentioning the enforced control of raw materials proposed by Dr. Walther Rathenau, director at the General Electricity Company. The first step came on 14 August 1914 with the setting up of the War Raw Materials Department (KRA) by the Royal Prussian War Ministry. This body regulated the distribution of raw materials in collaboration with the semi-State owned War Raw Materials companies. Those concerns which had received important war contracts at the right time clearly benefited. The various interests hampered coordination in the administration of raw materials and food. Between spring 1915 and summer 1916, KRA seized all available raw materials in Germany.

It was still a long road to a uniform leadership. In order to resolve the many and very complex logistical problems centrally, new ministerial departments were set up such as WuMba, (*Waffen- und Munitions Beschaffungsamt* – the Weapons and Munitions Procurement Office) created on 30 September 1916 in the framework of the Hindenburg Programme and made directly responsible to the newly created War Office. In June 1917 alone, WuMba employed a staff of 3,144.

Decisive for the continuation of the war was ammunition supply. In 1914/15 this had developed into perhaps the most important industrial problem of the war, and for the Entente too: the consumption of materials exceeded all forecasts and on the German side led to a munitions crisis. For example, the plans drawn up in peacetime foresaw that in case of war the 7.7-cm field guns 96 n/A would require 200,000 shells per month, and the 10.5-cm light field howitzers 98/09 would require 70,000 shells per month. As was to prove the case this fell well short of the need. By stretching all labour forces and machinery to the limit, by December 1914 German industry had succeeded in producing monthly 1,250,000 and 360,000 shells respectively. The problems began to grow, however, for artillery ammunition was only one aspect of the whole. The basic ingredients for the

Women were taken on by the armaments industry for the first time in the autumn of 1914. In the course of the war their work gained extraordinarily in importance and changed the way in which women saw their place in society. The photo shows two women involved in the manufacture and inspection of artillery shell casings.

manufacture of the commonest explosives –
shell-filling 88 (picric acid) and filling powder
02 (TNT) being unobtainable, substitutes were
employed, and even the problem of hydrogen
was solved.

After Haber-Bosch developed a process
to harvest hydrogen from air and had put
it into the major industrial frame, the paint
and fertilizer industries were combined into
the armaments industry. In the autumn of
1914 the monthly supply of nitro powder
was 1000 tonnes, in October 1915 it had
risen to 4750 tonnes and two years later to
10,000 tonnes, to which up to 4,000 tonnes
of ammonium powder must be added. These
deliveries made it possible by 1917 to load
almost 9,000 complete ammunition trains
for troops in the field. A further increase was
prevented by the now tangible shortage of
steel for shell manufacture: this led to steel
and iron being used for the manufacture of
cartridges and cartridge cases. The preparation
of propellant powder for the cases was only
possible by using wood cellulose in place of
cotton, which had to be imported.

The Cartridge Scandal

*Not only the Germans were poorly prepared for a long war. Although
British industry had invested heavily in the years before 1914, it had not
been awarded to domestic markets where capacity for assembly generally
and also in ammunition production was lacking. This had political
consequences. Responsibility for ammunition production lay in the hands
of Lord Kitchener, hero of Khartoum. After the British offensive at Neuve
Chapelle in March 1915, the Commanding General Sir John French told
a British journalist that the lack of shells was the reason for the failure.
This conversation had been confidential but the content found its way into
the newspapers with the widest circulations. French was relieved of his
command by Sir Douglas Haig and the crisis situation was now recognised.
Prime Minister David Lloyd George found himself confirmed in his
conviction that British industry was not in a position to prosecute a long
war with Germany and he did not believe that Kitchener was the right man
as War Minister to remedy the problem despite his wide popularity. In a
Cabinet reshuffle under new Prime Minister Asquith in May 1915, however,
Kitchener was retained as Minister for War but relieved of responsibility for
ammunition production.*

Gold for Iron: Mobilizing Civilian Society

The longer the war lasted, the worse the raw
materials situation became for Germany.
The naval blockade was taking effect, there

were shortages everywhere. Camel hair, for
example, important in vehicle manufacture,
was no longer arriving, and the Red Cross
called for "donations of ladies' hair", which
brought in several hundred tonnes. In
1917 by decree all tin and copper had to be
surrendered and the order was given to melt
down church bells provided not of great
historical importance. Many households
had already given away their valuables, but
gold and jewellery was now being collected
in under the motto "I gave gold for iron".
To finance the war (the costs of which had
become astronomical from 1916) people were
urged to subscribe to the War Loan.

The food industry had not prepared for a
long war as became more obvious in its second
half made worse by the absence of artificial
fertilizers, nitrates being required for the
production of ammunition. At the end of 1914
there had been major increases in the price
of foodstuffs, these increases led to the first
social unrest. Still in 1914, a State organisation
had come into being, the War Grain Society
(*Kriegsgetreidegesellschaft*), which began
to buy up supplies on the large scale: from
1915 the cultivation of grains covered great
areas, to be followed in October by potatoes
("*Reichskartoffel-Stellen*").

How tense the food situation must have been
in the early years of the war is demonstrated
by the "Swine Killing" in which between
eight and nine million pigs were slaughtered
because it was thought that feeding them might
cause reductions in food for the population
and troops. This was a fatal error, as was to
be highlighted in the years of hunger and
starvation which ensued later. The food
situation became critical in 1916, a poor potato
harvest led to food riots, and the winter of
1916/17 went down in history as the "turnip
and swede winter". As a result of malnutrition
in the workforce, industrial production began
to suffer.

In conclusion it must be remarked almost
as a miracle that the German Reich was in
a position at all to keep fighting until the
autumn of 1918. This would not have been
possible without the multitude of scientific-
technological innovations.

Commemorative photo of munitions workers, date and place unknown.

The requirement for hand grenades leapt with the changeover to trench warfare. In all, fifty to sixty firms were involved in the production, again using much female labour. The photo shows the production of egg-type hand grenades with a combustion time-fuze.

Chapter Two

MACHINE-GUNS IN THE FIRST WORLD WAR
The Multiplication of Fire Power

"Machine-guns were not an invention of the First World War, the development of quick-firing small calibre weapons goes much further back. In the 19th century amongst others it was the two canister-shot guns, the French Mitrailleuse (11.45 mm calibre) and the North American Gatling revolver gun (calibre 10.7 to 24.5 mm), which raised killing efficiency.

The story of the machine-gun cannot be told without mentioning the name of the engineer H.S.Maxim, one of the most accomplished inventors of his epoch. Along with others he made motors, pumps, fire extinguishers, carbon arc lamps, smokeless powder and a quick-firing gun. His invention of the water-cooled machine-gun with short barrel recoil in 1885 was of great significance for the development of fully automatic weapons. Contemporaries credited Maxim with

A revolver-cannon invented by the American Dr.R.J.Gatling patented on 25 July 1893 under number 502185. The picture shows a Gatling-gun of the Italian Navy.

"... exceptional razor-sharp intelligence and indefatigable tenacity in the persecution of the goals he set himself," even if he had not devoted his unusual mental capabilities to the service of progress. "If in future wars the toll of victims (…) will be perhaps tenfold what it is today, then it may well be that Maxim's inventiveness will have played no small part in creating this 'grandiose' effect," wrote a certain H.Giersberg in 1905 in the 12th issue of *Bibliothek der Unterhaltung*. As it so transpired, the machine-gun influenced military technology and tactics decisively in the First World War. Hand grenades, flame-throwers, mine throwers, infantry guns, artillery bombardments and armoured fighting vehicles – all were created not least in order to overcome the murderous effect of the machine-gun. Its introduction into the fighting forces came up against a lot of opposition, and a suitable tactic for the use of the weapon was not forthcoming until after the war had started.

An Idea Makes its Mark

Britain was the first major European Power to purchase 11.4 mm calibre Maxim MGs, primarily for use in her colonies. The results were compelling enough to convince the fighting forces of other States that this weapon should be taken up. In Germany, where the matter was met with some reservations, the question was asked which of the various systems appearing on the market in the interim was the most suitable – Bergmann, Colt,

Heavy machine-gun 08 on an MG sled 08 in temporary anti-aircraft attitude. The barrel jacket protected the sensitive barrel against splinters with cooling water. The increased weight was a disadvantage.

Gardner, Maxim or Skoda. Various trials were held, including two by Maxim, for the 11 mm cartridge M.1871. In December 1889 at Fort Zorndorf near Küstrin comparative trials were held with two Gardner-Mitrailleusen, the construction of the Maxim proving superior. However its purchase was contingent upon conversion to take the 7.92 mm cartridge of the magazine-reload rifle 88 then in process of introduction. In the following years this ammunition proved troublesome and as a result the Royal Prussian War Ministry decided against having machine-guns and abandoned the trials. Nothing further happened for two years.

At this time the Reich Navy Office could make its own decisions independent of the War Ministry. The Berlin firm of Loewe also had right of user of the Maxim patent, and manufactured 7.92 mm MGs and 3.7 cm machine-cannons on a Navy

contract. In the acceptance tests, the *Gewehrprüfungskommission*[1] was required to make the 7.92 mm cartridge serviceable for the machine-gun. Accordingly in 1894 it was not entirely unexpected when the trials with the Maxim MG were resumed by order of the Kaiser. A sled, new sights and other improvements were introduced. More comparative trials followed, this time with the air-cooled Hotchkiss MG and a water-cooled Skoda model. These trials ended in 1898 and the first trials of the Maxim MG were carried out by 1.Batallion/1.Masurisch Infantry Regiment 146 at Allenstein: in 1899 six MG sections held trials each with four guns. These went off successfully except that the horse-drawn MG and ammunition waggons proved inadequate. The procurement of replacement vehicles was based on field-artillery equipment. In 1900 six further experimental MG sections were set up and two MGs passed to the

Patent for an automatic machine-gun by H.S. Maxim and L. Silvermann dated 24 December 1895.

The weapon was a recoil loader with moveable barrel. Combining the recoil with a toggle spring, the feeding, loading and ignition of the cartridge, and also the removal and ejection of the spent cartridge cases were all performed automatically. The principle was outstanding.

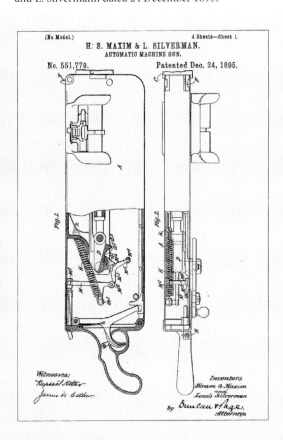

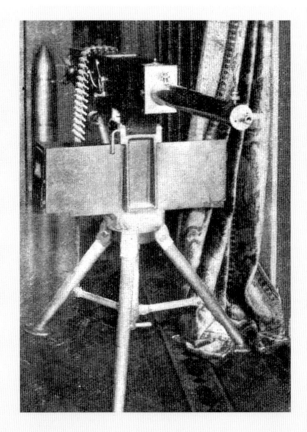

Infantry Shooting School. In the following year all MG formations were subordinated to the Inspectorate for Rangers and Riflemen. The first five MG sections appeared in the military estimates approved by the Reichstag on 1 October 1901 and so the Maxim MG was now officially a German Army weapon, thus ending more than ten years waiting time of development, trials, doubts and setbacks.

Before the First World War there could be no talk of unity in the assessments of the new weapon. In 1901 German General H. Frobenius characterised the machine-gun in his hand encyclopaedia of the military sciences as a small-calibre weapon which worked like a machine. "Its rate of fire (…) mostly exceeds the practical requirement and is for that reason of much lesser significance than its vulnerability to disruptive, inevitable influences in the field (…)". From the modern viewpoint, the recognised military specialist of the day

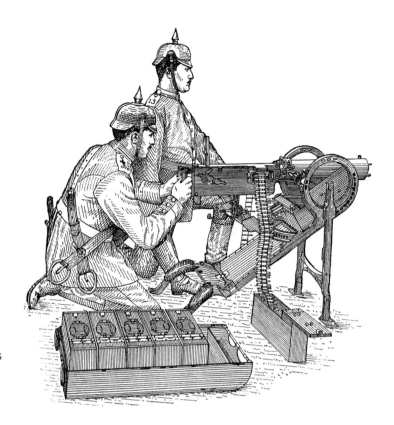

MG 01 transported by its crew, and in firing position. At this time the ammunition sled contained six boxes of ammunition each with 250 rounds. The gun (less sled) weighed 26 kgs, the cooler unit held 3.7 litres of water. The muzzle velocity was 645 metres per second, the theoretical rate of fire lay between 400 and 500 rounds per minute.

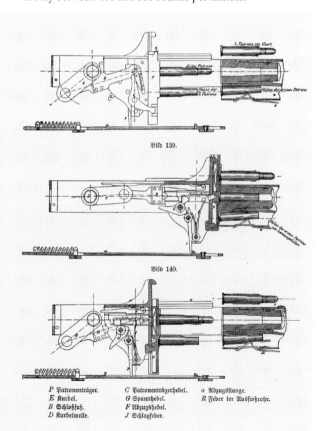

Bild 139.

Bild 140.

P Patronenträger.
E Kurbel.
B Schloßfuß.
D Kurbelwelle.

C Patronenträgerhebel.
G Spannhebel.
F Abzugshebel.
J Schlagfeder.

a Abzugstange.
R Feder im Ausstoßrohr.

provided unjustifiable reservations. It would be less than fifteen years before machine-guns advanced to be the most important infantry weapon thanks to their firepower.

The Tactical Application of the New Weapon

The uncertainty regarding the classification and tactical deployment of such a sensitive, complicated but also extraordinarily efficient machine which the MG now proved itself to be was highlighted in the third volume of the weapons training manual *Bibliothek des Offiziers Handbuch* of September 1903: "The most original and newest weapon of our Army is the machine-gun. Its specifications and shooting performance identify it as a hand fire-arm while by the manner of transport and manning it is linked to the artillery."

In general, MG's were seen as sensible weapons for the German colonies, for the Navy and fortress warfare, less for the field. Already in 1900 orders were placed for mobile tower chassis, notched and pivoting chassis, and splinter shields for use in fortress defences. From 1903 MG's were given a new sled with cranked elevating gear. Rules for exercises and shooting regulations were handed out. In 1908

came the final version of the MG sled. The contemporary MG 08 weighed only 66 kgs, an extraordinary advance. The barrel jacket, originally of bronze, was replaced by steel. The older models (01 and 03) were distributed amongst the fortress MG detachments of which there were sixteen in 1914, five of them stationed in the Western border region of Metz-Diedenhofen alone.

It was in the wars of those years, the Russo-Japanese War (1904–1905), the two Balkans Wars (1911–1912) and the Turkish-Italian War (1911–1912) that machine-guns were first used at the front. Although emphasised repeatedly that whatever happened in these military conflicts could not simply be transposed to Central and Western Europe, everybody did evaluate the experiences gathered. In the 1909 issue of *Vierteljahresheft für Truppenführung und Heereskunde* published by the Great General Staff in Berlin, several articles were dedicated to the implications of the Russo-Japanese campaign in Manchuria. The Japanese were reported to have said about the weapon, "Above all one must take out enemy MGs so as to prepare the breakthrough in attack." In defending, one should not open fire "until the attacker begins his advance. All such attacks

This photograph demonstrates the operational arrangement for the MG 08 in the period immediately before the First World War. The platoon has two MGs, in the background are the fore and rear parts of the horse-drawn gun waggon 08. Weapon and sled including four litres of cooling water weighed 64.25 kilos.

will peter out in the face of the effect of intact MGs." Notable ideas which did not implant themselves in the heads of the German tactical planners until years later.

The original German concept for the use of the machine-gun, and one of the reasons why it was subordinated to the Inspectorate of Riflemen, was that it should appear on the battlefield as a surprise just as riflemen did. After the reorganisation of the MG detachments the debate in the technical press as to the tactical application grew more heated. In 1911 1st Lt von Jecklin, Chief of the MG Company/2. Brandenburg Grenadier Regt 12, addressed the subject of infantry-MG attacks in the journal *Vierteljahresheft für Truppenführung und Heereskunde*. He pointed to the high expenditure of ammunition, the limited mobility, the difficulties of positioning the gun and its team in the terrain and deprecated it as a stand-by infantry weapon. Hauptmann Kretschmar, who served during the war in the rank of major as a Staff Officer of MG troops in an Army Corps, described the machine-gun in 1913 as "the strongest infantry firepower" but recommended that it should only be used to escape the effect of artillery. The basic idea was that the machine-gun was unsuitable to be used throughout a period of fighting: and it was forbidden to use it as the only weapon. The British and French thought differently but even so rejected having groups of MG detachments together at the front.

It does not seem to have occurred to the Germans, until they were finally influenced by the foreign reports of heavy losses on the battlefield, that machine-guns working in concert with the quick-firing guns introduced into the infantry in 1890 would strengthen the defences. The offensive concept however remained embedded in the arrogance of obsolete tactics. The later QM-General of Supreme Army Command, Ludendorff, is said to have expressed the opinion once: "With their MGs all they can do is make a mess of our marching columns."

Military progress could not be stopped however. In 1906 for example the Tsarist Army had over 100 MG companies while Germany at the same time had only 16 detachments. The time had come to expand the MG force.

Every infantry regiment and ranger batallion received one MG company with six MG 08 on MG sled 08, and every cavalry division one MG detachment. By 1 August 1914, 218 infantry regiments had 219 MG companies (the infantry training regiment had two MG companies): 113 reserve infantry regiments had 88 MG companies: 86 brigade-replacement batallions had 44 replacement MG platoons and the previously mentioned fortress MG detachments. Landwehr units were not provided with machine-guns. The total of available MGs was 4502, of which 2400 were brought up to the lines when the time came .

Machine-guns at the Front

In the tactical realm it was only a few weeks before the many unsolved problems of the pre-war period made themselves felt. The first to suffer was the infantry, advancing as if across the exercise fields in thick columns of riflemen. During the fighting at Mons and Framière in August 1914, the German infantry sustained heavy losses during the attempts to make their mark with the bayonet against skilfully distributed British MG nests in the terrain. A similar fate befell the French 69th Territorial Regiment at Bellenglise, north of St.Quentin, caught out on the flank of a German MG company. General Douglas Haig, from 1915 Commander-in-Chief of British troops in France and Flanders, wrote of the fighting at Orly on 8 September: "The enemy's artillery and cavalry did not take part in the fighting long whereas his machine-guns were deployed with great skill and determination; (…) and wherever our infantry advanced, they were taken under fire unexpectedly."

In the eastern theatre of war some of the MG companies fought closed up although a number of units such as the Landwehr Division commanded by von der Goltz, involved in heavy fighting at the end of August near Allenstein, had no MG at all. In the West the German Army had gone over to trench warfare by the year's end. The trench sectors at the time were not deeply laid out and the preferences of individual MG teams were given full recognition, their small requirements

MG 08 on MG sled 08 in temporary anti-aircraft attitude. Aerial targets could be engaged up to a maximum altitude of 1000 metres. Photo from 1915.

The tripod introduced in the summer of 1916 enabled the MG 08 to be used against both ground and aerial targets.

For firing from a trench, and especially for a quick change of firing location, the MG 08 was too heavy and unwieldy. The makeshift solution was to fire the gun resting on a sandbag.

Alternatively makeshift supports (above) or improvised tripod (below) for use against ground and aerial targets.

MG 08 with large MG splinter shield. Experimental versions were ready before the outbreak of war and serious production was in hand. The protection offered was good but in the trenches the gun was difficult to aim. Moreover the shape and size of the shield was quickly spotted and drew enemy fire, resulting in its general rejection.

a relatively large stock of MGs. From a total of 4502, the army in the field had 2438, the depots (including 465 as a reserve for repairs and spare parts), replacement troops, occupation troops and fortresses held 2064. Initially the replacements required were comparatively few so that by the end of the year the 1000 guns delivered had sufficed. In 1915 around 6100 new MGs were delivered; together with the large stock of captured MGs these were enough to compensate for losses and re-equip all units in the field up to strength. This not only meant units of the line, reserves and Landwehr, but also special formations such as independent MG companies and detachments, "musketeer" batallions, mountain MG-detachments, and vehicle MG platoons. At the end of 1915 the total stock of MGs including captured weapons was around 8000. The picture changed immediately after Colonel-General Paul von Hindenburg took over the Supreme Army Command on 16 August 1916. At once he and Ludendorff introduced measures to increase military striking power, primarily by the setting up of new divisions and increasing allocations of weapons, ammunition and equipment. MG production was tripled under the "Hindenburg Programme" of 31 August 1916.

The Hindenburg Programme

The Hindenburg Programme had the aim of expanding armaments production. By the spring of 1917 the production of powder, mortars and ammunition had doubled, and that of guns and MGs tripled. This required the extensive mobilisation of the female workforce. Moreover "business concerns not important for the war" were closed in order to release employees for work under the Hindenburg programme. The newly set up War Office under General Wilhelm Groener handled the coordination.

for space – as measured against the major firepower – limited the search for where to dig in. Unlike a line of riflemen, they could be withdrawn more easily from enemy fire of the same intensity. Even if half the MG team (with driver and waggon commander seven men) fell, the firepower could be maintained given enough ammunition and water. The main task of the machine-guns during an attack consisted of gaining fire superiority, in defence "… of overcoming the enemy at long range, since the firepower and the possibility of planned searching fire at these ranges (over 800 metres – *Author*) is far superior to the infantry," (see F. von Merkatz, *Unterrichtsbuch für die Maschinengewehrkompanie-Gerät 08*).

At the outbreak of war the German Army had

Until then the entire procurement had been the job more or less of the Spandau rifle factory through the *Feldzeugmeisterei*[2] substitutes for indispensable raw materials (amongst others brass, red brass, raw rubber and vulcanite) now played an important role.

The increases demanded would not have been achieved without co-opting private industry on the grand scale. Thus for the complicated gun locks the Erfurt rifle factory and eight other concerns were roped in. The assembly work continued at Spandau, but also here selected firms were appointed to assist. By November 1916 the monthly output of MGs had risen to 2300. This made it possible to reform some of the MG units set up at the beginning of the year, each with six MG 08 on hand carts, into MG sharpshooter-*Abteilungen* each composed of three companies. The rest were formed into other MG companies so that in the late autumn of the year the first regiments were at the front with three of these units.

The authorised strength of the divisions rose from 24 (as at 1914) to 108 heavy and 144 light MGs. In comparison, a French division had 108 heavy and 216 light, a British division 62 heavy and 192 light MGs.

The MG 08 on sled 08 weighed at least 62 kilos and was so heavy that it could not be transported entire. Battle experience and the re-use of captured British and French light machine-guns and the Madsen MG used by the Russians resulted in a light Maxim system MG being developed in Germany. After Army trials in 1915, it was introduced in the summer of 1916 as light MG 08/15 but not until the beginning of 1917 did it begin to arrive in any numbers to infantry companies at the front. At 13.7 kgs it was two-thirds lighter and so suitable for fighting off infantry attacks and also making them oneself, but with the bipod support it lacked the accuracy of the heavy MG. Another light MG, Modell 15 n/A, was also available, air-cooled and weighing only 13 kgs. For reasons of training and supply the War Ministry did not wish to dispense with the Maxim system. The Rheinische Metallwaren und Maschinenfabrik Düsseldorf turned out the water-cooled MG 15 (Dreyse) of which around 3000 were supplied to German troops in Palestine.

Operational Principles and Usage

Major changes came about in machine-gun tactics. In this connection the assessment of the experiences drawn from the Battle of the Somme by the General Staff of the Field Army (Ia/II Nr 175 gh.op) of 25 September 1916 is interesting: "Only a few machine-guns belong in the forward lines. The main mass of MGs is to be positioned in the lines to the rear and in the intermediate terrain so that the entire front

Defence against low-flying fighters on the field railway. Even here makeshift supports for the MG 08 were in use.

of the position, and the adjoining territory between our own lines and the nearest terrain to the rear is controlled by flanking MG fire. Set up at inconspicuous points. The choice of MG positions requires quite special care." The requirement for a wide field of fire arose from the need to withdraw the position from enemy observation. Of decisive importance for defensive success were no longer the riflemen of the infantry companies but the network of machine-guns distributed in the depths of the battlefield. "The arrangement of the machine-gun points and dug-outs form the framework of all infantry fighting lines. 100 metres and less is sufficient for the frontal field of fire."

Details of ammunition consumption underline the significance of the MG. It happened that MG companies used up to 35,000 rounds on days of major engagements. That was 140 boxes of belts (each with 250 rounds) with a weight of around 1164 kgs. During the war there was never any shortage of infantry ammunition. In March 1916 the monthly production reached 220 million rounds, was reduced to a quarter of that for a while and only after the Battle of the Somme at the end of the year was it set finally at 200 million rounds. In the spring of 1917 infantry ammunition with steel casings was introduced.

In a technical respect the MG 08 had proved itself. A report by the MG company of Inf. Regt. 114/29.Inf.Div. regarding the performance in the trenches stated:

> *"The Company had the opportunity to work with British, French and Russian MGs. German guns were given decisive preference. The superiority lies in their great reliability (…) and in the possibility of periods of enduring and accurate fire they provide."*

Hoped-for improvements were greater breadth of fire, better jacket armour, a splinter shield and an easier method of topping up cooling water. Special attention was paid in the report to the MG armoured chassis supplied by the Becker steelworks.

After the distribution of the light MG 08/15 (initially one, then three, finally six to eight) to the infantry companies, the heavy MGs were used mainly for targets at long range. These targets included troops on the march, assembly and readiness areas and rest areas up to 3.5 kilometres distant. At this range fire was indirect, for which purpose from 1917 Leitz and Zeiss telescopic sights, gunlaying, shooting and triangular measurement tables were issued. MGs received limiters for laying and training

Closed MG position of prefabricated blocks with MG 08 on sled. (**right**) Open MG position of prefabricated blocks, the MG here is resting on a makeshift base.

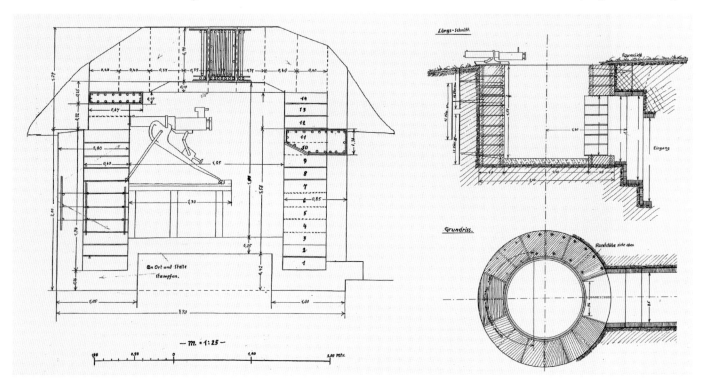

Training on the light MG 08/15. Accuracy of the MG 08 on MG sled 08 was better.

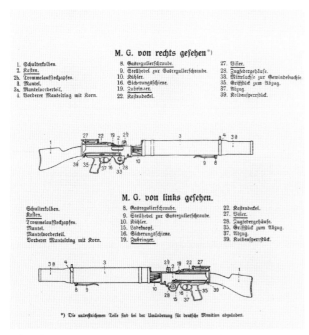

After the ammunition supply for the musket-batallions was exhausted, in 1916 the Rifle Testing Commission proposed replacing the Madsen light MG 03 with Lewis light machine guns captured from the British. They were converted to take the 8 x 57 German ammunition.

Madsen MG with German gunners. The Russian cavalry had been armed since the Russo-Japanese War with this light MG weighing only 10 kgs. The German Army used captured weapons of this type to set up two "musket" batallions which served on the Western Front from 1915.

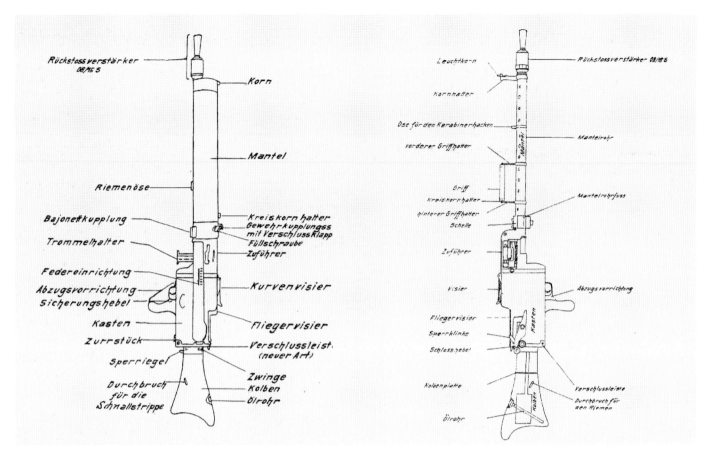

The light MG 08/15 developed from the design of the MG 08 but with smaller water jacket, bipod, butt and drum for 100 cartridges, had a two-man team. The theoretical rate of fire was 500 rounds per minute.

The light MG 08/18 was air-cooled, weighed only 12.5 kilos and was ready for introduction at the front as the war ended. Afterwards it was used in the rifle battalions of the Reichswehr.

Assault squad with tso light MG 08/15's – a typical photo from the fighting in the years 1917/1918.

The light air-cooled MG 15 n/A (Bergmann) was manufactured at Suhl and was issued as a priority to the German Asia Corps in Syria and Palestine in the autumn of 1917. Calibre 7.92 mm, rate of fire (theoretically) 500 rounds per minute, weight 12 kgs.

The French 8 mm light MG Chaucat mle.1915 had a 20-round magazine and weighed 8.2 kgs. Individual specimens made their way to the German Asia Corps in Palestine (see photo at bottom). Although it did not perform well, it was manufactured in large numbers in the United States for its expeditionary corps in Europe with a 7.62 mm calibre.

Franzøs. Maschinengewehr

German MG units occasionally received the French Hotchkiss MG mle.1914. These had a calibre of 8 mm, the cartridges were fed from a 30-round magazine, the theoretical rate of fire being 450 rounds per minute. Although at 25 kgs the weight was substantially below that of the German model, they were not particularly popular on the German side.

During 1915, German MG companies received the Russian heavy MG model 1910 (Maxim) suitable for German 7.92 mm ammunition. With the wheeled chassis and four litres of cooling water they weighed 55 kgs, their fighting value was equal to that of the German MG 08. Training on captured specimens provided no problems.

The heavy MG 08 on MG sled 08 with MG telescopic sight 12 without transversing stop. The theoretical rate of fire was 450–500 rounds per minute and the range 3500 metres. At 2,000 metres range dispersal of fire was around 41 metres when elevated and 170 metres when depressed.

British MG group with two heavy Vickers Mk.1 of 7.71 mm calibre. The water-cooled recoil loader (Maxim system) weighed 40.4 kgs including four litres of cooling water, and was substantially lighter than the German 08. Muzzle velocity was 792 metres/second, the theoretical rate of fire 400 rounds per minute.

the weapon. In *Vorschrift für das indirekte Schiessen* (…) available from March 1918, two kinds of fire were foreseen, sustained fire and harassing fire. The latter involved firing 18 to 50 rounds with short intervals. This meant firing over the heads of the German infantry. To avoid causing casualties in the German lines a trouble-free MG and a well trained crew with good knowledge of the terrain were required. These factors seldom coincided; nevertheless the heavy MGs were indispensable in an attack. The training regulations prescribed: "The machine guns subject to availablity must be involved in reducing the enemy superiority of fire power and bringing the attack forward to the enemy positions by pinning down the enemy." They had to be where it was decisive, which in open country could be a problem.

This endeavour had to be carried out with fire support from other weapons as follows. The light MG 08/15 had developed operationally into the mobile main fire power of the infantry companies. Used as the basis for the training of assault troops, from there the assault troop tactic had been worked out. Hopes of success in attempts to penetrate the deep echelons of the enemy defences depended no longer on the attack by light MG troops alone, but their combination with hand grenade-, light mortar- and flamethrower units.

The Machine Gun branch

At the end of the war there were around 2500 MG companies in the German Army, each company being equipped with twelve heavy MGs (up from six in 1914). In addition there were independent MG Abteilungen (= perhaps three companies, no apparent equivalent in English), single companies, platoons and teams. This huge increase was not least a consequence of the constantly growing demand.

As the war went on, machine-gunners were confronted with ever more tasks. These included engaging enemy aircraft flying at low level. An exhibition of this showed the many, often makeshift, gun mounts and sights for anti-aircraft MGs. In August 1917, 25 anti-aircraft MG *Abteilungen* were set up each with 36 MGs plus another 103 independent MG platoons. Equally important was the use of machine-guns

to defend against armoured fighting vehicles known to the British as "tanks". It was the British who had introduced mobile armour to the battlefield precisely as "machine-gun destroyers" in order to overcome MG firepower: and now from the intended victim was born the anti-tank machine-gun with special steel-core ammunition. In 1917 MGs with this type of ammunition were the most important means of combating the tank at close range. In a memorandum on anti-tank work dated 19 August 1918 it was envisaged how several well-camouflaged MGs with a large supply of ammunition (at least 500 rounds SmK) could unleash massed fire against the vulnerable spots of a tank. On 3 September 1918, however, a report by Armee Oberkommando 6 doubted whether SmK ammunition would have the desired effect against the new, improved British tanks. The use of MGs for this purpose therefore remained a solution of last resort.

The Part Played by 3.MG Company/2.Garde-Regt zu Fuss (1.Garde-Inf.Div) in the Battle of Aisne, Spring 1917

Hauptmann H.von Petersdorff, commander of 3.MG Company reported:

"During the first operation of my Company on the Damenweg near Hurtebise Farm between 21 and 28 April 1917, Gefreiter (Private soldier) Ptock distinguished himself in such a manner that he was awarded the Iron Cross, Second Class. There had been frequent shortages of ammunition because insufficient could be brought. Each time, Ptock would step up and fetch the supplies through the Ailette terrain under constant heavy artillery fire (…)

The MG team to which Ptock belonged was positioned with its MG as Company-leader's reserve within the Dragon's Hollow. This feature was occupied by the enemy at their end, and ran mostly below the enemy trenches. Suddenly the enemy saturated the Hollow with gas grenades while putting our exit under heavy fire from rifle-grenades and mine-throwers. At the same time Senegalese troops wearing gas masks and carrying hand grenades tried to force their way though the Hollow. The reserve MG opened fire at once and so kept the enemy at bay. Meanwhile serious disquiet had broken out amongst the reserve batallion lying in the Hollow, for a sly dog who had received a whiff of the gas through his mask shouted out: "We are all done for, the gas is lethal!" This was not the case and the bold MG team stayed by their weapon, supported by a number of wounded lying nearby in a nook. Of these men, the seriously wounded Grenadier Hubert Richter of 1.Company of the Regiment conducted himself outstandingly.

During Operation Semper talis two days later (25 April) leading to the capture of the Hurtebise Farm, Ptock again distinguished himself by his resolution, pluck and calm shooting.

On 28 April my Company was relieved from the advanced front line and placed as reserve for the regimental staff on the Boverücken. On 2 May 1917 my Company had to go forward again. Heavy fire was falling on the position day and night. Endless assaults by hand-grenade troops left our people with no peace, our MG nests in particular had to suffer mines and artillery fire. On 4 May, an MG of my Company led by Gefreiter Willy Ackermann, a man proven in many engagements, received a direct hit by a mine which buried the entire MG team. Rescue attempts began at once but were unsuccessful. The artillery bombardment grew more intense hourly. In the Hollow great blocks of rock were shaken free from the ceiling, our people of the reserve there being buried.

On 5 May the battle began. At ten that morning after hours of artillery bombardment the enemy broke into our sector in thick waves of assault troops. All our MGs became either buried under the rubble or otherwise unserviceable. Before our reserves could be deployed outside the Hollow, the French had already occupied the exits and were throwing hand-grenades down into the shafts. At this dangerous moment, only the reserve MG of Gefreiter Ptock remained serviceable. Not only did he clear a way through the Hollow exits, but he held up the French advance into the Aillette Valley, inflicting heavy losses on their troops.

The enemy now concentrated on Ptock's MG, but cold-blooded as ever under the hail of steel he changed his worn barrel and fired box after box of ammunition until the enemy attack faltered and no further waves ventured up. His MG was then hit and destroyed by a hit from their infantry, Ptock being wounded in the hand. With rapid determination Ptock took up a rifle lying nearby and was intending to fight his way forward when he found in the second crater into which he leapt a light MG in good condition, ready to fire and several boxes of ammunition. At once he took under fire the French troops in the field. The effect of the well-aimed bursts at such short range was devastating. The momentum of the attack was now broken. The enemy half-batallions, advancing from the Aillette terrain towards the Boverücken, also stopped short when they could not see their comrades following. There was no going back for them, they broke up in despair, and those which did not fall into our own hands were soon received behind the wire by our neighbouring sector of 4.Garde-Regiment."

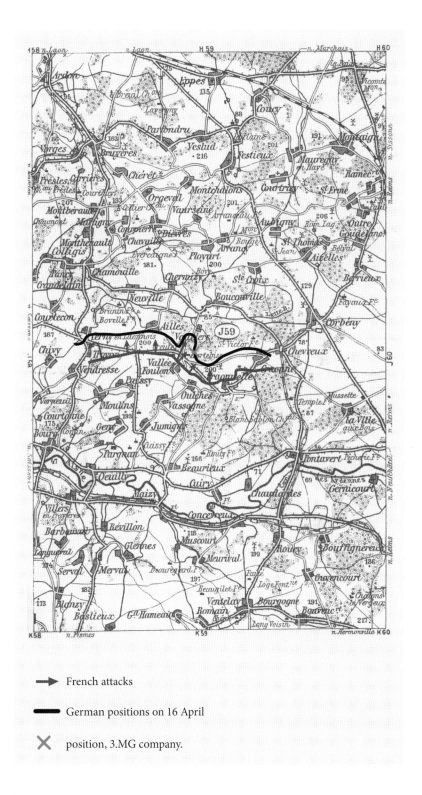

➡ French attacks

▬ German positions on 16 April

✕ position, 3.MG company.

Notes

1. *Gewehrprüfungskommission*, between 1879 and 1920 the authority for the testing and approval of hand firearms.

2. *Feuerzeugmeisterei*, between 1898 and 1919 the authority subordinate to the Royal Prussian War Ministry under the command of a Major-General or Lieutenant-General (the Feldzeugmeister) who handled all matters concerning weapons, ammunition and equipment for the Army.

Chapter Three

TRENCH WARFARE AND GEOLOGY

From "the roundabout way of achieving one's purpose" (Moltke) to the Science of Annihilation.

If there is anything typical of the First World War it is trench warfare. By the beginning of 1915, the war of mobility begun so optimistically on both sides had degenerated into a system of fixed fronts lasting for years and dominating the course of events. In connection with the development of trench warfare, military geology rose in significance as a branch of geology with special emphasis on the earth's crust.

Trench warfare existed in earlier times. It was what General-Feldmarshall Helmuth von Moltke called "the roundabout way of achieving one's purpose." First one used defence for sparing one's energies, and then after that struggle had yielded its advantages, one went over to the attack which consumed one's energies. Looked at in that way, trench warfare was limited by the time factor. Defence was and is not a means to win a war against a stronger foe, but it can break the attacker's strength, or at least weaken it, thus changing the relationship of the respective strengths. The dominating principles before the First World War for the German Army were formulated in the *275 Feld-Pionierdienst aller Waffen* outline of 12 December 1911:

> *Field fortifications make it easier for weaker forces to resist a stronger opponent in order to attack him later elsewhere with stronger forces; to gain time or hold an important location. They make it possible to hold captured areas, and establish departure points for later attacks.(…) Moreover they do not need to influence the decision-making of commanders, especially not to impede the joy of the unstoppable advance or become the grave of aggressive thinking.*

This over-emphasis on offensive thinking was not unique to the plans of the German military. A whole-hearted attacking spirit dominated the military thinking in other armies. Nevertheless by the end of 1914 trench warfare had arrived at every front, introducing the struggle to hold bits of territory and positions which had been reached in the war of mobility without having the ability to be decisive.

The Failure of the War of Mobility

At the beginning of September 1914 the German offensive came to grief on the Marne. After that, the hope of a quick victory receded into the far distance. The war of mobility continued only towards the north-west, the opposing belligerents reaching the North Sea coast more or less in a state of exhaustion after two battles in Flanders (end October/beginning November 1914). Under its new commander-in-chief General Erich von Falkenhayn, the German Supreme Army Command held fast to the idea of breaking through to Calais. That led to the first Battle of Ypres in the course of which it became clear that the German Army was no longer capable of achieving the aim. The Allied defenses proved stronger …

The thrust and energy of the attack was expended in the tactical area before a decision could be forced in the operational respect. The strength of the defences lay above all in the firepower of their machine-guns, of which both

A battlefield after weeks of artillery shelling. The trench frontline is difficult to make out.

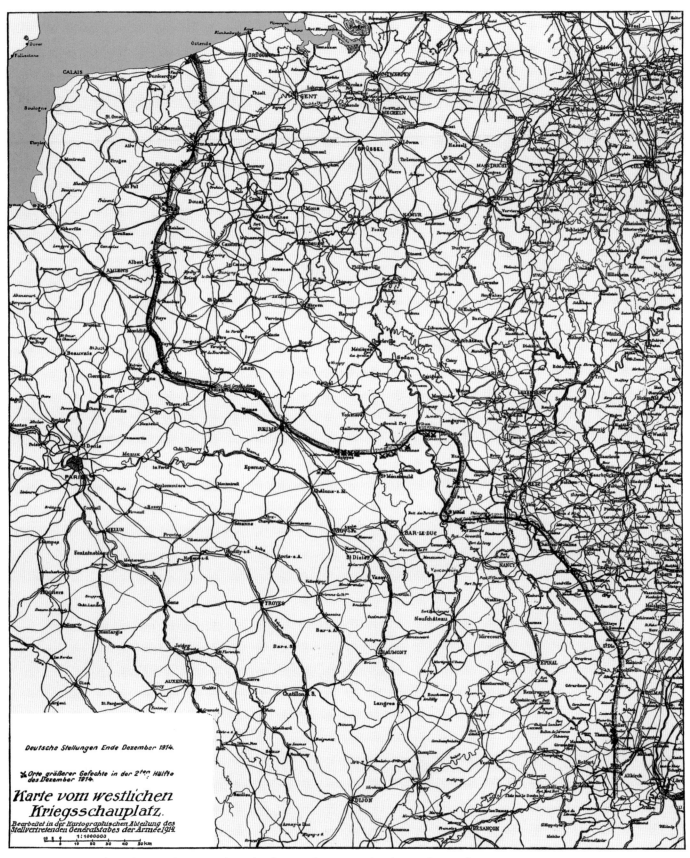

Map of the Western front showing the extent of trenches forming the German frontline, end December 1914.

the French and German infantry regiments had only one MG Company each at the outbreak of war. These were installed with forethought on the battlefield and skilfully camouflaged.

Another strength was the hidden artillery. Means of detecting its position such as identification by light and sound did not exist at this time. Lucky hits were the only way of knocking out artillery and therefore had no lasting effect on their ability to participate in defensive fighting.

At the Battle of the Aisne on 13/14 September 1914, the German 1st and 2nd armies went on the defensive and, not least by means of numerous local counter-attacks, repulsed British and French attacks. At that, on the night of 13 September the French commander-in-chief, General Joseph Joffre, ordered "… since it is now a matter of methodical attack (i.e. attacks on a fortified position -Author) as soon as each position is captured, it must be fortified." This order marked the beginning of trench warfare.

Once the fronts had reached the North Sea coast, the threat from the flanks disappeared.

Since the wars of mediaeval times, field commanders had always aimed to go about the enemy flanks and so attack from the rear. The German Army training regulation of 29 May 1906 mentioned why that also had validity currently for the massed army of the present: "With good use of its firearms the infantry at the frontline is very strong and requires relatively fewer men there. Its weakness is in the flanks." Trench warfare with its endless frontline had no flanks, and this strengthened the defences.

However, the defences suffered heavy losses; many of the German units had lost half their operational strength by mid-September 1914. This was on account of tactics learnt in peacetime but no longer valid because of machine-guns; by advancing in fixed lines frontally combined with the lack of staggering and camouflage, troops were exposed to the full force of enemy fire.

Latterly the greater firepower proved advantageous for the tactical defence and influenced manpower needs. The enemy had

Infantry of 26 Reserve-Div. during the fighting in the winter of 1914 at Artois, west of Bapaume. As laid down in the infantry training manual, the troops are moving up uniformly and together, heading directly for the objective and maintaining contact with each other, a tactic no longer current at that time. From a sketch by Helmuth Stockmann, published in the *Illustrierten Zeitung Leipzig* No. 3747 (War issue No. 38), 22 April 1915.

first to overcome the staggered trench system: that was and remained the aim in the West: the related problems were little changed in principle throughout the war.

Necessity dictated the composition of the forces for attack. In order to give the initial onslaught the necessary weight, infantry and artillery units had to be combined in large numbers. This ruled out the element

German infantry excavating a dug-out. Its position and measurements correspond to field fortifications of the pre-war period. A photograph from the autumn of 1914.

German trench with shelter and earthed-up parapet. Photo from spring 1915.

Construction soldiers during a rest break. They belonged to the military workforce and were formed up into units at the outbreak of war. Their "weapon" in trench warfare was the spade, ten million of which were issued to the German Army in the First World War.

of surprise. In April 1917 before the French could move out of their 100-kilometres long sector near Soissons and launch an attack east to Rheims, they had to assemble 1.5 million soldiers, 3,300 guns and 200 assault vehicles. They used 33 million rounds of artillery in an unbroken barrage over a ten day period to "soften up" the German trenches. The attack began on 16 April but collapsed completely in the face of the defensive fire. The Germans had noticed the build-up for the attack early on and strengthened their defences accordingly. This example shows that the defences had sufficient time for counter-measures, to strengthen the trench lines in depth, for camouflage, to bring up reserves and to prepare everything at the expected focal points of the attack. Even the ammunition supplies were adequate. Incidentally the shortage of ammunition in the first year of the war had occasionally been the cause of a damping down of the fighting. The peacetime supplies were expended and the growing demand outstripped the fresh supplies. This was also a factor favouring the freezing of the fronts and the transition to trench warfare.

At a Loss in the Face of the Circumstances: The Strategy of Attrition

The opposing forces lacked means and ways to bring about a quick and definitive military outcome. The former art of war failed them. In its place came battles of war materials. These continued to grow in size but failed to deliver the success hoped for. The crisis point to which the art of war had now come, with what perplexity the participants gazed upon the circumstances, can be summed up by the decision of the German Supreme Army Command to attack the French at Verdun.

Behind the French sector of the Western Front there are reachable goals for us which the French High Command is obliged to defend to the last man. If they do so, French manpower will bleed out, for they cannot avoid defending it irrespective of whether we reach it or not. If they do not defend it and it falls into our hands, the effect on morale in France will be enormous."

Erich von Falkenhayn.

Both Supreme Army Command under von Falkenhayn and the Allies miscalculated with their repeated attacks in Flanders and on the Somme. Both sides sustained very heavy losses. Advantage lay with the side which had the greater reserves, and that was the Entente. This art of warfare involved a war of attrition which aimed to exhaust the enemy's fighting strength. The decisive area of the war was shifted to other fields – to the politicians, industry and morale. In fact, all efforts to revive the war of mobility failed. In the West all the Entente achieved was to force back the German lines frontally from September 1918.

Elements of Trench Warfare

a. *"Stellungsbau"*

The German word "Stellung" in military terminology, strictly a "tactical position", has various meanings:

1. Every tract of territory, every locality including a village or town, where a German unit was fighting. Every advance and retreat, every lateral shift of position was a change of "Stellung".
2. It also meant any place where German troops were assembled to engage the enemy, such as an interception-position, readiness-position, flanking position or a barrage-position.
3. In the sense of a field fortification, "Stellung" also meant a more or less expanded defensive position suitable for holding in the longer term (Stellungskrieg=positional warfare). Initially infantry slit trenches would be dug. These would be gradually extended and interconnected. A continuous line would not come into being until the war of mobility had been abandoned. If time was available, strongpoints would be built for heavy infantry weapons, MG nests and artillery emplacements. In principle these would be free of standardisation schemes and designed to suit the tactical situation and terrain. The positions for artillery had to be surveyed. Obstacles had to be erected to protect the positions, bunkers, shelters, communication and

access trenches, drainage ditches etc. The positions laid out initially formed the basis for the main battle front, but in order to conceal its actual course from the enemy and disperse his fire, advanced trenches would be dug with outposts. The choice of every position was carefully weighed with regard to tactical considerations, for example on a forward facing slope or a back slope. Water courses, swamps or precipitous slopes offered additional protection. Blocking trenches running diagonally on the flanks provided additional lateral defence against penetration of the defensive system by enemy forces. Rearward trenches were laid five kilometres behind the foremost line, committing the attacker to new, time-consuming advances of his artillery. The forward trenches were manned relatively thinly, but in strength in the deeper echelons. Normally, everyday life in trench warfare was quiet, bellicose activity was limited to reciprocal unrest. Small scale operations were launched mainly as armed reconnaissance or to obtain local advantages.

In the winter of 1914 the trenches fell far short of these yardsticks. During the bitter fighting in the Champagne from 16 February to 16 March 1915 for example, the German defenders occupied trenches of defective construction and not interconnected in the deeper field. Nevertheless VIII.Army and VIII Reserve Corps were able to resist the attacks of the French 4.Army. In this case, however, the artillery played a major part in the succesful German defence by accurately targeting the attackers' exit points.

b. *Infantry trenches*
In the pre-war service instructions a distinction was made between infantry trenches for kneeling and standing riflemen. The former would have a depth between 90 centimetres and 1.1 metres, the latter 1.4 metres. For upper body protection, bulwarks for breast and back were designed. Shoulder bulwarks at distances of from eight to ten metres were to be laid to protect the trench occupants against flanking

fire, but also shell splinters and hand grenades. These would usually be installed when the trench was dug, but if not sandbags, boxes, baskets or barrels filled with earth, gravel or stones could be added later. If enough time and building materials were available, trenches would be reinforced with shelters. Where building materials were in short supply, it was left to the troops to improve their cover by excavating protective niches. There were also cover trenches and communication trenches. Cover trenches, dug about fifty metres behind the foremost front line, accommodated the complement of the foremost trenches in platoon strength. The communication trenches connected the infantry and cover trenches with the observer and field-telephone centres, the medical posts and the batallion commander's observation post laid much farther back.

Interestingly, even in 1915 field fortifications were still not considered a connected line but as independent group positions (batallion groups), although the trend was to pay heed to the changed circumstances, and reaction followed. Defensive installations were "in trench warfare (…) to be arranged in depth, i.e. several trenches (at least two) to be dug one behind the other." The forward line was now the battle trench, if possible 2.5 metres deep,

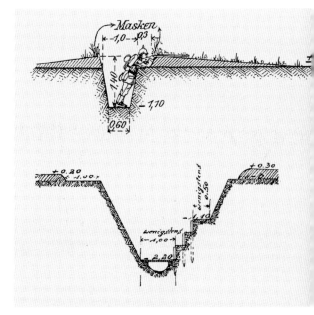

Comparison of infantry trench 1914 (above) and 1916 (below). (Masken=masking vegetation: wenigstens=at least)

The fitting out of infantry trenches took many forms depending amongst other things on the tactical situation, the lie of the land and vegetation, and the ground conditions. (Photo centre right reads "Infantry trench 40 metres from the enemy).

German infantry trench with 5-cm cannon in armoured cupola with chassis and captured Russian Maxim "Modell 1911" machine-gun. The photograph was taken in May 1916 on the Western Front near St. Hubert. The German Army administration ordered 200 of these armoured cupola from the Magdeburg firm Gruson in 1890. Originally intended for fortress defence, after the outbreak of war they became surplus to requirements. A large number of them were used as anti-assault guns in the trenches.

Schematic representation of an infantry trench with communication and cover trenches. (Wolfsgruben= see chapter footnote) Horchposten=listening post: Unterstände=protected rooms: Beobachtungsstand=spotter post: Bombensicherer Unterstand=bomb-proof bunker: Abort=toilet: Verbandsraum=dressing station: Verbindungsgraben= communication trench: Munitionsraum: magazine: Offiziers Unterstand=officers protected room: Fernsprecher-Stelle=telephone post: Deckungsgraben=cover trenches: Wohn und Schlafraum=living and sleeping quarters: Zugangs-Strasse=access road

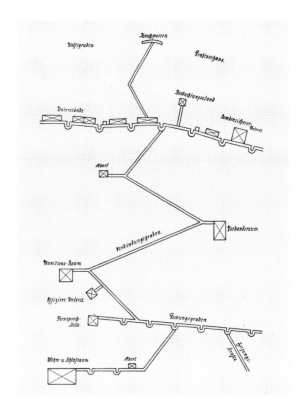

one metre wide at the foot and over two metres wide at the parapet. The cover trenches lay farther back and received defensive installations and protected rooms.

There were traffic trenches and accommodation trenches. In principle when trenches were being dug, long straight lines were to be avoided. The "closed-up flanking of all parts possible of our positions" took on great importance. This was the path towards the goal. This goal was clearly formulated in Part 1a "General Matters Regarding Construction of Positions" in the *Sammelhefte von Vorschriften für den Stellungskrieg*, issue of 13 November 1916:[1] "In principle, the terrain is to be defended using all natural advantages (villages, woodlands, quarries, ravines etc) so that stubbornly defended sectors are fortified in such depth that the loss or abandonment of individual parts does not endanger the

Where possible, mainly in the hinterland, machines were used for trench digging. The photograph shows a French excavator.

overall situation. On the side nearest the enemy a deeply staggered and strongly developed position is to be created. It will consist of a trench system of several interconnected and non-parallel lines at distances of between 150 to 300 metres. The lines are interconnected by numerous communications trenches. Approach trenches, of which there cannot be too many, provide the connection from the rear. All trenches are to be laid in such a way that the enemy cannot possibly see into them from any angle. A limited field of fire suffices."

Back slope positions, therefore positions close behind the line of the horizon, were preferred since they were out of the line of sight of enemy artillery spotters. There were naturally exceptions – one of these was the observer posts for the German artillery, which would then have to be laid on the slope facing the enemy. This meant that the foremost infantry trenches had also to be laid on the front slope with the second and third line of the trench system farther back.

Machine-guns were of great importance to protect the infantry. The previously mentioned regulations stated: "The skeletal structure of all infantry battle lines are the MG sites and protected rooms. 100 metres or less suffices for the frontal field of fire. The concealed MGs must be able to fire on the obstacles and the area in front of them as well as between the individual lines and flanking positions, and if possible over them all, and should be sited accordingly in the field."

The improved quality of the positions can now be seen clearly. The defensive power to resist was no longer based on the building up of the most forward front line, which generally tended to be flattened by the enemy artillery in the softening up period before an attack. Because trenches to the rear were on the whole not exposed in this way, it was these which were built up to accommodate most of the crews including the MGs.

c. *Sappen*

The word *Sappen* means a short trench dug towards the enemy's position, frequently to instal a listening post. In trench warfare there were many variations, but all from the most advanced front line into No-Man's Land. Makeshift *Sappen* were created by burrowing and using the disturbed earth as a cover. Others intended to be of longer term duration would have protection in the form of wattle or boarding along the trench walls. At the trench head the listening post would need particular protection provided by armoured cupolas or armour shielding.

d. *Protected Rooms*

In contrast to hastily erected refuges, protected rooms were built to be splinter-, shell or bomb-proof. For protection against shell- and bomb hits, there were two possibilities: rooms dug up to five metres deep or concrete subterranean bunkers. The former were laid as galleries lined with aprons of wood in layers or corrugated sheet iron. The disadvantages of these rooms lay in their depth in the ground, which made rapid evacuation difficult for the crew: additionally they were exposed to the

Dimensions of principal building materials for excavated protected rooms/bunkers

Description	Bomb-proof observation post with protection for the head against splinters	Concrete bunker
dimensions (length x breadth x height)	2000 x 800 x 1700 mm	4000 x 2900 x 2000 mm
concrete/reinforced concrete	36 m³	155 m³
Corrugated iron, bent	–	8 piece
Corrugate iron, straight	–	12 m²
carrier	40 m railway metals	50 m T-carrier N.P.20
planking	1.5 m²	–
armour sheet	–	1 piece

"Heavy MG 08" bedded on improvised turntable in an underground room.

Protected position for a Heavy MG 08 " operated seated, room 1914 (left). Box for ammunition belt was at "a": "b" is a flattened hollow: the hatched area is raised ground providing protection. For comparison, sketches of a 1916 bomb-proof MG post (top sketch right) and another with removable armour plate (bottom sketch right).

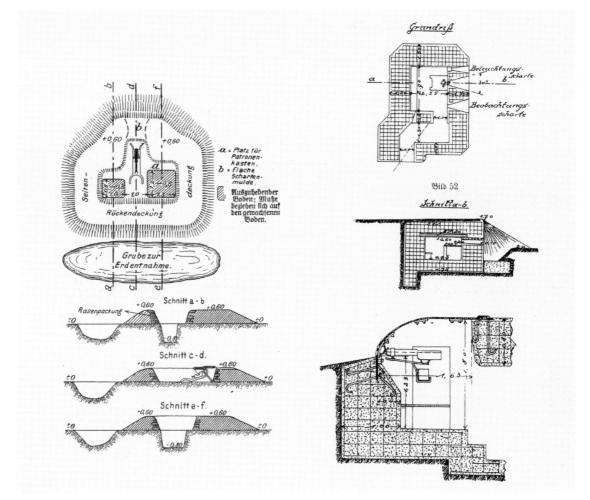

Protected storage for a heavy MG in a niche in the trench wall.

Group fighting position, 47.Landwehr-Division near the Aisne. This back-slope situation was advantageous.

Sappen trench-head showing observation post with protective shield of rolled steel 6 mm thick and weighing 13.2 kgs. It came in various versions.

A large concrete underground bunker under construction in the Vosges. Concrete structures provided very good protectioon against the effects of artillery. Photograph taken in 1915.

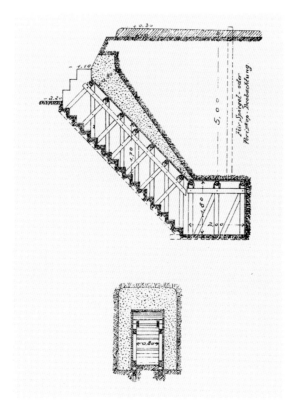

Sketch of a subterranean bunker with concrete exit and fitting for observation periscope.

Protected artificial cave of corrugated iron sheets and sandbags. Photo taken on 17 September 1916 in the position "Warsaw" in Flanders.

danger that the entrance could be buried under earthspill and rubble.

The occupants of underground concrete bunkers, even better if it was reinforced concrete, had the advantage of quicker readiness for action. This had to be weighed against the greater expense of construction, for example the cost of transporting-in the various building materials including wood for the shoring up and water, which also had to be brought in.

Schurzholz (wooden aprons) came in three sizes: (Size I) 80 cms broad x 1.2 metres high and 50 mms thick: (Size II) 80 cms x 1.6 metres x 60 mms thick: (Size III) 1.2 metres x 1.8 metres x 80 mms thick. Aprons were manufactured in the pioneer park and delivered. Four to seven aprons were required for each metre of gallery. Corrugated iron sheeting was between 80 cms and 1.25 metres broad and 1.2 to 1.3 metres high.

The Engineee Committee issued a *Betonierungsanleitung für das Feld* (Manual for Concrete Structures in the Field) on 21 July 1917. In the forward lines generally, posts or protected rooms of concrete, iron or beams were favoured which offered space to only a limited number of men. In the lines to the rear deeply excavated installations able to accommodate a large complement – one to two groups – were preferred but which in all cases had to be combined with fighting posts. Here the danger of being buried under the debris caused by artillery fire was not so great as in the forward lines. Large protected rooms offered more comfort and better living conditions. "With regard to the health and inner feeling of security of the fighting troops this is of an importance not be underestimated," the manual advised. Each man should have 1.5 square metres room, and if possible be able to rest on plank beds, mattresses or in hammocks. There should be internal comforts with pasteboard or corrugated iron, flooring, ovens, chimneys, ventilation piping, benches, tables and the like. Iron rations for six to ten days were to be stored: a nearby spring was desirable. It had proved advantageous to have the field kitchen in bomb-proof rooms, and the same went for the dressing-stations and magazines. Besides good protection and the

Everyday life for soldiers on a quiet sector of the front. In the background is a concrete bunker for the crew.

best view over the battlefield sector, company and batallion command posts should guarantee good connections to all subordinate units. The infantry and artillery used *ground observation posts*. These had to be concealed especially carefully while being bomb-proof and offering a good vision.

Great value was placed on the arrangement of the protected rooms with a view to

German concrete bunker in Flanders destroyed by French artillery. Photo taken on 15 August 1917.

immediate defence. This purpose was served
by MG posts and stretches of trench. Since
these needed to be bomb-proof they were rarely
situated in the most forward line. Therefore
machine guns were set up in protected
partitions in the parapets where they had at
least some degree of protection against artillery.
When the enemy launched an infantry attack,
the MG crew would bring the gun to the most
secure position against rifle fire. MG posts
proof against bomb- and rifle-fire were situated
in a flanking position set well back but in an
advantageous position as regards their field of
fire.

e. Artillery positions

The importance of artillery grew constantly
in the First World War. The great increase in
casualties it inflicted was caused primarily by
its mass effect and secondly by a lengthening of
the range. This effect and the grouping together
of large numbers of guns made it a preferred
target for the enemy. Artillery emplacements
were selected for tactical criteria based on the
guns but taking into account the possibilities
of protection for field guns, howitzers and

15-cm heavy howitzer of a Landwehr foot-artillery
batallion in a firing position. Photograph taken at the
beginning of the war.

mortars. The previously mentioned manual
Vorschriften für den Stellungskrieg issued on
13 November 1916 prescribed: "The artillery
must be set up at a favourable distance from
the enemy corresponding to the operational
purpose. It must be able to fire deeply behind
the enemy's lines. The great range of our guns
should not result in the artillery being placed
well to the rear, but on the other hand the

German 10.5-cm
light howitzer
98/08 in an open
position destroyed by
enemy artillery.

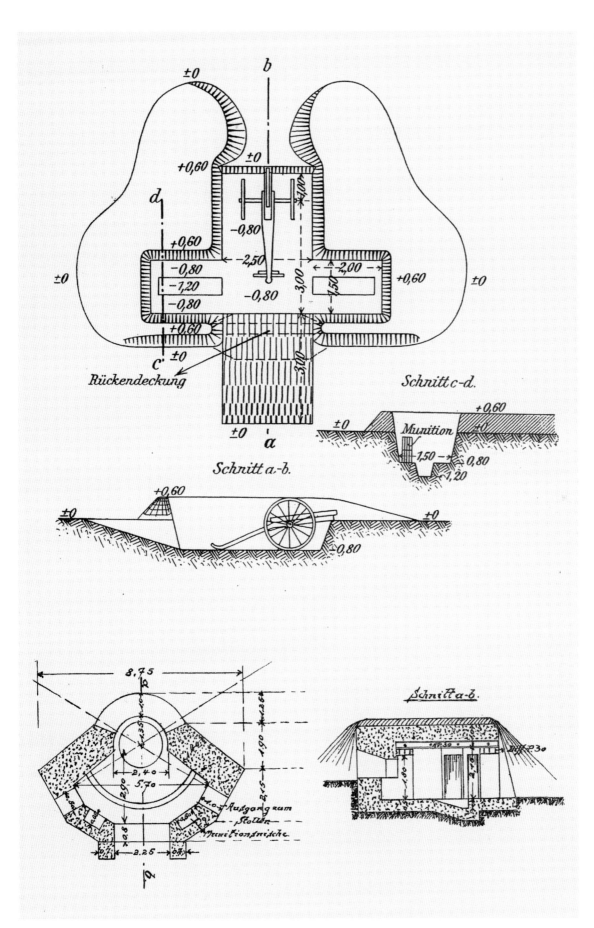

Comparison of gun emplacements for 7.7-cm light field gun, above in 1914, below in 1916.

Concrete emplacement for a 10.5-cm light field howitzer after completion and after installation of the gun. Emplacements of this kind offered good protection but needed careful camouflage. The range was limited.

Concrete gun emplacements were also used by the naval artillery on the Flanders coast.

"There should be internal comforts of pasteboard or corrugated iron, flooring, ovens, chimneys, ventilation piping, benches, tables and the like."

batteries should not lie within the spread of artillery fire aimed at the infantry. Protection suitable to the terrain, especially shell- and bomb-proof structures for the gun crews and ammunition, are necessary."

It was worth the effort to construct battery positions using concrete and camouflage, protected behind obstacles with the guns spaced irregularly. At the same time each battery was to be arranged with an eye to close defence, which became problematical against tanks. This required the siting of some guns detached from the main position so as to fire from open ground. For artillery battles, alternative positions had to be prepared in advance, and basically this also applied to observer posts.

f. Obstacles

Obstacles proved their military worth in past wars, particularly in fortress warfare. They are mentioned again in the D.V.E. No.275 Field-Pioneer Service of all Weapons, outline of 12 December 1911: wire obstructions, tree- and

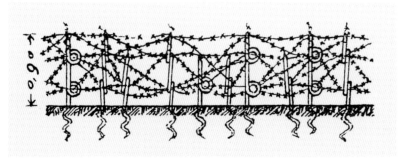

Barbed wire entanglement with iron screw-in stakes. These often had to be installed under the close and watchful eye of the enemy. To screw-in the stakes, an iron bar was inserted through the eye and turned. This also had to be done lying down.

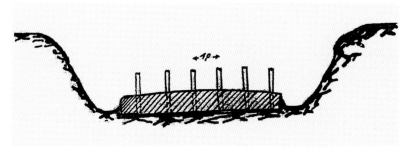

Tank trap of upright railway metals embedded in concrete.

branch entanglements, trenches, Wolfsgruben,[2] water dams, makeshift barricades (waggons, furniture, agricultural equipment) and mines with a time fuze, the so-called "Fladdermines".

Barbed wire fencing was relatively recent. It came into use in the mid-19th century in the United States to enclose cattle pasture and had awakened the attention of the military. From then on it belonged to the arsenal of fortress warfare. It rose to great importance in the First World War, during the course of which it was used in great quantities. Unlike tree and branch entanglements it was not dependent on vegetation. At the beginning of the war simple and reinforced wire obstacles were known, the latter being of stakes 1.5 to 2 metres tall laid irregularly across a terrain up to ten metres wide. Also used were wire hedges and – to close the gaps – rolls of barbed wire.

From this comparatively modest beginning, during the war an effective obstruction of wire staking was adopted. Wooden stakes only 50 to 90 cms in length were linked to iron screw-in stakes. This kind of obstruction was usually set up about 40 metres ahead of the German most advanced lines.

There would be several strips five to ten metres wide linked to each other by diagonal fencing: there were even laid in the depths of the German trench system.

Other uses for wire and barbed wire were as snares and mantraps while wire rolls were made up in the pioneer parks into *Spanish riders*[3] and the roof-shaped Lochmann fast-wire obstacles. They were also stockpiled in the parks. To prevent enemy egress by water, wire obstacles were erected on rafts which froze in winter. Wire grilles facing towards the enemy but slanting back were designed to prevent hand grenades from entering a trench. Experiments were also made to electrify wire obstacles.

In view of the wire development, tree- and branch entanglements lost in importance. They were in any case too susceptible to artillery fire. As a completion measure for all common obstacles, remotely detonated observation mines were recommended. Their construction, maintenance and detonation remained the province of the pioneers. Mines with self-activated detonators had apparently not proved

German trench with shallow depth barbed wire entanglements.

British Mk-IV tank (female) overturned in a camouflaged trap laid in a German trench system.

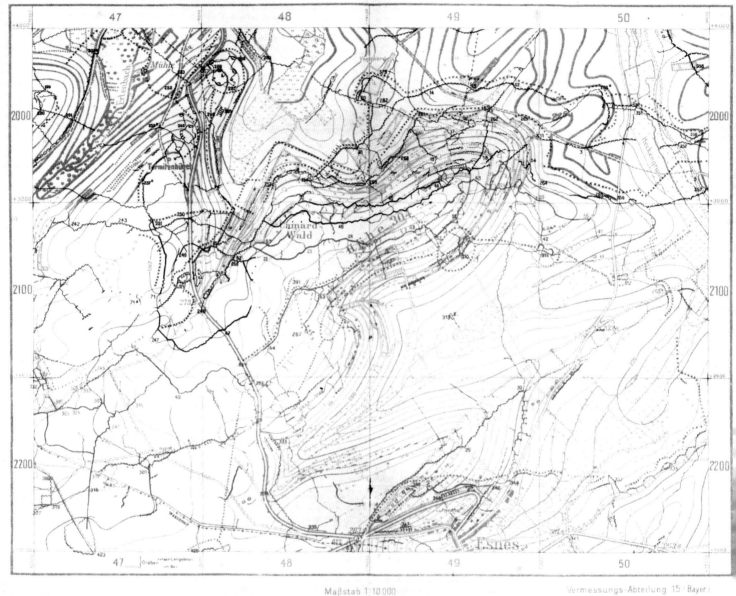

Bavarian Survey Detachment-15 map showing the German and French trench systems around Height 304 north of Verdun, situation as at 31 May 1916. 54.Infantry-Division fought here from 18th to 29 May.

a viable proposition although this was blamed on their tendency to detonate during heavy shelling by enemy artillery.

A favourable new role for mines arrived with the introduction of the tank since tank attacks were not preceeded by artillery shelling to soften-up the enemy positions. In the summer of 1918 there were two types of anti-tank mine at the front: *Holzkisten*, wood boxes containing a mine (the medium heavy type fired by a mortar) with trigger detonator, and *Blechkästen*, waterproof metal cans with a battery charge weighing 15 to 30 kgs with pressure detonator.

Other devices for passive anti-tank work were kilometre-long trenches with almost vertical walls, three to four metres wide and up to four metres deep, but these could be overcome by tank crews by the use of thick bundles of fascines.[4] Many ideas existed for making barriers: for example, six railway metals in concrete and not protruding more that 75 cms, and finally camouflaged tank traps or exploding craters.

g. Mine Warfare

Mine warfare was also a part of fortress warfare especially from the end of the 17th century. The opponents went through tunnels towards each other; the attackers intent upon blowing up defensive positions, the defenders set upon stopping them. It was practised on the large scale in the First World War. Part 2 of the German manual *Sammelhefte von Vorschriften für den Stellungskrieg* under the heading "Mine warfare" and issued on 19 April 1916 states: "If the distance from the enemy and the ground- and water circumstances are favourable for an underground operation, the possibility of an encmy mine attack must be borne in mind. The only defence is a mine system developed to plan with an advanced tunnel and at its head a listening gallery." It was quite wrong to wait until the enemy had extended his tunnels below the German position: "It is very important to deprive him of first claim and to tunnel under his own position in order to blow it up. The mine attack is the best defence."

In order to achieve that, several more or less parallel tunnels would be bored and lined with wooden panels to prevent cave-ins. These tunnels would be connected by galleries running at right angles. This work exposed the pioneers to great physical and mental pressure on account of the heavy manual labour required in the very narrow tunnels, the poor lighting and ventilation and the constant fear of being buried alive.

Once the tunnelling was concluded, the demolition chambers would be filled with powerful explosive charges. In general the weight of these varied from 0.8 to 13.4 tonnes, but charges of 20 tons and over occurred occasionally. The German side mainly used a safety explosive, but employed sometimes the more difficult to handle black powder,

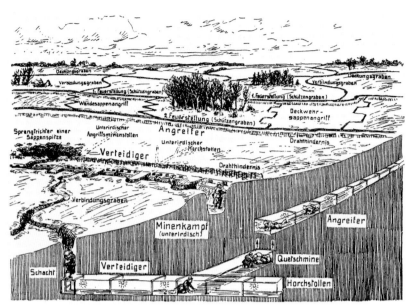

Simplified representation of mine warfare in the trenches on the Western front.

or a 1:1 mixture of the two. For better effect *Sprengkörper* 88 or 02 would be added. Large charges were packed in waterproof individual parcels each weighing 25 kgs. Then the demolition chambers would be sealed off with sandbags. Detonation was performed electrically by wire. To provide an example the 0.8-tonne charge would create a crater of 21 metres diameter and ten metres deep. This would be immediately attacked by stormtroops and developed for defence purposes. By 1916 the German side did not have any extensive

A French pioneer officer listening to German tunnelling work. Through the stethoscope he could pick up vibrations and the echo audible underground.

Crater caused by an underground mine, a photograph from the year 1916. Notice its dimensions in relation to the makeshift shelter at the nearer edge of the crater.

A German listening post. Listening equipment would enable even enemy conversations to be overheard. The most important work, however, was to monitor the progress of the enemy's tunnelling.

experience with the use of liquid air. The lack of poisonous explosive battlefield gases and the low price were seen as advantageous, the difficulty in handling a disadvantage.

Listening observers played a special role in mine warfare. Their reports provided information on enemy tunnelling activity and enabled counter-measures – the setting off of collapsing mines – to be undertaken. The operators used amplifying apparatus to hear sounds at long distance; at the *sappen*-head stethoscopes or listening equipment of the Edelmann, Schmidtmann, Knieriem or Waetzmann systems were employed to hear sounds at distances up to 80 metres.

An idea of the drama of mine warfare is conveyed by a report appearing in the August 1936, of the magazine *Kriegskunst in Wort und Bild*:

"In May 1917, Saxon Pioneer Company 324 at the Yser Canal near Ypres was given the task of tunnelling. Tunnelling activity was lively from friend and foe; every week smaller or larger explosions took place.

On 5 May, 2.platoon of the Company was in the foremost trenches under the command of its livewire leader, Sergeant Max Pucklitsch (…) 2.Platoon had orders to dig defensive tunnels and listen out for enemy tunnelling so as to warn the Württembergers in the surface position against surprise explosions. (…) He himself (i.e. Pucklitsch-the author) was at the very head of our tunnel where he had set up the listening equipment. He was just about to make a fresh attempt at listening when the iron tip of the listening device encountered resistance in the otherwise soft ground. Upon investigation he found sandbags which could only have been placed there by the enemy. These were carefully removed and large explosive charges found with 12 detonator caps and detonating wires ready for use. A terrible danger for the infantry in the trenches above and the pioneers working under the ground below!

Sergeant Pucklitsch did not panic. Calmly and with a clear head he followed his training. First he cut the wiring himself and removed the dangerous detonator caps. That cleared the greatest danger. Then he carefully removed the explosive charge, about twelve metric hundredweight of it. The pioneers now came to more sandbags protecting the enemy tunnel. Pucklitsch moved these only far enough to create a crack between the sandbags so that he could see into the tunnel.

Whilst dismantling the sandbag barrier there was a draught of wind which attracted the attention of two enemy pioneers, who approached cautiously. At that moment the remaining sandbags fell forward leaving Pucklitsch and his pioneers facing the enemy, who quickly retraced their footsteps to a refuge in their tunnel.

What should Pucklitsch do now? Penetrate deeper into the enemy tunnel? That seemed fairly pointless and would not bring any great result. Pucklitsch decided quickly that before counter-measures could be taken it was best to blow up the enemy tunnels from his own tunnel which ran on below the enemy position.

The decision was bold and Pucklitsch went to work with caution. It was clear to the platoon leader that he could not do it all by himself fifteen metres below ground. He reported his decision at once to the infantry holding the position on the surface and to the commander of his Company, requesting approval for his plan. Meanwhile he made all the preparations himself.

Pucklitsch had some of his men occupy the enemy tunnel, but had shooting windows created between the sandbag wall for his pioneers to keep the enemy back with rifle fire. In haste the pioneers then dragged the enemy explosive to the head of their own tunnel to join six hundredweights of their own explosive. All the pioneers worked feverishly while up to the ankles in water.

Finally everything was ready. The infantry above notified that they were in agreement with the plan and had abandoned their trench, but so far Company had not given permission (…) Sergeant Pucklitsch therefore took it upon himself to detonate the explosive! It was audacious, showed his readiness to accept responsibility and was also within the terms of his instructions – his task was to protect the German infantry against enemy subterranean explosions, and that he was now about to do to the best of his ability by beating the enemy tunnellers to it.

Sergeant Pucklitsch detonated the explosive! With a gigantic tumult his powerful charges went up and destroyed a substantial part of the enemy position."

Geology Affecting Military Operations

Military geology, *Wehrgeologie* in German, is, like military geography, an area of military science. The idea behind it is to make geological knowledge useful for military purposes. The principles were laid primarily in the 19th century, and the first positive application was inspired by Russian officers during the Russo-Japanese War of 1904/1905.

"Take care what you say in conversation! !The enemy is listening!"

At the outbreak of the First World War, the German Army had made no preparations to use geology in warfare. The geologist Major Dr.W.Kranz wrote in 1918: "At the end of 1912, on the basis of many years' practical application of geological knowledge in fortress construction, I submitted an official proposal for the permanent employment of military geologists in the construction, maintenance and defence of permanent fortifications. When at the beginning of 1914 the Army considered whether to allocate part of its budget to geologists, they could not see the need, for they thought that even in trench warfare events would happen so quickly that the attachment of a geologist did not enter the question. Events were to contradict this objection fundamentally."

Therefore such military-geological activity as there was collapsed with the freezing of the fronts into trench warfare in the late autumn of 1914. From the autumn of 1916 geologists were attached to the War Survey Service (*Kriegsvermessungswesen*)and subordinated to Staff officers for survey duty with the Army High Commands. Until the war ended, survey posts existed at Command level for leading geologists, who were also competent for the specialized leadership of the geological posts at Army Corps and Divisions. Moreover geologists were to be found in independent survey detachments. If required, groups of geologists would be positioned along the front

The Messines Crater

One event convinced the German Army in hindsight of the need for military-geological advice: the subterranean explosions by the British at the Wyschaete Bend on the Flanders Front near the Belgian village of Messines. The British had succeeded in undermining the German positions. They had dug 25 tunnels – for this purpose they forming special Companies of mineworkers – and filled the chambers with a total of 538.2 tonnes of explosive. These were detonated on 7 June 1917, nineteen of the charges (420.3 tonnes) being exploded. The trench system above it was totally pulverized. Although the Entente was not able to break through on the Ypres Front, the experience made a lasting impression. The small lake which formed in the crater is still there today. Thirty-eight years afterwards in 1955, one of the charges which had failed to go off in 1917 finally exploded.

and in advisory posts. These included experts in spring- and hydraulic engineering, well-borers and sketch artists. At the same time preparations were made to attach the military-geological structures to the pioneer arm. The latter drew the greatest help from their work.

A report by the head of the *Kriegsvermessungswesen*, Major (General Staff) S.Boelcke in September 1917 makes clear the reason for the change: in the Staffs and at the fronts it was being recognized that in trench warfare the nature of the ground was an important tactical factor. Military-geological knowledge as to the favourability of ground conditions simplified the selection and construction of positions and installations of all kinds. This led to a savings in work costs, made for reductions in the workforce while building materials could be found and utilized in the area surrounding the position. Mine warfare would not have been possible without geological knowledge. The following examples make no claim to being comprehensive, but provide an idea of the significance which applied military-geology achieved in war policy.

a. Determination of the physical nature of the rock(-types), of the rock strata, tectonic disturbances, of the steadfastness of the soil, water courses and the possibilities of workability. These were important for all structures, not only trenches and protected rooms or for mine warfare. The laying of roads and paths, tracks for the field railways, airfields, artifical swamps and water obstacles, the bedplates and platforms for heavy and the heaviest guns and mortars; all these were dependent on this science.

b. Knowledge of the behaviour of the various types of rock and earth surfaces under artillery fire.

The effect of shells on various types of ground and soil were influenced by the fuze (impact or delay types). Independently, swamps and morasts, soft sand and loam weakened the explosive effects while firm sand, shingle, firm matrix, hard loam and clay reinforced them. On the other hand, deeply excavated bunkers in the rock were not frequent victims to artillery while the splinter effect on this bedrock was outstanding.

c. Knowledge pertaining to the soil layers provided information as to the distribution of ground water. This showed that trench laying was not to be planned on the basis of tactical considerations alone. Measures for obtaining potable and other usable water (e.g. for concrete mixing) as well as ways of clearing ground water from the trenches and flood precautions could be deduced.

d. Obtaining raw- and building materials to construct a position, including natural rock, bricks, clay and cement was also dependent on the composition of the terrain. Fossil fuels were also required to heat the countless bunkers, protected rooms and other shelters in the front area. Because of high transport costs only exceptionally would these be shipped in from the rearward areas. The help of geologists was needed for a search in the immediate vicinity, to assess the quality and device the means of extraction.

e. The results of the geological survey regarding the conductivity of the sub-strata were of great interest to the signals corps. Of primary importance were the requirements of ground telegraphy (Etel) in which electric current was energized over two poles and could be detected at some distance by sensitive equipment. Most suitable were constantly damp strata of rock thinly spread on, below or near dry rock. In the deployment of landlines for telephonic conversations one had to be aware that when the water level was high a far greater range was possible, but the enemy could still overhear. Before laying telephone and telex lines the advice of geologists would be sought if it was the intention for to use the lines long-term in trench warfare. Without insulation, wiring would be eaten away by humic acid: this could be avoided by laying it in humous clay, peat and wood-humus.

f. The acoustics of earth and rock strata were important for the listening posts in mine warfare, which had the task of obtaining information on attack and defence underground. Further defensive measures would be undertaken based on observation and analysis of the direction and intensity of the noises of enemy subterranean activity.

Schützengraben angelegt in _Feinsand_ und _undurchlässigem Lehm_ (Unterer Grünsand und Ton der Kreideformation) - _Wände nicht standfest_, derGraben zerfällt, über der undurchlässigen _Grabensohle sammelt sich das Regenwasser._ Ursprüngliches Grabenprofil _gestrichelt._

g. The expansion of shock waves following the detonation of underground mines influenced the radius of the destruction, for example in mountain warfare. German assault troops could therefore be prepared for what awaited them in the enemy position.

All this information had to be made available to the fighting troops in a generally comprehensible form. For this purpose the geologists in the survey detachments issued commentaries, reports and guide papers. A most important means of communication was a multitude of special maps often in colour. For example, there were building-ground and building-material maps, maps for earthbound telegraphy, ground-water, mine- and avalanche maps. Rockfall maps and maps showing the splinter effect of shells in this or that area

Geological comparison material for the fighting front, 1918. Herein are displayed the disadvantages of ignoring the geological characteristics of the sub-strata with respect to trench laying. Dr. Schuster's text reads: "Trench laid in fine sand and impermeable loam (lower green-sand and clay of chalky formation) – walls unstable, the trench deteriorates, rain water collects over the impermeable trench floor. Original trench profile marked with dotted lines."

In the Wyschaete Bend at the beginning of 1916, the British began their preparations for a mine attack on the German positions between St Yves and north-east of St Eloi. On account of the complicated geological situation, from March 1916 they relied on the advice of two specialists. Up to the day of the attack, 7 June 1917, the miners dug tunnels totalling 5,464 metres. The schematic diagram shows the various geological layers.

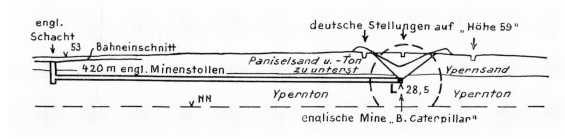

Key: Stollen=tunnels; vorderste englische Stellung=most advanced British position; Schacht=shaft; Ladung=explosive charge; toniger Paniselsand=clayey panisel sand; Basiston=clay base; Ypernsand=Ypres sand; unten wasserführend=water bearing below; Ypernton, trocken=Ypres clay, dry; z.T.schwimmend=occasionally floating sand.

This sketch shows the British mine "B.Caterpillar" below the German position on Hill 59, north-west of Meesen. On 7 June 1917 a total of 31,752 tons of ammonal was detonated.

Key: engl.Schacht=British shaft; Bahneinschnitt; railway line; 420 m engl. Minenstollen=420 metres British tunnels; deutsche Stellungen auf "Höhe 59"=German trenches on Hill 59. Soil strata as above.

were mimeographed by the presses of the survey detachments. The appearance of a new weapon, the tank, led to the introduction of another map in which the expected "easiest routes of passage for tanks" in the terrain were represented. These provided the basis for the development of artificial passive defence (tank ditches, tank traps, mine barriers).

Logistics

The war in the trenches was tied to an enormous achievement of labour. At its zenith in October 1916 the German trenches alone stretched for 2,200 kilometres (700 kms in the West, 1000 kms in the East and 500 kms in the South). If one allows three trenches along the front each for the opposing sides this works out at 15,600 kilometres, and with communication- and other trenches 31,000 kilometres. This in turn corresponds to about 60 million cubic metres of earth, not forgetting that many trenches had to be re-dug, and many

cubic metres of earth were also excavated for protected rooms, tunnels and tank ditches.

600 million sandbags were transported to the front. Put together this would form a three-metre high and two-metre wide wall 2,500 kilometres in length (the distance from Brussels to Palermo in Sicily is 2,556 kilometres).

1500 railway trains each of fifty waggons were needed to ship iron to the front for the construction of protected rooms and bunkers amongst other things, the necessary railway metals having to be built up and tracks expanded first. Where no normal gauge railway existed, narrow gauge lines were laid. There have never been so many Army field railways as in the First World War, all run by railway troops. The Germans installed in their positions 180,718,000 square metres of ceiling pasteboard. The consumption of barbed wire took on unimaginable proportions. It rose within a single year from 2,000 tonnes in July 1915 to 7,000 tonnes in July 1916: a total of 600,000 tonnes was laid altogether.

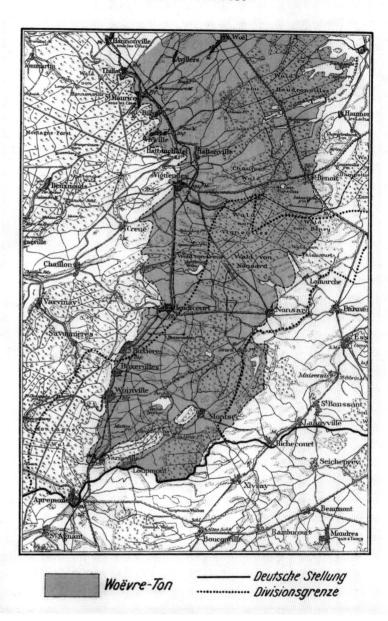

"Report on Attempts with Ground-telegraphy in the various ground types in the 17.Army Region" made between 24 April and 18 May 1918. The geological work in this case was commissioned in particular for listening and ground telegraphy stations and was undertaken by the Geology Group at Stoverm 17 in collaboration with Akonach 26.

Verbreitung des Woëvre-Tones.

Maßstab 1:100 000.

Woëvre-Ton — Deutsche Stellung — Divisionsgrenze

This map is an appendix to the "Guideline for Trench Building in the Wovre-Clay" issued by Survey Detachment 2. La Woevre is a territory in the Meuse Departement, Lorraine, between the Meuse and Moselle heights, its soil is of chalk and impermeable clay. It was bitterly contested in the Battle of Verdun in 1916 and in September/October 1918 was again the theatre for defensive fighting by Army Division C.
Key: Deutsche Stellung=German frontline
Divisionsgrenze=divisional limits

The Siegfried Line

In a communiqué dated 22 November 1916 circulated to General Staff officers, the German Supreme Army Command provided a basic overview of how it saw the progress of the war up to that time and its future intentions. In the extract "The Character of the War has Changed" they were of the opinion: "On the whole, the war from the military point of view has become one of attrition. Our enemies, numerically superior, are trying to wear us down." Because Germany was not in a position to change the nature of the war at that time, it had to attempt to alter the balance of forces to its advantage from its defensive position. In effect, the aim remained to achieve the decision by great attacking battles. "From these considerations," Ludendorff wrote after the war, "there(…) arose the decision to pull back our front by straightening its bulge into France." This decision was extraordinarily difficult to make. Ludendorff: "In it lay the admission of our weakness, which would encourage the enemy and have a demoralizing effect on ourselves." Therefore the order to prepare positions to the rear which had been given to the Army Group Kronprinz Rupprecht

Trench system under artillery fire.

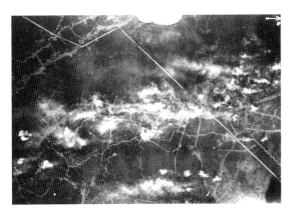

von Bayern long before the communiqué of 22 November 1916 had primarily military motives. Work on the plans for the Wotan, Siegfried, Hunding and Aisne Lines had begun there at once. Beginning in October 1916, the net-like trench system took four months to construct taking the most recent view of the trench war into account.

At times, between 70,000 and 100,000 men from the rearward units were involved in building the new stretch of line, but also prisoners-of-war. Problems with the supply of building materials and heavy frosts delayed progress. Until the retreat to the Siegfried Line at the beginning of March 1917 the defence was maintained with continuous trenches, numerous concrete bunkers and broad obstacles. MGs and mine-thrower positions, observation points and battery emplacements for the artillery in great numbers were available to the withdrawing units. Not all targets were achieved: there was a lack of accommodation and ammunition rooms to the rear. Dressing stations and the signals network reached a high standard. Notable were the shell-proof sheltered field wells for water supply. Veteran troops had a poor opinion of some of the defensive sitings from the point of view of choice of location and expansion. The depth of the defensive zone was not sufficient. The expected pause for rest was

Shortening the Front

The Siegfried Line shortened the front from 186 to 141 kilometres, releasing 13 divisions. The laying waste of a strip up to fifteen kilometres broad in the forefield impeded the approach of Allied forces, increased security against enemy break-throughs and created simultaneously the exit points for our own operations of attack.

foreseen for further efforts in this regard.

The order for the retreat from the front bulge to the line east of Arras, west of Cambrai, the Nord Canal, St Quentin, La Fère Vailly followed on 4 February 1917 under the cover name "Alberich". Operation *Alberich* took place between 9th and 16 March. Although the Allies were hard on the heels of the eastwards-retiring Germans, everything went as close as possible to the plan. British attacks caused concern at the seam from the former front line to the Siegfried Line, and there was heavy fighting at the beginning of April between Escourt and Noreuil where the more active French got to close quarters.

The fighting on the Siegfried Line at the beginning of March 1917 north-east of Bapaume is described in the history of the Lehr-Infanterie-Regiment. This was part of 3.Garde-Infanterie-Division which itself was not transferred to the threatened front until mid-April.

"The first impressions in the new battle area were gained. The British had here, as previously, proved their outstanding soldierly qualities, their field outposts had defended their positions to the bitter end and they had never shied away from man-to-man combat. The Siegfried Line, the wonders of which gained in the telling mouth to mouth, passed muster here to the sober inspection of the old veterans. The handbook wire entanglements ahead of our own positions were almost our undoing. After the obsolete facilities in Lorraine we were completely surprised by the wide, open trench profiles. Even the deep protected rooms aroused confidence except that there were not enough of them. The lack of labour had resulted in much remaining at the planning stage. A more forward occupied terrain with bunkers and field outposts lay between our own line and the enemy. The trenches had received only a few rounds and we found them to be almost undamaged. However it would not be long until the Siegfried Line showed us a quite different face only a little farther to the north...

On 4 May we received orders from Division to relieve 27.Infanterie-Division at Bullecourt and Riencourt. Hard but laudable days in the history of the regiment were to follow.

II/L.I.R. had already been transferred on 30 April as Group-reserve to Raillencourt and Sailly. The alarm was given at 0530 on 3 May to move up northwards. It had to resist the first assault from within the regiment.

In the Siegfried Line, Bullecourt, situated at some height, was a bastion-like jumping-off point to the south. The most advanced German line framed this village in the west, south and east and then ran for about two kilometres eastwards from its northern edge before making a sharp right turn. About 700 metres behind the centre of the West-East line was the southern edge of Riencourt. The intention of the British was to advance to Riencourt and if possible also capture Bullecourt by attacks on the flank and rear, having up until now found it a hard nut to crack by frontal assaults. Then they wanted to advance along the Arras-Cambrai highway.

Using much heavy weaponry and an enormous force of infantry they succeeded in making a dent 1500 metres broad in our line extending 300 metres north of 2.trench line of the Siegfried Line and embracing the eastern part of Bullecourt. It was apparent that they would not be satisfied with this partial success. With their own kind of tough energy – especially in defending – they developed this nest and used it as a base for very unpleasant flanking MG and rifle-grenade fire. Especially disturbing was the position they set up in the deeply incised sunken road which ran between Bullecourt and Riencourt. Since all connecting routes between the two had been flattened by their heavy artillery, any traffic by day from and to Riencourt was as good as impossible. It was essential to get everything back fully under the control of the Siegfried Line(…).

On the whole, trench warfare was fairly quiet here. Apart from their sporadic, small patrols, the British launched no infantry attacks. One of our assault troop undertakings by II. and III./L.I.R. in the morning hours of 1st May under 2nd Lieutenant (Reserve) Stephan of 10.Company led to the capture of a British soldier.

The enemy artillery made regular, but in the opening days not substantial, artillery bombardments especially targeting the hinterland territory. At Pronville and Inchy it was occasionally heavy. Because of the almost total lack of shell-proof bunkers in those localities, a direct hit would have caused serious casualties. Early on 26 April the baggage train at Marquion suffered some losses. The cellars of the houses which had been quickly fortified were not altogether reliable, but initially the enemy was firing only light and medium calibre. At Inchy for example, he was apparently concentrating on the eastern part of the village. The readiness batallion and the district commander in the western part had a roof over their heads by day even if this was often a little uncanny.

The British expenditure of ammunition increased slowly but surely, probably in support of larger attacks farther north. We began to suspect that we would soon be ripe for the witches' cauldron there. For the time being, often enough we had the nights free to stand in our foremost advanced strip and watch the huge fireworks display to our right in which a coloured halo of starshell framed the ghastly symphony. Blood-curdling and a terrible thing upon which to reflect that in this horror men were disputing every inch of ground in attack and defence. When would this fall to out lot?"

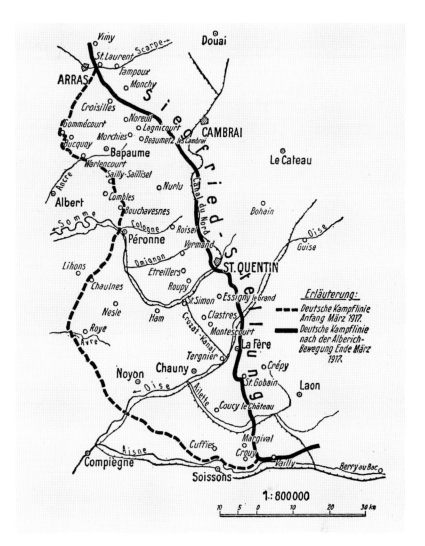

1.: 800 000

In November 1917 the Siegfried Line was the theatre for the tank battle at Cambrai. On 21 March 1918 it was the exit point for the attacks by 17. and 2.Armies in the framework of the German spring offensive in which they pressed forward westwards as far as Thory and Villers-Bretonneux. Nevertheless, the offensive failed. At the beginning of September 1918 the Line was reoccupied by German troops, but finally abandoned one month later.

The section of the Siegfried Line between Arras and Soissons in March 1917.
Key: dotted line= German battle line, beginning March 1917; thick line=German battle line after the Alberich movement, end March 1917.

Notes

1. Part 1a of this issue replaced that appearing in the 20 June 1916 issue.
2. Wolfsgruben: Concealed, sharply converging depressions in the ground with sharpened stakes at the bottom.
3. Spanische Reiter: Wooden trestles 2 metres in length wrapped in barbed wire.
4. Fascines: 3–4 metre long thick bundles of shrubs, bushes or brushwood bound with wire or osier twigs and used by tanks to overcome trenches, waterways or swampy paths. For method of use see sketch, Chapter 5.

Chapter Four

THE RISE OF ARTILLERY
The Big Guns Hold Sway

Before the First World War the purpose of the artillery, whether light or heavy, was to do no more than support the infantry effectively, and afterwards it became the task of the heavy artillery to clear the way to enemy bases and fortified positions and support the light artillery – the field artillery – in battle against the enemy artillery. During the war years that did not change essentially. What changed was the numbers of artillery groups and units. They doubled, the heavy artillery trebled, and they grew to decisive size in the battles of materials.

The rise of the artillery is closely linked to the fast pace of industrial and technological progress in the second half of the 19th century. Advances in metallurgy and manufacturing techniques, in optics, chemistry, physics and mathematics together with discoveries in the area of ballistics led to far-reaching changes in the armaments, equipment and organisation of the armed forces. In the artillery sphere this began in 1843.

Improvements in All Components

The Swede, Baron Wahrendorff, invented the rifled breech loader which solved the difficult problem of sealing the breech against the propellant gases. Combined with the transition to extended barrels it set up a milestone in the history of artillery. Not until 1861, however, was the Prussian artillery able to apply the principle with its 6-, 12-, and 24- pounder cannons. Other advances were the introduction of gun barrels made of cast steel. As against the former bronze barrel of common construction, the better material allowed an increase in gas pressure in the barrel, accordingly now providing a range of 4,000 metres as against the former 1,600 metres.

Lead-jacketed explosive and incendiary shells with mechanical fuze device and canister-shot were introduced. The cartridges came in cloth bags containing propellant charges of black powder with a hemp pressboard for a gas-proof seal of the interstices between barrel and breech. The shrapnel shell with powder-combustion time fuze was introduced rather later. As against the smooth bore muzzle-loader the shell weight had more than doubled and accuracy was greatly improved. In 1864 Prussia introduced the sliding wedge breech which brought about an increase in the rate of fire. A significant improvement in gas-proofing was the installation of Broadwell rings in the barrels.

Progress in ballistics, particularly internal ballistics, proved that propellant charges of black powder did not explode but burnt very quickly at firing. This knowledge influenced the form of the powder, and in 1872 a transition was made to prismatic black powder. This raised the average gas pressure in the barrel, increasing the muzzle velocity, the flatness of the trajectory and the range. A further increase in efficiency was the limit set with regard to barrel stresses. In Prussia the changeover was made to elaborated barrel construction with the introduction of the 8-cm and 9-cm field cannon C/73.

This was a convincing success: in 1884 the greatest range was 7,600 metres. Artificial barrel construction was also advantageous for the utility and durability of the gun barrel. If the accuracy of bronze barrels began to fall off

Photograph of the fighting at Verdun in the spring of 1916. "Steady destructive fire at Fort Douaumont and Dead Man Hill."

Example from 1861 for a lengthened gun barrel of Krupp crucible steel with rifled breech loader.

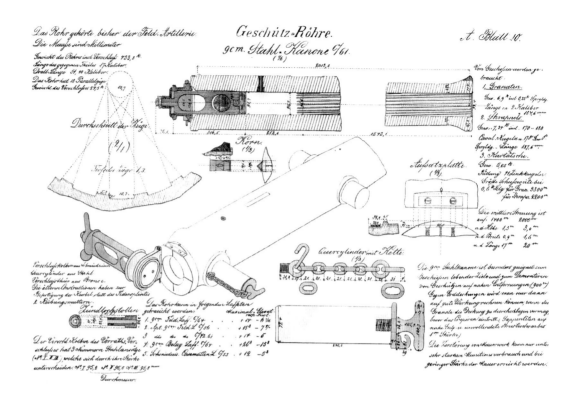

Feldgranat-Zünder C/73. in der schweren Feldgranate C/73.

Nadelbolzen.

Vorstecker für 15 cm Langgr. m Hbl.

Example of mechanical fuze device for the heavy field shell C/73 from the year 1873.

after 1,100 rounds, the C/73 barrels were not adversely affected even after 5,000 rounds with greater loading. Because of the higher stress factor wooden mounts were no longer suitable and were replaced by metal mounts.

In 1882 shells with lead jackets were replaced by thin driving rings of copper. This prevented lead contamination of the barrel and gave the shell a better splinter effect. From 1881 double-detonators were employed. A further real advance in the progress of artillery technology was the introduction of smokeless nitrocellulose powder in 1886. It had several advantages. The troublesome smoke development on firing disappeared: the powder itself was not so sensitive to humidity as black powder (which in turn benefited muzzle velocity and the uniformity of shell performance). Because of the higher energy content of nitrocellulose powder, the weight of the propellant was reduced to a third or a quarter. The powder delivered in the preferred form – e.g. in packets or pipes – burned more uniformly.

The stability of the gun mount provided a further increase in shooting efficiency. It

was still the case that after each round had been fired the gun rolled back and the crew had to spend time and energy bring it back to its former position. Fortress and siege guns were too heavy for this activity and recoil wedges were laid behind the wheels. A solution was found in the application of special barrel-recoil brakes which several designers had been working on before the turn of the century. An example here is the Darmancier System of 1899, a spring tension mount with glycerine brake. By far the best idea was that of the engineer K.Hausser who prepared a memorandum on the subject in 1888.

This gained no recognition from the firms of A.G. Grusonwerk, Magdeburg-Buckau and F.Krupp, Essen, but finally Privy Councillor H.Ehrhardt of Rheinmetall, Düsseldorf, took up the design and built a serviceable barrel-recoil gun. It was introduced in the winter of 1896, turned down by the Artillery Testing Commission, improved and re-introduced, and was now condemned as being too heavy. The dogged objection by the military to the barrel-recoil is explained by the fact that only on 22 March 1897 after long experimentation

The 7.7-cm field gun C/96 which entered service with the German Army in 1897 after years of testing.

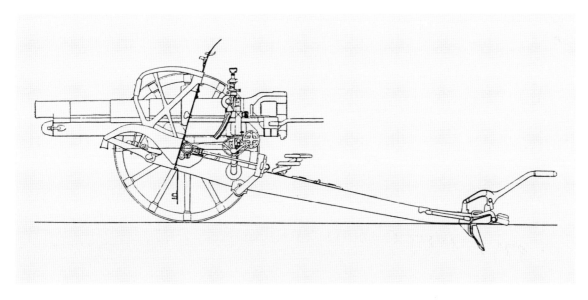

The 7.7-cm field gun 96 n/A with barrel recoil, trail spade, splinter shield and field-gun panoramic telescope is an example of the barrel recoil guns developed to avoid having to re-position the gun after firing each round.

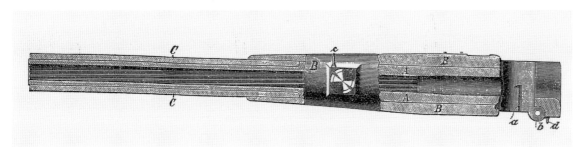

The barrel of a 10-cm siege gun as an example of elaborated barrel construction (A) inner barrel lining with rifling; B=jacket; a=flute; b=appendage for breech thrust crankshaft; c=sight; d=retraction loop

Brass shell casing: (A) with detonator cap, (B) as example for a propellant charge of nitroglycerine powder (C) The casing has seven partial charges of propellant for the 10.5-cm light field howitzer 98/09.

and trials was the 7.7-cm field-gun C/96 introduced officially. In contrast to the old model C/73 it had undoubted advantages; it was easier to move, had better ballistics, faster rate of fire, had a self-clamping breech and metal cartridges in place of bags. All it lacked to become a quick-firing gun was a barrel recoil brake. When fired it bucked and returned to the ground with the traverse gear positioned off-centre. One year later the French introduced their 75-mm field gun mle.1897 to which the C/96 was inferior. The French gun remained perfectly still after firing because the barrel ran back in the cradle. It had better ballistics than the German model, had a faster rate of fire (15–18 rounds/min) and longer range. Modernisation of the C/96 was unavoidable. The new gun with barrel-recoil brake was introduced in January 1905 as "7.7-cm Feldkanone 96 n/A". Together with the introduction of the barrel-recoil

gun the traverse apparatus (eight degrees) was refined. Optical gunsights and modern optical equipment led to a further increase in accuracy and speed in laying and training the gun against more distant targets. This laid the ground for the use of modern barrel-recoil guns. At the same time, for the purpose of increasing the rate of fire, the changeover to cartridge ammunition took place with *Röhrenpulver 05* powder which had no muzzle fire. The new propellant powder for the light field howitzer and the guns of the Army foot artillery were brought out in 1909.

The introduction of the barrel-recoil gun for the foot-artillery was a complicated process involving many setbacks. The photograph shows the 21-cm experimental mortar L/10 (Krupp) of the eight delivered and tried out at the Foot-Artillery Firing School at Jüterbog.

KAISERLICHES PATENTAMT.

AUSGEGEBEN DEN 14. APRIL 1893.

PATENTSCHRIFT

№ 67921

KLASSE 49: MECHANISCHE METALLBEARBEITUNG.

HEINRICH EHRHARDT IN DÜSSELDORF.

Verfahren zum Lochen und gleichzeitigen Formgeben von Eisen- und Stahlblöcken in erhitztem Zustande.

Patentirt im Deutschen Reiche vom 28. Januar 1891 ab.

Zur Herstellung eines schmiedeisernen Hohlcylinders nimmt man ein Stück Quadrateisen a, Fig. 2, dessen Querschnitt, diagonal gemessen, gleich dem Durchmesser des zu erzeugenden Hohlcylinders ist. Das Stück Quadrateisen wird im roth- oder weißwarmen Zustande in die Matrize b, Fig. 1 und 2, gebracht, deren Hohlform der Form des zu erzeugenden Hohlcylinders entspricht, und ein spitzer Dorn c, Fig. 1, vermittelst eines Hammers oder einer Presse in dasselbe eingetrieben, wobei der Deckel d, Fig. 1, als Führung dient. Der Durchmesser des Dornes ist so gewählt, daß das durch ihn verdrängte Material die vier segmentförmigen Zwischenräume e, Fig. 2, ausfüllt; dabei ist berücksichtigt, daß eine gewisse geringe Stauchung des Werkstückes stattfindet. Dadurch, daß das vom Dorn verdrängte Material seitlich ausweichen kann, dringt der spitze Dorn sehr leicht in dasselbe ein. Der so hergestellte Hohlcylinder mit geschlossenem Boden ist in Fig. 3 und 4 dargestellt. Das Durchlochen desselben, wenn der Hohlcylinder nicht mit geschlossenem Boden Verwendung finden soll, findet mit einem stumpfen Dorn f, Fig. 3, in der gewöhnlichen Weise statt. Die nach dem beschriebenen Verfahren hergestellten Hohlcylinder können unter anderem zu dünnwandigen Röhren oder Ringen ausgezogen bezw. ausgewalzt werden.

Zur Herstellung eines prismatischen Hohlkörpers erhält die Matrize die entsprechende prismatische Hohlform und zur Verwendung gelangt ein Stück Rundeisen bezw. Stahl,

dessen Durchmesser gleich demjenigen des eingeschriebenen Kreises der Prismengrundfläche ist.

Im übrigen ist das Verfahren genau wie oben beschrieben. Das Werkstück wird in der Matrize centrirt und der vorhandene Spielraum durch das vom Dorn verdrängte Material ausgefüllt.

Bei Herstellung längerer Hohlkörper kann man nöthigenfalls von beiden Seiten einen spitzen Dorn eintreiben, wie in Fig. 5 angedeutet.

In gleicher Weise lassen sich auch Blöcke von unregelmäßigem Querschnitt lochen und gleichzeitig in eine bestimmte Form pressen. Bedingung ist nur, daß das Werkstück von der Matrize einen entsprechenden Spielraum für das vom Dorn verdrängte Material vorhanden ist.

In Fig. 6, 7, 8 und 9 ist beispielsweise der Dorn g von ovalem Querschnitt angenommen. Der Querschnitt des zu lochenden Werkstückes ist aus Fig. 7 und derjenige des gelochten Werkstückes aus Fig. 9 zu ersehen.

Um den ovalen Querschnitt zu einem runden, aus Fig. 10 punktirt ersichtlichen umzugestalten, kann man beispielsweise einen runden Dorn von entsprechend großem Querschnitt eintreiben.

Die Matrize besteht aus dem einen Theil i, welcher oben durch das Verbindungsstück k und unten durch die Platte l abgeschlossen wird. Der Deckel k dient gleichzeitig als Führung für den Dorn. Die Führung des letzteren

(3. Auflage, ausgegeben am 11. Januar 1906.)

kann übrigens auch bei Dampfhämmern oder anderen mechanischen Hämmern oder bei Pressen durch das Gestell des Hammers bezw. der Presse herbeigeführt werden, wie dies z. B. in Fig. 11 angenommen ist. Soll das Werkstück m von dreieckigem Querschnitt in eine runde Form übergeführt werden, so kann der Dorn n zu diesem Zweck an dem Bär eines Hammers oder an dem bewegenden Theil einer Presse angebracht werden. Auch ist der Fall möglich, daß der Dorn mit dem Gestell der Presse fest verbunden ist und die Matrize mit dem Werkstück an dem Gestell der Presse geführt wird, oder daß beide Theile, Dorn sowohl als auch Matrize, an dem Gestell der Presse Führung und Bewegung in der Dornrichtung erhalten.

Um die Führung und die Anlage des Werkstückes besser zu sichern und die Ausbauchung der freiliegenden Flächen desselben zu befördern, kann die Matrize an den Stellen, an welchen die Führungskanten des Werkstückes

dieselbe berühren, mit einer Wasserkühlung versehen sein. Zu diesem Zweck sind bei der in Fig. 6, 7, 8 und 9 dargestellten Matrize die Hohlräume o o mit Wasser gefüllt. Bei den in den Fig. 11 und 12 bezw. 13 und 14 dargestellten Matrizen dienen die Hohlräume p p bezw. q q zur Aufnahme von Wasser zum Kühlen der Matrizen.

PATENT-ANSPRUCH:

Verfahren zum Lochen und gleichzeitigen Formgeben von Eisen- und Stahlblöcken im erhitzten Zustande unter Anwendung einer Matrize und eines Lochstempels in der Weise, daß die Innenwände der Matrize dem Werkstück eine bestimmte Lage zum Lochstempel geben, das Werkstück aber im Querschnitt um so viel geringer, als der Querschnitt des Matrizenhohlraumes gewählt ist, als zur Aufnahme des vom Lochstempel zu verdrängenden Materials erforderlich ist.

Hierzu 1 Blatt Zeichnungen.

Berichtigung zur Patentschrift 67921, Klasse 49.

PATENT-ANSPRUCH:

Verfahren zur Herstellung von Hohlkörpern, darin bestehend, daß Metallblöcke oder Stäbe von drei-, vier- oder mehreckigem Querschnitt, bei welchen Werkstücken die Materialfasern parallel zu seinen Kanten gelagert sind, in eine Matrize derart lose eingesetzt werden, daß die Kanten des Stabes an den Wandungen der Matrize anliegen und eine Endfläche desselben auf dem Boden der Matrize aufruht und daß alsdann von der entgegengesetzten Endfläche ein Dorn centrisch in das Werkstück parallel zu dessen Kanten hineingepreßt

wird, wobei der Dornquerschnitt gleich der Summe der Querschnitte ist, welche zwischen Werkstück und Matrize verblieben sind, so daß das durch die Kanten gehaltene Werkstück ohne wesentliche Stauchung, theilweise oder in der ganzen Länge in der Weise gelocht wird, daß das Material desselben nach den Wandungen der Matrize hin verdrängt wird, wodurch die Matrize in einer dem eindringenden Theil des Dornes entsprechenden Länge voll ausgefüllt wird, ohne daß das Werkstück von seiner freien Endfläche aus einen Stauchdruck erfährt.

BERLIN. GEDRUCKT IN DER REICHSDRUCKEREI.

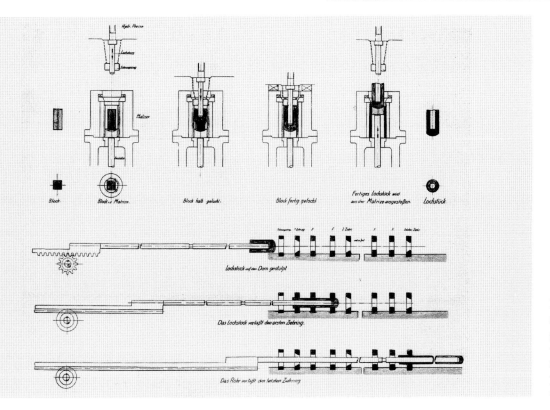

Ehrhardt's patent for a tougher steel for gun barrels. After the war began there were not enough heavy presses to meet the enormous demand.

New Explosives

There had been comprehensive changes in the field of explosives. Gun cotton, which had replaced black powder as Shell-filling C/83 proved a failure. After a short period of use the number of shells detonating in the barrel began to escalate, and by reason of its hygroscopic characteristic it could not be stored satisfactorily. Here the chemists were quickly of assistance. In 1886 they discovered the explosive properties of picric acid used to dye silk, wool and leather. This was introduced as Shell-filling C/88, but was only the forerunner for other high explosives, among them trinitrotoluol (TNT), introduced as "Filling powder 02" and Ammonal. The Swedish chemist Alfred Nobel did well out of modern explosives. Amongst his discoveries were dynamite (1867), explosive gelatine (1875) and nitroglycerine powder (1890). The table below shows the energy content in comparison to the mixture of black powder in modern explosives:

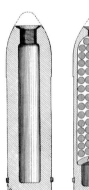

Explosive shell (left) and shrapnel shell with thin driving rings.

Comparative Energy of Explosives

Explosive	Velocity explosive gases (m/sec)	Volume increase (litre/kg explosive)
Black powder	400	280
Shell filling C/88	7250	675
Filling Powder 02	6800	690

Filling shells with the new higher-energy explosives resulted in cast-steel shells disintegrating at detonation into numerous tiny and therefore fairly useless splinters. The new requirement was for a ductile, resistant steel. The problem was solved by Ehrhardt's patent of 28 January 1891 "Procedure for spiking and simultaneous shaping of iron and steel blocks in heated condition" (see illustration of patent). Only after the outbreak of war did the disadvantage of the procedure make itself known, for the number of available heavy presses was insufficient to meet the enormously increased demand for ammunition, and substitute shells of lesser efficiency had to be called upon.

Long before the war the artillery branches of Germany and Austro-Hungary had adopted a unified shell which combined the effect of high explosive with shrapnel. As so often is the case when combining several functions into one, problems arose, in this case in the logistical field. The heavy artillery placed special value on thin-walled shells with a large explosive charge, so-called "mine-shells". Before the war the Germans had put much effort into placing heavy and the heaviest mortars and howitzers in their fortress and siege parks. This was considered a matter of especial urgency. The heavy calibres were to assist in swiftly overcoming the fortifications on the French eastern border. This was seen as the guarantee for a short and successful war against France.

There had been numerous innovations related to shell fuzes, such as improved dual purpose fuzes, sensitive impact fuzes and shell fuzes with adjustable delay setting. New safety precautions had also been introduced to artillery fuzes to protect against pre-detonation in the gun barrel.

Artillery Technology in the First World War

Artillery formed part of the armaments race between the leading industrial nations. The influence of science and technology, and the tangible headway made by private concerns in the weapons and equipment field in the 1870s, accelerated advances despite differences and misunderstandings. Numerous inventions raised the effectiveness of artillery as the principal fire power of the land forces. The most important technological building blocks were brought together and in the harsh conditions of warfare were developed in quantity and quality. Pressing changes were needed in training, organisation and artillery tactics.

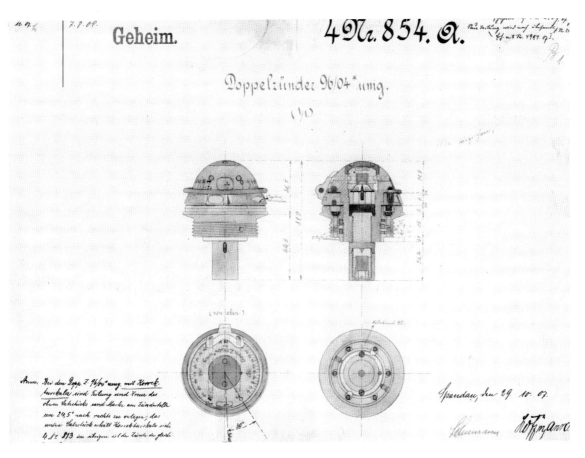

Example with patent for a dual purpose impact/ delay fuze, a modified Doppelzünder 96/04. It was used in action with the 7.7-cm field gun 96 n/A field-shrapnel or field-shell cartridges.

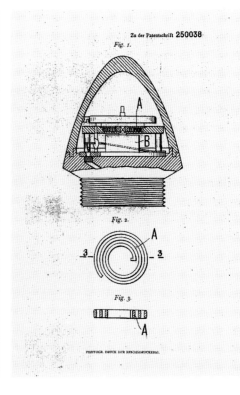

The German Artillery at War

Since the turn of the century, the field- and foot-artillery of the German Army – not without internal resistance – had been equipped with modern barrel-recoil guns. In the field-artillery, light, mobile field guns dominated. They had a short range and limited shell effect, being intended for direct, flat trajectory fire. The 15-cm heavy howitzer and 21-cm mortar, both steep-trajectory guns, were at the forefront of the foot-artillery. There were also other steep-fire guns available for bombarding fortifications. The stocks of flat-trajectory guns was not large. In 1914 the flak-artillery was at the early stage of its development: there were only eighteen guns, then classified as "anti- observation-balloon guns". The coastal artillery of the Imperial Navy was distributed amongst the fortifications on the Baltic coast and North Sea coasts and islands such as Amrum, Borkum and Heligoland. A large number of these guns were considered obsolete.

Within a few weeks of the outbreak of war it was clear that the military concept of the intensity and probable duration of the fighting was unrealistic. The losses in men and materials were of unexpectedly high proportions. The Front came to a standstill and devolved into trench warfare in the Western theatre of war first, as a result of the exhaustion of the respective opposing armies. From the simple infantry trench there developed a deeply staggered defensive system. The firepower of the MGs held the field and was decisive for the steadfastness of the defence.

Initially the artillery was the only fighting arm in a position to pin down defences. Accordingly ammunition supply was increased. In the Battle of Verdun (February to December 1916) this development reached a highpoint. The battlefield, with a surface area up to thirty kilometres wide and ten kilometres deep was ploughed and reploughed by 21 million German and 15 million French shells and transformed into a moonscape. Only deep infantry trenches, protected rooms, bunkers and tunnels offered protection against artillery fire. The foremost trenches were only thinly held. Compared with the losses of the first months of the war and measured by the expenditure of ammunition, the losses were relatively low. This resulted from deeply

The 7.7-cm field gun 96 n/A after firing. The barrel is at the farthest projection to the rear after recoil. Seen behind it is the rear section of the ammunition waggon 96 n/A. The photograph was taken in the autumn of 1916 at Reserve-Field Artillery Regt.58 in Rumania.

During the First World War the French armaments industry delivered more than 17,000 75-mm field guns mle.1897 of which 5,145 were still in service at 5 November 1918.

During the Batle of Verdun in the Louvemont Gorge a 42-cm mortar (short Marine-Kanone 14 L/12) wrecked by a shell exploding in the barrel. Photgraph taken, spring 1916.

The 10.5-cm fast-loading cannon L/35 on wheeled chassis was one of the guns on temporary loan from Imperial Navy stocks. The gun, weighing 4.18 tonnes, was always used with wheel-belts, firing base plate and recoil-chocks.Thirty were converted for use in the field.

staggered trench systems. In the rear sectors of the Front, troops and equipment stood ready to make counter-attacks. Daily, especially at night, there was a lively traffic between the Front and the hinterland. Fresh troops came forward as reliefs, rations, ammunition and equipment were brought up. The transports were the target of long-range flat trajectory guns, in short supply at the outbreak of war because Supreme Army Command had given priority to heavy steep-trajectory guns. Every active Army Corps had gone into the field with a foot-artillery batallion which gave them superiority over the Army Corps of the enemy.

What this superiority looked like was reported upon by M.Schöne, former sergeant on the Staff of 1.Batallion/2.Königlich-Sächsisches Fussartillerie-Regt. Nr.19. His batallion had arrived at the front with sixteen 15-cm (5.9-inch) heavy howitzers and on 23 August 1914 was in a firing position three kilometres east of Dinant.

The explosive effects of the heavy 15-cm howitzer and 21-cm mortar shells were impressive and their ability for indirect fire was of advantage in trench warfare. However, their range was not sufficient for the all desired tasks. Another circumstance had fatal consequences: the field artillery guns were of light construction and mobile, advantages which were significant while the war remained one of

"Our spotter posts lay on the road embankment just west of Gemechenne; gradually we could make out individual infantry trenches from there and fired on them. On the other hand, for some time it was not possible to pick out the very skilfully hidden enemy artillery. A French Rimailho battery (15-cm howitzers) inflicted heavy casualties on the l.F.-Batt (light field howitzer battery – the author) Leonhardi (5./48) (5.Battery/Reserve-Field Artillery Regt. Nr.48) which had drawn up in fairly open meadowlands. Our batallion also received its baptism of fire here. All efforts to identify the location of the French battery were at first unsuccessful. Then suddenly came the shout from the batallion spotter post: "I have them!" This was from the excellent batallion auxiliary spotter Sergeant Leupold who had seen the brief flash of the enemy salvoes through the scissor-telescope. Now we had won the game. Battery Wolf (2.Battery/Foot-artillery-Regt Nr.19 – the author) received the order to destroy the French battery. Their fire ceased after a few rounds and the l.F.-Batt breathed a sigh of relief.

Then we saw that the Rimailho battery was attempting to leave. As a result they

suffered the most enormous losses, of which the batallion was able to convince itself the next day when passing close by the enemy battery position. Our shelling had wrought fearsome devastation."

mobility. By the end of 1914 that was all past. Range and shell effect had been lost, as can be seen from the tactical-technical comparative table of the German and French field guns.

Even the range of the 10.5-cm field howitzer 98/09 did not meet requirements, although its shell effects were convincing. There now arose amongst all the belligerents a competition for longer range, and in Germany four paths were followed:

a. Modernisation of the current gun models with their projectiles, cartridges and shell casings as well as propellant charges. In June 1915 the 7.7-cm field gun arrived at the front on a howitzer chassis (elevation of the barrel up to +40º); in the spring of 1916 the 7.7-cm field gun 16 with a longer barrel followed. The same went for the 10-cm gun,

the 10.5-cm light howitzer, the 15-cm heavy howitzer, the 21-cm mortar and the 42-cm mortar. The latter received a 30.5-cm barrel L/30.

b. Employment of naval guns: the lack of heavy far-reaching cannons (heavy flat trajectory fire) was overcome by the use of fast-loading naval guns on wheeled chassis. Krupp alone supplied 150 15-cm heavy cannons. In 1916 railway and railway-bedded cannons followed. The largest calibre was the 38-cm cannon L/45.

c. New heavy field guns: While the 18-cm experimental howitzer failed to make the gracde, the firms of Krupp and Rheinmetall succeeded in turning out heavy flat-trajectory guns based on the 1913 design for the heavy 15-cm gun. These were accepted officially in 1916. The Krupp 15-cm gun was the first to be planned *ab initio* for motorized towage.

d. Modifications in the Manufacture of Shells: Numerous problems were encountered in the struggle to increase range and shell effect by improvements in the ammunition. The design and manufacture of the expensive unified shell fell by the wayside: the value of

Tactical-Technical Comparative Table of the German and French Field Guns

	7.7-cm light field gun 96 n/A	**75-mm field gun mle. 1897**
Calibre	77 mm	75 mm
Barrel length	2080 mm=L/27	2588 mm=L/34.5
Elevation	-12.9/+15.2	-110/+200
Traverse	80	60
Muzzle velocity	465 m/sec	535 m/sec
Rate of fire	12 rounds/min	15–18 rounds/min
Maximum range	7800 m	5800–9500 m
Weight, firing position	1020 kg	1140 kg
Weight for towage	1910 kg	1970 kg
Weight of HE shell	6.85 kg	5.5 kg
Weight of HE content	0.25 kg	0.695 kg
Weight of shrapnel shell	6.85 kg	7.24 kg
Hard lead balls	300 x 10g	290 x 12g

Comparison German Artillery Weapons 1914 and 1918

	1914	1918
Field artillery	**1069 batteries**	**2800 batteries**
7.7-cm field guns and 10.5-cm		
light field howitzers	6326	11204
Flak guns	18	120
Mountain guns	0	100
Infantry escort guns	0	200
Anti-tank guns	0	1150
Heavy (Foot)-Artillery	**201 batteries**	**1160 batteries**
15-cm heavy field howitzers and 21-cm mortars	2300	7600
13-cm guns	16	120
15-cm guns	0	232
Railway guns	0	120
42-cm mortars	7	20

shrapnel, well proven in mobile warfare, was now disputed. In trench warfare explosive shells with an increased charge were preferred. The great leap in the expenditure of ammunition brought the war economy to its limits of capacity. Shells of grey cast iron, thicker-walled and of lesser value, were being manufactured: they had less explosive and less effective splinter action but a greater propensity to explode in the gun barrel. Not until the changeover to pressed steel shells was a viable solution found for mass-production. Problems of materials and completion hampered the production of driving bands and detonators.

It required a tremendous effort to meet the demand for propellant powder and explosive. At the end of 1914 the field artillery was asking for 2.5 million shells monthly, the heavy (foot) artillery 1.66 million. In particular, filling the unexpectedly high demand for explosives for

Examples for Increases in Range

Gun	Shell	Range	Shell	Range
7.7-cm field gun 16	HE	9100 m	C-shell	10700 m
10.5-cm light howitzer 16	HE	8400 m	C-shell	9700 m
10-cm gun	HE	11400 m	Haube	13100 m
Long 15-cm heavy howitzer 13	HE	8500 m	Haube	8800 m

38-cm (15-inch) fast-loading cannon L/45 "Max" on railway bedding turntable. In October 1918, one gun was operational with the Army, Sächsische 38-cm Kanonenbatterie 1050, the naval coastal artillery in Flanders had others.

ammunition of the heavy and heaviest guns caused substantial problems.[1]

The introduction of poison-gas ammunition was a completely novel way to increase shell effect. During the war shells were developed with altered configuration for longer range. These were the C-shells of the field artillery with a slender head. The heavy and heaviest artillery were given hooded streamlining (*Haube*) shells which had lesser air resistance and consequently a longer range.

Star shells came into use as a special munition to illuminate the battlefield by night. For close-combat, canister shot was re-introduced. Its effective range was 600 metres. After the first appearance of tanks at the Somme in the autumn of 1916 the field artillery was supplied with armour-piercing ammunition, the so-called "Cannon-shell 15 with armoured head".

The infantry, whose firepower had been substantially increased during the course of the war (e.g. with 7.6-cm light mortars) also received other artillery such as transfers-out of 7.7-cm field guns 96 n/A from artillery units. The purpose of this gun in the infantry role was to take out nests of resistance by direct fire at close range. Special infantry-gun batallions were formed for the purpose towards the end of the war.

Special Guns

Numbered amongst the "special guns" are anti-tank guns. At first guns of the field- and flak-artillery were employed. They were absented from their true role, the artillery battle and anti-aircraft defence. Therefore industry was given contracts to design special anti-tank guns. By the end of the war, the fighting fronts had received 600 such guns, which went first to the mortar batallions.

Certain parallels can be seen in the development of guns to defend against aerial objects. In 1906 the War Ministry asked the Artillery Testing Commission to determine which field- and foot-artillery guns were suitable for such purpose. After comprehensive research it was found that the role was best suited to a special barrel-recoil gun mounted

The weight of the hooded projectile for the 38-cm fast-loading cannon L/45 was 400 kgs of which 32.8 kgs was the explosive charge. The projectile had a muzzle velocity of 1014 m/sec and a range of 47.5 kilometres (29.5 miles).

on a central pivoting chassis. At the beginning of the war they were few in number, at its end there were 2576, some of them conversions from obsolescent or captured guns.

At the outbreak of the First World War the German armed forces – except for police troops in the colonies – had no mountain guns. As the war went on mountain gun batteries and sub-batallions were formed. By 1918 there were about 100 mountain guns in service.

The requirement for special guns burdened the industrial capacity, already stretched to the limit. The monthly production in the summer of 1914 was 120 guns for the field- and foot-artillery, and had risen to around 2900 in the summer of 1918.

Artillery in warfare made not only enormous demands on ammunition but also resulted in rapid wear and tear on gun barrels. Thus in July and August 1916 in the West around 1600 field- and 760 heavy guns had to be replaced. Enemy fire accounted for 15 percent of these losses, the rest was caused by intensive firing activity. The numbers of shells exploding inside the barrel was very high. Between mid-February and the end of May 1916 in 5.Army sector, 57.3 percent of the 637 field guns in action at the front were

Amongst the special guns coming into use during the First World War were anti-aircraft guns (flak). One of the these was the 8.8-cm motor-drawn Krupp Flugzeugabwehr kanone L/45 here shown mounted in firing mode. By November 1918, 169 guns of this type had been delivered.

Also amongst the special guns were anti-tank guns. The picture shows the 3.7-cm Rheinmetall Tankabwehrkanone. In 1918, 600 of a total of 1020 ordered had been delicvered. The shell could penetrate 20 mm armour steel at a range of 100 metres.

The 10-cm Kanone 14 with a maximum range of 13.1 kilometres was already on order before the outbreak of the First World War. It was a foot-artillery weapon, after 1917 a heavy artillery weapon. The first battery with four 10-cm Kanone 14 was operational in May 1915.

In transport mode the Krupp 15-cm Kanone 16 weighed 14,405 tonnes and was dismantled into two parts for transport. An all-wheel drive 100 hp tug was used for the purpose. The price to be paid for the substantial increase in range was a gain in weight so great that it could no longer be horse-drawn.

The 21-cm Mörser
L/12 mortar was
introduced in
February 1912.
In July 1914 there
were 256 of them
available. Each shell
weighed 120 kgs: the
gun had a range of
9400 metres.

A 21-cm Mörser
with an L/14.6 barrel
lengthened to 3062
mm had a range of
10.2 kilometres. They
were manufactured
from 1916, each
battery had three.

lost in this way, and 26 percent of the 880 heavy guns. The life of a gun barrel was limited. It varied from 2000 rounds from the 15-cm gun 16 to 12,000 rounds from the 15-cm heavy howitzer. The limits were soon reached. Many heavy howitzer batteries had the experience of having to replace all gun barrels within an eight week period. Occasionally there were no replacement barrels available and captured guns made up the numbers. Of the 5074 heavy guns at the beginning of 1916, about 600 had come from captured stocks.

Other factors to improve effectivity of artillery use resulted from the areas of general organisation, re-distribution of weapons within the regiments, training and firing experience. Operational experience, bought at a high price in losses, changed the face of the German Army artillery. In this respect the *Schiessvorschrift für die Artillerie*, issued by the Chief of the Army General Staff on 1 December 1917 in collaboration with the War Ministry, is notable. "This recently published *Schiessvorsschrift* replaces issue 3 of the Training Regulations for the Field-Artillery (*Ausbildungsvorschrift für die Feldartillerie*) (Berlin, 1917) and that for the Foot-Artillery of 19 November 1908. The basic principles considered important by the revision are set out herein and indications are shown as to where the previous Regulations are modified. (…) These changes pave the way for the urgently wanted unification of the regulations for light and heavy artillery. Simplification is to be striven for. The sections "Firing instructions" and "Regulations for Aiming" are valid for both branches with only very minor differences. Special value is placed on uniform terms to be applied between the two artilleries. To every artillery commander of mixed artillery groupings this will alleviate fire control and supervision of the men, and artilleristic communications between the men themselves.(…) The term "Field- and Foot-Artillery" is to be replaced by "light artillery" and "heavy artillery"(…)".

Reorganisation

In October 1914, in connection with the reorganisation of ten reserve field-artillery regiments, it was decided that each regiment should have three *Abteilungen* and to reduce the number of guns per battery from six to four. This rearrangement was caused by the simple shortage of field guns and howitzers. In December 1914 a further sixteen field artillery regiments were formed. These had only two *Abteilungen* each (with four batteries each), one *Abteilung* having twelve 7.7-cm field guns 96 n/A and the other twelve 10.5-cm light field howitzers 98/09. The field artillery now preferred howitzers for the first time.

By the spring of 1918 there were some batteries with six guns again; these were installed at positions without vehicles or horses.

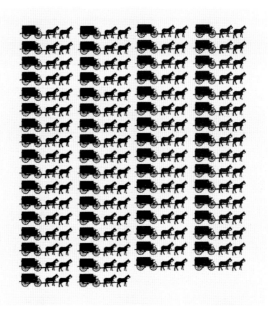

Ninety-eight batteries, each with eight captured guns, were operational on the Eastern Front. Six field-artillery regiments with vehicles for towage were also formed at the same time. This new quality was hoped to lead to faster transfers to artillery points of main effort. These *Schwerpunkte* were the focus for numerous organisational measures such as the assembly of artillery units into groups and sub-groups. Corresponding to the planned purpose they were organised under a uniform command and centralised with the artillery command located with the High Command of the attacking army. Without this form of organisation, artillery bombardments running like clockwork would not have been possible.

At the beginning of the war, the foot-artillery had batallions with four heavy 15-cm howitzer- or 21-cm mortar batteries. Some also had 10-cm cannon batteries. All batteries had four guns. This changed as the war went on. Batteries with 13-cm cannons and 21-cm mortars now had only three guns each, those with the new 15-cm cannon 16 had only two guns each. The heaviest steep- and flat trajectory batteries had one gun each.

Firing Procedures and Reconnaissance

The foot-artillery adjusted better to the changed conditions in the technique of firing, and even acted as instructors for the field-artillery.

On average in one day in 1916, four 15-cm heavy howitzers of a foot-artillery battery fired up to 1600 shells, each of which weighed 43 kilos. That corresponded to 55.9 tonnes. In order to bring up this quantity of ammunition, 66 heavy field waggons 05 were required, each bearing a one-tonne load of 23 rounds. Seen statistically, a battery fired 67 rounds or 2.3 tonnes of munitions per hour; and since the life of a gun barrel was a maximum of 10,000 rounds, a gun needed a new barrel after scarcely four weeks. These figures highlight the dimension of the problem.

The devastating effect of German artillery fire on a Russian gun position.

German tethered balloon prior to an ascent. Balloon platoons carried out artillery-spotting work: extended observation of the enemy battle lines, reconnaissance of enemy batteries, fire direction during the fighting, calibration of guns and photography.

Before 1915 mobility, coming to readiness to fire swiftly, and firing from open positions had been the priority factors. This was not valid in trench warfare. The foot-artillery procedures, developed in fortress warfare, were closer aligned to the new conditions. This did not imply that long-proven field-artillery – now called "light artillery" – procedures were to be abandoned. Heavy guns were only suitable to a limited extent to offer direct fire from open firing positions in attacking battles.

In trench warfare, at first the respective opponents took another way characterised by emphasis on indirect fire, lengthening the period of firing and greater concentrations of artillery. Three examples of this: in September 1915, during the Allied offensive in the Champagne and in the Artois, there were 4085 guns in action, in February 1916 during the German attack on Verdun 1925 guns, and finally in July 1917 in the Allied attacks in Flanders 3525 cannons, howitzers and mortars.

Both sides adapted their defences. Thus the new regulations issued by German Supreme Command *Grundsätze für die Führung in der Abwehrschlacht* (Principles for fighting Defensive Battles) issued in 1917 provided for elasticity with counter-thrusts and counter-attacks. Useless hanging-on to strips of terrain was to be avoided. Firing all day long robbed the attacker of surprise and enabled the defender to alert his reserves. It churned the territory into areas of craters of very difficult passage. The artillery had to be used more intelligently. Therefore the Germans developed better firing procedures.

The artillery received important support for its deployment from the Survey Service (*Vermessungsdienst*) whose reliable maps showed the favourable firing locations for the batteries. Light- and sound-measuring batteries helped to identify enemy artillery positions. Tethered balloons with cable and telephone leads linked to command posts on the ground were indispensable for a constant observation of the enemy battle lines, to identify the enemy batteries and to calibrate the German artillery.

Artillery spotter planes also served this purpose and fire direction by use of phonographs (dictating machines) and other accessories. Great value was placed on the evaluation of aerial photos for the identification of enemy positions, particularly those of the artillery, but also for other activities which were a prelude to enemy attacks and offered rewarding targets for the German guns.

At the outbreak of the First World War, Germany's ally Austro-Hungary was in the process of reorganising its artillery and introducing new, more efficient weaponry. Especially impressive was the heaviest artillery, e.g. the 30.5-cm (12-inch) motor-drawn mortar, and mountain artillery with partially superior German equipment. The industry of the

Special Firing Procedures

The Pulkow *procedure gave effective fire without previous calibration which guaranteed to the German attack the element of surprise.*

The Bruchmüller *procedure worked out the infantry advance (beyond splinter range) to provide simple artillery cover. There was also a double-barrage with splinter shells and gas shells.*

Both procedures played a significant part in the intial German success in the West in the spring of 1918. The artillery no longer worked alone with its guns and huge quantities of ammunition: surprise and mobility were now added.

Danube monarchy was not adequate to meet the great demand for guns and ammunition. Noteworthy quantities were not available until 1915, which proved disadvantageous for this branch of service throughout the entire war.

Between 1914 and 1918 the German artillery alone fired 290,760,000 shells valued at 16.1 million Gold Marks (today about 80 million euros). In those days these amounts were hardly imaginable. To give a rough idea of the relationship: a pound of white bread in Nuremberg – where the firm of Zündapp was an important manufacturer of detonators – cost 24/100ths of a Mark at the outbreak of war.

During the war period, 65 of every 100 fallen soldiers was killed as the result of artillery fire. Where artillery was highly concentrated, such as at Verdun in 1916, the tally was 75 in every 100. During the Franco-Prussian War of 1870/71 – and the commanders of both sides could look back only to that war for their assertion – the loss rate due to artillery fire had been 7.5 percent. The artillery fire of the First World War put anything that had gone before into the shade, and the numbers of guns and the quantities of ammunition fires reached enormous proportions.

The Artillery of the Entente

At the outbreak of war the French had over 4,780 75-mm field guns mle 1897, of which 3,792 were at division or corps. Their range was increased from 8500 metres to over 11,000 metres. On the other hand heavy guns were few and far between: of the 308 in service many were already

A battery of French
155-mm field
howitzers in an
open firing position.
Officially this gun
was known as "Canon
de 155 C mle.1915"
and "1917 Schneider".
By 5 November 1918
the heavy artillery
regiments had 1980
of them, including
the 390 howitzers
delivered from
St.Chamond.

New to the artillery
stocks of the French
Army was the 155-
mm cannon mle.1917
with a range of 15,900
metres, manufactured
from 1917. In firing
position it weighed
8956 kg. The fighting
troops had 224 of
them on 5 November
1918.

On its bedding plate, the 370-mm (14.56-inch) mortar "Filloux" weighed 28.6 tonnes. The shells with streamlining cap stood about 1.7 metres tall and weighed between 400 and 540 kgs. Maximum range lay between 10.5 and 10.7 kms. In January 1916 there were three of them, in November 1918 ten guns of this type.

The 370 mm howitzer mle.1915 on railway chassis using an 1887 naval gun barrel weighed between 127.5 and 134 tonnes. Of the eight guns available at 1 January 1918, four were captured by German forces in the spring of 1918.

British field guns were officially designated "18-pounder Field Gun Mk 1": the British traditionally used shell weight instead of a metric measurement for the calibre details. The calibre of this gun in millimetres was 83.8, this was the largest calibre at the outbreak of war, and at 8700 metres (9514 yards) also had the longest range.

British ammunition dump on the North-west European Front.

The most important representative of the heavy field guns in the British Army were the 6-inch field howitzers Mk-1 and Mk-*. Ready to fire they weighed about 4250 kgs. Maximum range with the 100-pound heavy shell was 8700 metres (9,514 yards), the range in 1918 with the lighter 39 kg (86-pound) shell introduced that year was 10.4 kilometres (11,374 yards).

A 15-inch heavy howitzer Mk.I deployed during the fighting on the Flanders Front near Arras. It was manned by British naval gunners. The weight on the firing position was 94.5 tonnes: the maximum range was 10,794 yards. The shells weighed 1400 pounds. Ten howitzers of this type were built.

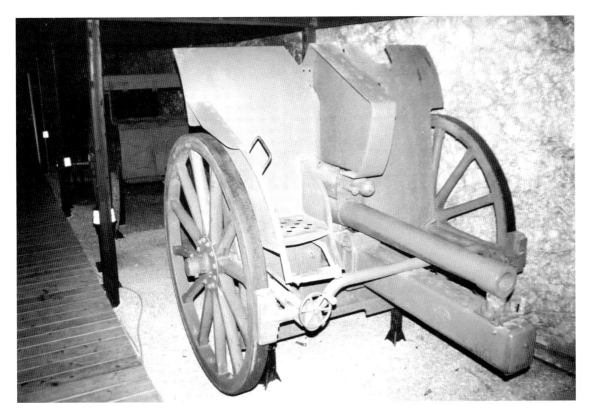

The Italian field gun model 1911 weighed 1073 kgs on the firing position and fired its shells weighing 6.3 kg up to a distance of 8400 metres.

152-mm cannons
L/40 of the Italian
heavy artillery built
between 1891 and
1899. They weighed
13.3 tonnes and could
engage targets at
12.5 kilometres range.
This photograph was
taken at the end of
October 1917 after
the breakthrough by
German and Austro-
Hungarian forces at
Flitsch and Tolmein.

Russian 76.2-mm
guns captured during
the fighting in East
Prussia and displayed
as trophies in Berlin.
The heavy gun
weighed 1040 kilos
on the firing position
and fired a 6.58 kg
HE shell at a muzzle
velocity of 593 m/
sec. The greatest
range was at first
6600 metres, and rose
later to 8750 metres.

obsolete. 7000 guns formed part of fortress and fortification defences. They were not mobile and only with great effort could they be shifted to the front when trench warfare began. By November 1918 the composition of the French artillery had changed radically. Of its 10,119 guns, 3377 were of heavy and the heaviest calibre, and with regard to their numbers and firepower they made an overwhelming impression. In organisation the artillery branch was separated into field-artillery and heavy artillery.

In Britain, field artillery had undergone a process of renewal in 1904 and 1910 respectively. A 3.29-inch field gun and a 4.5-inch light field howitzer had entered service: of the latter there were 1225 at the war's end in 1918. The greater part of the heavy guns in 1914 made up the siege artillery and were mostly obsolete. The branch of service, separated into field-artillery and heavy artillery as in France, required reorganisation and, as in other countries, improvised.

Long-range naval and coastal guns were provided with field mounts. From 1915/16 newly manufactured guns arrived at the front:

3815 cannons and 3723 heavy howitzers of 127 or 152.5 mm calibre and 1290 heavy howitzers of 203.2 and 233.7 mm. There were also guns of the heaviest weight on railway mountings. The efforts made to introduce motorised tractors for towage must be acknowledged as must the first armoured self-propelled chassis for 152.4-mm heavy howitzers, the so-called "gun carriers" in 1918.

The Russian field artillery at the outbreak of war had the ballistically most efficient field-gun of the genre in the 76.2-mm field gun 1902. On 17 June 1917 they had 7621 of them. Their light 122-mm howitzer based on the French design and its ammunition also impressed. The heaviest Russian guns were of German manufacture from the turn of the century, afterwards their guns were completed at the Putilov works to French blueprints. As the war went on, the Russians had increasing problems replacing their losses at the front, and they attempted to close the gap with imports from Britain and France.

Italy had also used German and French artillery technology before the war. An

Long 15-cm heavy field howitzer 13 during the German offensives in the spring of 1918. Between 1916 and the war's end 1550 guns of this type had been delivered. The weight on the firing position was said to be 2250 kgs, the weight of shell 40.3 to 42.3 kgs. Maximum range was 8800 metres.

interesting home design was the "Cannone da 75 mod.1911" Dèport – known as the Dèport Cannon with a mount which was used successfully to engage both and ground and aerial targets. There was a backlog in the area of heavy artillery so that naval gun barrels, some with unsuitable mountings, were thrust into service. Italy had the great advantage of being able to fall back on the war experience of her allies when eventually she entered the conflict. During the war, proven guns imported from Britain and France found their way to the front.

Up to the time when the United States entered the war on 6 April 1917, guns on order – amongst them guns with spreading tail chassis – had not been completed. For that reason the US Army Expeditionary Corps used British and French cannons, howitzers and mortars.

Involvement of 2.Battery/Foot-Artillery Batallion 119 during the Great Offensive at Chemin des Dames in May 1918.

Report by Captain (Reserve, ret'd) Reckhaus

"The following account depicts the mass bombardment in the framework of the 1918 May Offensive at Chemin des Dames by 28.Inf.Div., and especially the experience of the prepared nuisance fire and subsequent artillery barrage by my battery.

We had a planned bombardment almost lacking any opportunity of being observed, and refined down to the last detail so as to eliminate any chance of error: in other words a disciplined massive barrage. It was necessary to take great care in its preparation; it was to be carried out conscientiously and with punctual adherence to the schedule. The aim of the plan was to wipe out the targets by organised massed fire, or at least paralyse them totally, from along large sections of the front.

The basic concpt was as follows: initially there would be 160 minutes of destructive fire on all important targets, especially artillery, destroying resistance as a prelude to 300 minutes of uninterrupted bombardment to give our infantry advancing behind it the chance to occupy territory without incurring great losses. For this bombardment all batteries would align the farthest forward possible and coordinate their fire per timetable.

The general preparations were undertaken by 18.Inf.Div. as the attack division from the

positional division. This involved identifying where to station our battery positions 2 to 3.5 kilometres from the enemy's most forward front line, to indicate spotter posts and limber parks on boards with numbers for the purposes of survey and preparation of the battery plan by the survey troops. The latter had to work with the most painstaking accuracy, because there would be no prior calibration of the guns and only the direction of fire was to be marked on the plans. The zero line had to be established and sufficient plans on the 1:25,000 and 1:50,000 scale drawn up.

Some weeks before the day of the attack the attack divisions and all the reinforcement artillery was assembled and distributed by the divisions into anti-infantry batteries, anti-artillery batteries and long-range batteries (changes in style-the author). Every anti-infantry battery was given a 100–150 metre broad strip for the bombardment.

2.Battery/Foot-artillery-batallion 119 equipped with four 15-cm heavy field howitzers 13, was attached to 28.Inf.Div. and camped in the Sisson woods. These were exhausting weeks filled with the preparatory work with the battery and observation posts. The work couould only be done by night and taken ever possible precaution against detection. Every man had to be conscious of it that the element of surprise alone guaranteed the success of the great stroke. Especially difficult was the bringing up of ammunition which, as with all traffic to the firing positions, could only be done by night along the few approach roads. The planned firing positoins lay close together. The distance between guns was as short as possible. Every battery had to store about 3,000 rounds: splinter-, blue-cross gas-, green-cross choking gas- and smoke shells. It was necessary additionally to wrap the horses' hooves and ammunition waggon wheels in order to reduce noise as much as possible.

The battery plan was delivered for the preparation of the firing lists. The zero line and an auxiliary line were determined and the particular barrel influences for each gun worked out at the Lappion firing range. The influence of weather would have to be evaluated on the day before the attack. The actual weather conditions had to be reported during the firing at x+150 for each principal target and then each two hours afterwards to make out plan really effective.

All these theoretical and practical preparations required four whole weeks in which our hopes were high in our woodland camp. The battery crews visited each other daily. Officers and NCOs attended artillery lectures to acquaint them with the firing procedures. By day the men worked to perfect the firing lists, by night they cursed at storing ammunition and developing the position as far as that was possible. Everything went well. The thickly occupied woods were hardly ever molested by enemy fliers. Everything pointed to surprise being complete. The group order iof 26 May informed us: "Y-Day is 27 May. X-hour is 0200. The assault therefore begins at 0440.(…) All timepieces are to be synchronised. The shell flight times to our first target, Stefan II, are known. The first salvo will impact along the whole front at 0200. The weather conditions will be reported immediately. The corrected range, traverse and quadrant elevation will be given to the battery commanders.

Command (watch in hand!). First loading! Target I. Salvo! Fire! The barrels empty, tension is relaxed. In accordance with the plan reproduced below the battery continues destructive fire from 0200 to 0440 hrs.

The trench situation of the enemy main position is laid out in depth, four strips Stefan 1 to 4. Adolf means two artillery positions at 7500 to 7900 metres range 1500 metres east of Jumigny. Each target will receive the intermittent fire of two to four batteries.

A deafening hammering lasts until 0430. Left and right, to the front and rear, everywhere hammers and hisses. The enemy batteries and trenches are so heavily bombarded that nothing stirs over there. Each of us gives his all over the next seven and a half hours. As according to turn, 2.position, artillery 1500 metres east of Jumigny, battery reserves including command posts south of Craonne, 2.position again and then a line of trenches of the principal resistance line at Cheveux are taken under fire with ranges of 2800, 7800, 2800, 2500 and 2200 metres.(…)

At x+150=0430 hrs command: "Prepare for Walter-Bombardment. The foremost trench

Plan for Destructive Fire from x until x+160 (0200 until 0440 hrs)

Time periods	Target	Ammuntion Type	Number of Rounds
X – x + 10	Enemy position, strips 2 u. 1 = Stefan 2	up to 2 blue(-cross), splinter	52 rounds
X = 95 – x + 115	Enemy position, strips 2 u. 1 = Stefan 2	up to 2 blue(-cross), splinter	52 rounds
X + 115 – x + 150	Enemy position, strips 1 = Stefan 1a = 5a	splinter	85 rounds
X + 150 – x + 160	Beginning point for the bombardment, enemy position, strip 1, northern edge	splinter	28 rounds

The destructive fire according to the plan began with Stefan 2 (2.position). Below is firing list.

Firing List

Time	Salvo!	Battery	Fire!					
		"Then each guns fires as per table!"						
		IV	III	II	I	Number of rounds heavy field howitzers 40 incl. opening salvo above	Blue-cross gas shells
x	range 1	2495	2485	2515	2525		
bis x + 10	range 2	2445	2435	2465	2475		
	range 3	2545	2535	2565	2575		
	Glw.A.S.	9—	9—	9—	9—		
	traverse: Grundrichtung						
	range 1	572+	572+	572+	572+		
	range 2	592+	592+	592+	592+		
	range 3	552+	552+	552+	552+		

x+10kdo: Prepare for target Adolf!

Austro-Hungarian 30.5-cm mortar M.11 (Skoda) aroused much interest shortly after the outbreak of the First World War. It was involved in shelling the Belgian border fortifications and besides its firepower was very manoeuvrable. 58 models of the type had been built by 1916.

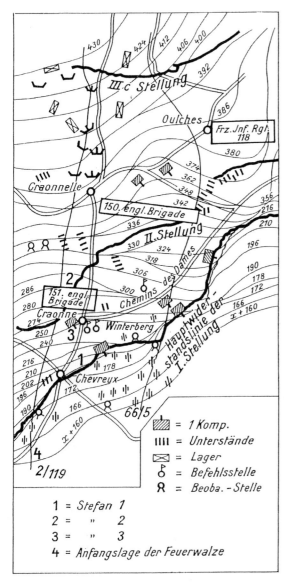

Relief sketch for the organisation of artillery fire in the 2.Battery/Foot-artillery-batsallion 119 sector on 27 May 1918.

IIIc/II Stellung = IIIc position
Frz.Jnf.Regt.118 = French Inf.Regt 118
engl-Brigade = British brigade
Hauptwiderstandlinie der I.Stellung = Main resistance line of 1.position

Key:
1.Komp = 1.Company
Unterstände = protected structures/bunkers
Lager = compound, dump
Befehlsstelle = command post
Beoba-Stelle = artillery spotter post

in the first position at Cheveux at the shortest range (2000 metres) was taken under fire. At x+160=0440 hrthe last rounds fell on the foremost bombardment curve, i.e. in th foremost trench of 1.position.

…The battery fired at a trench extension, the Dreising-trench, from 0440 to 0446 hr, a spit of trench that was latterly occupied by two MGs.

At x+172=4.52 hr we crushed the main resistance line of 1.position, wandered fire into the 2.position zone over obstacles, trenches with the reserves gone; at x+280 we left 2.position, wandered fire over the strongly developed Kaninchenberg between x+306 and x+330 and at x+386=0816 hrs fired at ammunition bunkers. Between x+386 and x+392 we covered two batteries recognised over the last two days as still operational, also at x+244. At the following and last bombardment our fire wandered through 3.position and the material store at maximum range. The infantry quickly followed the bombardment, and as we could see through the scissors telescope when it got light, only encountered sporadic opposition. The last rounds had to have ceased by this time. The shooting during these hour of physical toil were similar to firing at the artillery range. Officers and men, all in the best of spirits, gave everything , body and soul, in order to meet the parameters. No enemy counter-fire was perceived. The first British Pows appeared near the battery at 0900 hr."

Note

1. The HE shell for the 7.7-cm field gun 96 n/A weighed 6.85 kgs, the explosive charge 0.25 kgs. The shell for the 15-cm heavy field howitzer 02 was 40.6 kgs and took a 4.6 kg explosive charge.

Chapter Five

TANKS

The Road to Cambrai

Armoured vehicles were known from before the First World War. They were called "land-torpedo boats", "land ships" or "motorized guns". They were ideas and projects, the odd one here and there appearing as a prototype. The military saw no need for them – not even after the outbreak of war and not even at the turn of the year 1914 when the war of mobility froze into trench warfare.

In order to break through the enemy's defences, his concealed weaponry – MGs, mortars, artillery guns – had to be overcome. This required a major operation and was seldom successful. As an alternative, discussion in Britain turned very quickly to "an armoured vehicle", "(…) motorised, bullet-proof and so armed that it could overwhelm machine-guns and be sufficiently mobile cross-country to cross infantry trenches and climb trench parapets." This at least was how Lt-Colonel E.D.Swinton of the Pioneer Corps suggested it in his proposals and memoranda submitted to the War Ministry between October 1914 and June 1915. He saw the technical solution in the tracked towing machine offered by Holt-Caterpillar. The most prominent opponent of the "MG-destroyer" was no less a personality than Field-Marshal H.H.Kitchener, victor over the army of the Mahdi at the Battle of Omdurman in 1898, and since 6 August 1914 Minister for War. Only after several setbacks and with the support of the Admiralty and the newly created Armaments Ministry did the advocates of Swinton's ideas finally make some progress in the development and construction of the new weapon. In November 1915 the first prototype, "Little Willy", was introduced. It failed to convince. At the same time a wooden model was ready which was closer to Swinton's proposal in June 1915. At Hatfield Park, London in January 1916 the prototype of the first heavy British armoured vehicle known as

known as "Mother-Tank" made its debut. It already showed the later famous rhomboid-form with the high leading wheel forward and the caterpillar track running around the entire profile. After firing experiments with German MGs and ammunition, driving trials followed over a terrain in which German-type positions and obstacles had been copied, and finally the armament of the vehicle was tested. On 2 February 1916, the first tank was exhibited to the War Minister Lord Kitchener, the Minister for Armaments Lloyd George and other representatives from politics, the military and industry. Kitchener remained a sceptic. The civilian ministers were enthusiastic and even the officers from the front were in favour of the new weapon. The advocates had their way. 20th Armoured Vehicle Squadron of the Royal Naval Armoured Car Division was made the nucleus of the future tank corps. The cover name "tank" was used for the new weapon at the same time and would soon become a universal term.

The Entente Gallops Off

The first series of heavy British armoured vehicles received the designation "Tank Mk-I". The original order for 40 was raised to 100, and then in April 1916 to 150. 75 of these were armed with two 57-mm (2.2-inch) cannon L/40 and three MGs, the other 75 exclusively with MGs. They were divided into "male" and "female" based on the armament. Besides explosive shells with impact fuzes, canister shot

The French answer to the question what would destroy the MGs on the battlefield was "Chars assault" (assault waggon). There were two models, the "Char Schneider" and the "Char Chamond". They made their debut at the Aisne on 16 April 1917. 176 tanks stood ready, 124 saw action and 66 were destroyed. The one in the photograph is a "Char Schneider".

could also be used in close combat. Even before the first tank left the works, the new C-in-C in France and Flanders, General Douglas Haig, demanded the new "wonder weapon" for his planned offensive on the Somme. This raised the spectre of placing at the front, drop by drop, a technologically immature and tactically unproven weapon, thereby sacrificing the element of surprise.

In France as in Britain only a few personalities had spoken out in favour of developing an armoured fighting vehicle in the interests of upgrading the hitting power of their attacking units. Foremost was Colonel (and later General) J.B.Estienne. The French presented their own models, the "Chars assaults" at the front for the first time in April and May 1917, but long before the first operational use their shortcomings had been obvious, prompting Estienne to obtain from the industrialist Louis Renault his cooperation in building a lighter, fast tank, the "Char lèger". This was shown for the first time in March 1917, and in May 1918 just over a year later there were already 216 of them in stock.

In Germany the idea of using armoured fighting vehicles at the front had been accepted only with great reserve. Uncertainty as to what direction the work should take impeded the German development, and in any case at that stage of the war there were insuperable economic problems for mass production. Therefore the most promising design, the heavy fighting vehicle "A.7.V" was only available in small numbers in the spring of 1918. Local designs also existed in the United States and Italy, and some prototypes reached the testing stage. Ultimately the Allied belligerents decided to obtain tanks from the two leading producers, Britain and France, or pave the way to build under licence.

The Development of the Heavy Tank Mk-IV

During the Battle of the Somme in the second half of September 1916, the Mk-I demonstrated the usefulness of the tank. However, the fact that of 49 completed tanks only 32 had made it to the Front and only 14 of these had seen any action gave rise to doubts as to their reliability

in operation. There were other drawbacks. Three crew were involved in steering it. The tail wheels had proved superfluous. The speed and radius of action of the Mk-I were limited. The armour did not provide reliable protection against the steel-core ammunition (SmK) used by the German infantry from March 1917. The slightly improved Models Mk-II and Mk.III together with the Mk-I represented the range of British tanks in the first half of 1917. With the advent of the Mk-IV the others were all converted into unarmed "supply tanks", some fitted with sleds for transport, and used to bring up ammunition, fuel and replacement parts.

The Mk-IV had been ordered in October 1916 immediately after the first tank operations on the Somme. The experience gathered up until then had been included into the design. Accessibility to the motor and its reliability in functioning had been improved. A 6-cylinder Daimler engine had been installed in the forward part of the tank with the two-speed gearbox behind. Chains imparted the rear wheel drive. The vehicle was steered by coupling or uncoupling the left or right drive. To assist progress over soft ground wood or iron shoes or "spuns" were fitted one metre apart to the tracks. A feature of the Mk-IV were the two carrier rails on the roof for an anti-ditching beam or fachine-bundles which

In order to cross anti-tank ditches up to four metres wide in front of the German lines, Mk-IV tanks carried several tons of fachine-bundles. These were dropped into the ditch and then the tank moved slowly forward until the front of the hull inclined downwards to rest against the rear wall of the trench. The tank kept going, the rear of the hull fell back until the tracks encountered the bundles of fachine brushwood and provided sufficient purchase for the tank to climb out of the trench.

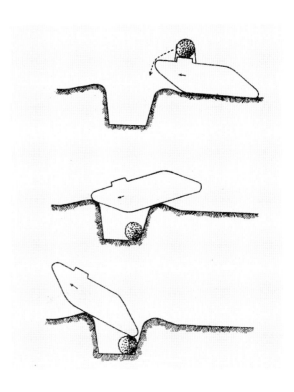

For the heavy fighting at Arras also known as the "Easter Battle" which lasted from mid-March until the end of April 1917, 60 reconditioned Mk-Is were made ready. They were distributed between five Companies, from eight to twenty tanks each, their purpose being to support three armies along 25 kilometres of front.

The tanks made their first attack on 9 April 1917. Over the next few days they made a significant contribution to the success of the attack in the 3rd and 5th Army sectors. In the 1st Army region they stuck in the mud.

34 of the 60 Mk-I tanks took part in the fighting. Of these, 17 (therefore half the total) received direct hits from artillery. How many remained stuck in the mud is not known: some fell into German hands.

The "Char lègere Renault" was the most modern tank design anywhere in 1918. The first 30 models saw action at Chaudun on 31 May 1918. Six weeks later 135 were involved in the fighting at Soissons. The tactical efficiency of these light tanks contributed substantially to the French successes.

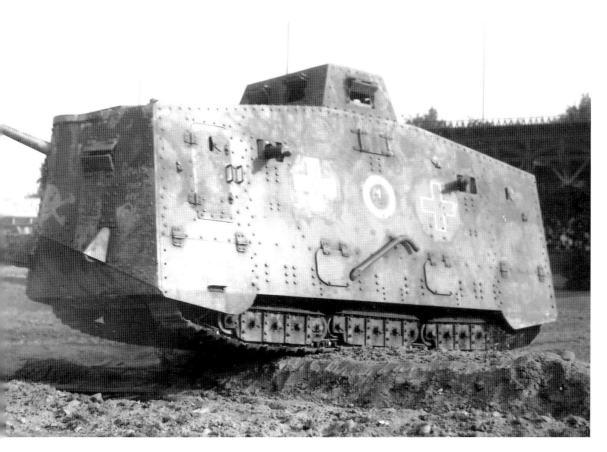

The A.7.V. was the first German armoured fighting vehicle. Only 20 were built. They became available in October 1917. Four A.7.V.'s and five captured heavy tanks took part in the "Michael Offensive" on 21 March 1918.

A Mk-IV (male) tank in the exhibition halls of the Belgian Tank Museum, Brussels.

Mk-IV (male) tank in
the Royal Armoured
Corps Museum,
Bovington Camp,
Dorset.

Side profile diagram,
Mk-IV tank.
Key: Radiator
ventilator: ventilator
motor: starting crank:
hinterer Turm = rear
turret: anti-ditching
beam: air flaps: fuel
intake. **Schrank**
= locker, chain
tightener, accelerator
pedal, throttle lever:
Lichtdynamo =
dynamo for lighting:
driver's seat: dynamo
for exhaust, principal
motor. **Anlasser**
= starter: end of
gearbox, hydraulic
gearbox, gear-motor
drive, fuel tank.
Spannrolle = tension
wheel, driving
chain: track drive-
wheel, track control
aperture, cooling-air
discharge, hook.

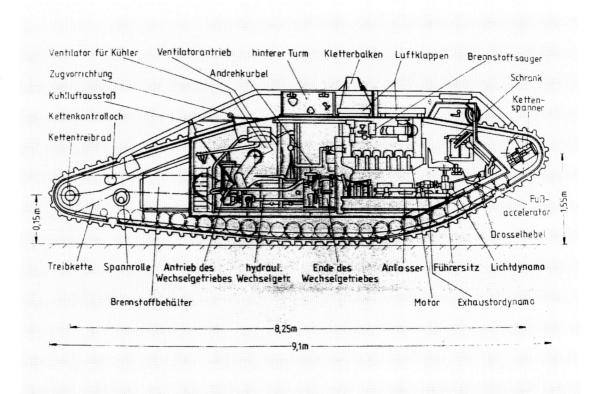

Technical and Tactical Details, Mk-IV Tank		
	Male version	**Female version**
Weight	28 t	27 t
Crew	8 men	8 men
Length	8.050 metres	8 metres
Breadth	4.011 metres	3.2 metres
Height	2.46 metres	2.46 metres
Ground clearance	42 cms	42 cms
Breadth of track	35 cms	35 cms
Fording depth	1 metre	1 metre
Climbing ability	1.2 metres	1.2 metres
Angle of climb	22°	22°
Overhang	3 metres	3 metres
Speed	6.7 km/hr	6.7 km/hr
Speed cross-country	0.8–3.2 km/hr	0.8–3.2 km/hr
Range	56–72 kms	56–72 kms
Fuel tank	318 litres	318 litres
Motor	4-stroke-Otto 6-cylinder	4-stroke-Otto 6-cylinder
Output	105 hp	105 hp
Revolutions	1000/min	1000/min
Coolant	water	water
Drive	rear	rear
Gearbox	2-speed	2-speed
Armour	6–12 mm armour steel	
Armament:	(male): 2 x Hotchkiss L/23 57-mm cannon, 4 x Lewis MG 7.71 mm calibre: 332 rounds/Hotchkiss: 6272 MG rounds.	(female): 6 x Lewis MGs 7.71 mm calibre: 30,080 MG rounds.

could be ejected by a release mechanism inside the tank into a trench or wall to be climbed. These bundles could cause problems since they were prone to break loose when the tank moved violently.

The armour was improved: twelve millimetres of thick special steel to protect against German SmK ammunition which would now only penetrate at the closest range with a favourable angle. The fuel tank at the rear with 318 litres capacity was given double armour. The differing armament between the two versions of tanks

was retained in the 2:3 relationship. "Male" tanks were equipped with two 57-mm guns and four MGs, "female" tanks had six MGs. The former had the task of destroying German MG nests, the "female" tanks would then harrass the retreating German infantry with their MGs. The ammunition they carried was enormous, 30,080 rounds.

The modified Hotchkiss MGs had been removed from the Mk-I to Mk-III tanks, and the 7.71-mm Lewis MG installed on the Mk-IV. On the "male" version in place of the

Mk-IV ("male" tank
No. 2083. In this
left side profile can
be clearly seen the
cannon window with
horizontal roller
shield in which the
57-mm gun could
be raised vertically.
Behind it is the shield
for the Lewis MG
although the weapon
itself has been
removed. The crew
hatch farther back is
open.

Mk-IV ("female")
tank without number,
name or batallion
insignia. The left-side
cannon window with
the two horizontal
roller shields are
easily recognisable.
The Lewis MG's were
inserted vertically.
Both weapons have
been removed, the
crew access hatch
below is open.

Photograph from the heavy fighting in Flanders, mid-October 1917. The Mk-IV "female" tank shown hopelessly bogged down in mud has signs of apparent artillery direct hits.

57 mm Hotchkiss cannon L/40 (= 2280 mm) a shorter barrelled L/23 gun was fitted (= 1324 mm), the shooting performance of which was very satisfactory. It had a shorter barrel recoil, a great benefit for the crew within the tank with such cramped working conditions, and it reduced the side profile of the tank, thus making lighter work of manouevring in difficult terrain and especially crossing trenches, ditches and shell craters.

The Mk-IV was also distinguished from its forerunners by the lateral weapon arrangement. The smaller tank had two MGs with viewing slits per side with crew access hatches below, viewing slits for the "male" tank in the sides were larger for a 57-mm L/23 cannon fitted either side with a large field of fire fore and aft together with a Lewis MG either side located behind a bullet shield. The third MG was in the front with the driver, the tank commander manned the gun when the occasion arose, the fourth MG was kept in reserve. A crew access hatch 90 x 50 cms in dimension was located at the rear. In contrast to the earlier versions

the "male" type had a more pronounced slope outwards lower down. This served to improve manouevrability on battlefields with trenches and other obstacles.

The motor was designed to have a specially shaped crank. Batteries now provided the internal lighting. Observation was made through slits and hinged flaps. Mirrors for indirect observation were occasionally fitted and also a commander's periscope. Armoured masking was fitted before the tank battle at Cambrai as protection against splinters, and lead-splinters from the 7.92-mm rounds.

Signalling between tank crews was achieved by means of coloured discs and handlamps, to the Staffs using carrier pigeons. There were also special armoured radio vans. The first of these were deployed during the major offensive in Flanders on 31 July 1917.

The War Ministry had ordered 1050 Mk-IVs, 1220 were delivered. Series production began in March 1917 behind schedule. The original plan was for 240 Mk-IVs ready for the attack at Arras. This total was reduced to 96. In the end none arrived at the front, and recourse was had to 60 repaired older models. A little more than half of these rolled up to the German lines on 16 March, 17 of them with their artillery expended.

The Mk-IV came to the battlefield for the first time on 7 June 1917 in connection with the great mine explosion at Wytschaetebogen. This was 2.Tank Brigade with 60 heavy tanks of this type. They encountered serious problems in the craterland of mud and mire, 26 of the force being unable to extract themselves. Otherwise the Mk-IV proved itself.

For the renewed attack near Arras on 31 July 1917 the British High Command could now fall back on three tank brigades with 216 Mk-IVs, two (female) Mk-IV radio tanks and 36 supply tanks. These were attached to the three Army corps of 5th Army. The Army reserve was one batallion. A ten-day softening-up period by an artillery force of 3535 guns deprived the operation of surprise. The tank brigades, spread along a 25-kilometre long frontline, bogged down again in craters and mud and, condemned to immobility, suffered 51 percent losses to German artillery fire. Their disoriented crews were bombarded with gas shells, and were exposed to shell splinters and lead splinters which the German infantry aimed at vulnerable spots on the tanks (including the observation slits and flaps).

The Tank Battle of Cambrai, November 1917

The commanders of the Allied land forces judged the war situation in the second half of the year 1917 as unfavourable. Russia had left the alliance. Italy had suffered a serious defeat at Venice. In addition the French Army had recognized weaknesses and had not been successful in the spring and summer battles. What was needed before winter set in was a military success to consolidate the Entente position. The USA had declared war on Germany on 6 April 1917 and the arrival of American troops was hoped for in the spring of 1918.

In this situation the commanders of the Royal Tank Corps seized the initiative. The specialists had pointed repeatedly to planning errors in tank operations; the unfavourable terrain and the distribution along long sectors of the front. Another disadvantage had been

the lack of all surprise. They suggested now a surprise attack with the following aims:

1. The German troops in the immediate area of the attack would be wiped out, demoralising the units in the neighbouring sectors of the front.
2. The bringing up of reserves and intervention divisions from the neighbouring sectors or the hinterland would be prevented.
3. Confidence of the German troop commanders in their front units would be undermined.

The key to success was speed. Despite their technical flaws, tanks were at a stage of development in which they were able to operate with surprise and fast. The Royal Tank Corps commanders convinced the British High Command of the rightness of their views. They had the support of a memorandum dated February 1916 authored by the now Colonel E.D.Swinton which contained important pre-conditions such as:

a. The suitability of the terrain for a tank attack,
b. A massed attack by tanks against a narrow sector of the front.
c. The preservation of the element of surprise by renouncing a week-long artillery softening-up period and
d. The use of the tanks' manoeuvrability, firepower and armour.

The Situation

A suitable terrain was quickly found. At the end of October 1917, the British High Command decided to attack and breach the German Siegfried Line south-west of Cambrai. In accordance with their most recent principles for the development of trench systems, not until March 1917 had the Germans occupied it in the framework of their planned retreat. Early in the spring the Allies had devised plans to attack there. Nothing had come of them but the preparations would now work to their advantage. The future battlefield would lie between two canals, L'Escaut (Scheldt) in the south-west and Canal du Nord, still under construction. The terrain was composed

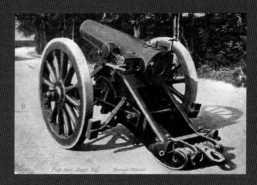

Mörser in Feuerbereitschaft

SOLDATENLEBEN.

Feldartillerie-Scharfschießen.

Der Kaiser u. der große Generalstab in der Gefechtslinie.

Geschützexerzieren.

Kruppscher Schießplatz Meppen — Feldgeschütz in Feuer.

3 cm Panzer-Lafette.

Les Chars Renault en manœuvre au Camp de BOURG-LASTIC

Angriff einer Maschinengewehr-Compagnie.

Maschinen-Gewehr-Kompagnie

Backen des Brotes in fahrbaren Feldbacköfen.

Essen-Ausgabe
an der Feldküche.

Das Zubereiten des Mittagsmahles
an der Gulaschkanone.

Kleine Bagage beim Überschreiten einer Ponton-Brücke.

K. S. 1. Train-Abteilung № 12
Proviantwagen, vierspännig.

Scheinwerferzug.

Truppen-Uebungsplatz Zeithain.

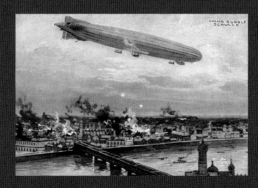

Tanks attacking the Siegfried Line south-west of Cambrai on 20 November 1917. The sketch was prepared by a war correspondent of a British illustrated magazine based on eye-witness descriptions. To the left is Havrincourt Wood, in the background to the right the village of Flesquières.

of ridges, streams, gullies and ravines. The Bourlon Massif rose behind the German Front. The villages of Moeuvres, Havrincourt, Ribàcourt and Banteux immediately before the Front were all totally destroyed, but in comparison to Flanders less scarred by artillery fire. The Germans considered it to be a quiet Front, a place to rest divisions. They had no intimation that the British were planning a major attack on the Cambrai front – they thought that the British were working to reinforce their positions and obstacles. The Germans allowed themselves to be deceived, and so the hoped-for surprise would succeed.

The British 3.Army under General J.Byng was responsible for the attack, and the following units were subordinated to him for the first tank battle in history:

- III and IV Army Corps, each with three divisions,
- A cavalry corps with three divisions,
- The entire Tank Corps with three brigades, each of three battalions.

Over 1000 guns and 160 mortars were to be used. The breadth of the sector to be attacked was approximately ten kilometres in length.

Moving Up

The moving forward of the three tank brigades was carried out with great care. They arrived at the Front by train from training camps and depots. Twelve tanks with crew and equipment made up one trainload, the tanks rolled off the train under their own power to the assembly area. All movements were made under cover of darkness. The last tanks arrived on the night of 18 November 1917.

There was a total of 476 fighting vehciles in all: 378 heavy Mk-IV tanks, 9 Mk-IV radio tanks with apparatus to set up a radio station, 1 telephone tank with cables and equipment, 2 pioneer tanks Mk-IV with anchors to rip up wire obstacles, 54 Mk-I and Mk-II supply tanks each with five towing sleds and 32 Mk-IV tanks in reserve.

The nine tank batallions had a reserve of one to six tanks each and at least 42 tanks per batallion: these batallions were formed up into three tank brigades.

Batallions G, D and E made up 1st.Tank Brigade and were attached to IV Army Corps in the north-west sector of the attack strip.

2nd Tank Brigade (A, B, and H Batallions) and 3rd Tank Brigade (C, J and F Batallions) joined III Army Corps in the south-westerly direction.

The tanks were divided into two groupings, except in the centre where in the sectors of 6th and 29th Inf.Divs. there was a third grouping with twelve tanks each from Batallions A and H.

On 20 November the commanding officer of the Tank Corp, General W. Elles, was aboard Mk-IV tank "Hilda" for the attack.

The Plan of Attack

A planned artillery barrage lasting several days was dispensed with. There was to be no artillery

A "male" Mk-IV without identifiable markings. This photgraph was taken after the battle. Where the German batteries succeeded in taking the tanks under direct fire they inflicted heavy losses on 20 November 1917, as for example at Flesquières.

fire until 20 November. Special emphasis was placed on cooperation with the infantry. For this purpose one week before the beginning of the offensive there was a field exercise around an old trench system near La Flaque. After the broad swathe of wire entanglements had been rolled down and the up to four metres-wide anti-tank ditches crossed, the tank sections had the job of advancing with the infantry into the German positions, paving the way for them and thus increasing the confusion in the enemy lines. Each section received specific targets. After these had been reached, the tanks woluld veer left and right and drive along the German trenches, flanking them. The idea of this was to drive the enemy into the protected housing and bunkers where they would be rewarding targets for the British infantry.

After reaching a line beginning north-west of the village of Havrincourt and running west of Marcoing south-west towards Le Pavé, the next task of the tanks was to prevent the German infantry becoming established and secure the new formation of the British units. The Germans were not to be in the position to build a fresh defensive line. To engage surviving enemy strongpoints to the rear of the British attacking units, some tank sections had been detached for "mopping up". Not until all these objectives had been achieved would the Army High Command accept that the pre-conditions had been met for the cavalry units to move in.

The basis for the cooperation with the tanks was the same as that with the infantry. If the breakthrough succeeded, infantry and cavalry together could capture tactically important points ahead of the British lines. Cooperation with the pioneers was seen mainly in getting the pioneers forward and protecting them during the dismantling or bridging of obstacles. The use of aviation was a fixed component of the attack plan. For this purpose signal lamps and a special code using single letters were prepared.

The objective was set out by the Commander-in-Chief, 3rd Army in the Attack Order for 20 September 1917 as follows:

"The aim of the operation is to break through the enemy defensive system at a single stroke with the support of tanks, and push cavalry through the gaps in order to win further territory. After breaking through the enemy trench system it is intended to send the cavalry corps ahead in order to capture Cambrai, Bourlon Wood and the bridges over the Sensée River. 1st Cavalry Division will send a detachment to Sailly and Tilloy to cut off Cambrai and link up east of Cambrai with the cavalry corps coming from England.(…) The success of the operation depends on whether we can occupy the bridges over the St Quentin Canal at Massnières and Marcoing and break through the last enemy trenches so as to get our cavalry forward before the enemy can bring up his reserve divisions for a counter-attack."

Tankschlacht bei Cambrai
Lage am 20. November 1917 und englischer Angriff bis 20.11. Abds.

Zu „Der Kampf gegen Tanks"   Karte 1

The Tank Battle of Cambrai
Situation on 20 November 1917 and British Attack until the evening

Key:		German
British	Position, that evening	Advanced line of trenches
Division	Tank movements that day	Main front line
Infantry Brigade	Attack positions of the tank batallions	SI and SII Siegfried Line
Cavalry Division	Destroyed "female" tank	
Direction until that evening	Destroyed "male" tank	
Main front line	Reconnoitred and situation clarified.	
	Destroyed tanks in terrain.	

The Key Element of Surprise

The key to the success of the operation was the element of surprise. And the British achieved it completely. On 16 November the Commander-in-Chief, 2.Army, General von der Marwitz, had advised Army Group *Kronprinz Rupprecht* at Mons: "Major enemy attacks against this Army Front are not expected in the near future." Furthermore two scouting parties of assault troops sent out on 18 November who returned with British prisoners brought no information regarding an imminent attack by massed armour.

At 0715 hr on 20 November 1917 the British artillery suddenly began a violent bombardment of the 2.Army trenches from Arras to north of St.Quentin. The main concentration of effort lay on the German defences around Havrincourt, Flèsquières and La Vacquerie. The smoke and dust of the explosive and smoke shells reduced visibility very substantially. After a short while, fire was laid on the German lines farther to the rear. Ten minutes before the commencement of the artillery preparation 204 Mk-IV tanks of the first grouping was set in motion. Soon they materialized from the swathes of smoke and mist in front of the German trenches, rolled effortlessly over the wire entanglements up to 30 metres wide, dropped fachine bundles into the anti-tank ditches and crossed them quickly. Attacking in several waves, the tanks reached the infantry trenches, veered left and right and drove along parallel to these. With their MGs and cannons they silenced all resistance. An officer of the Norfolk Regiment reported:

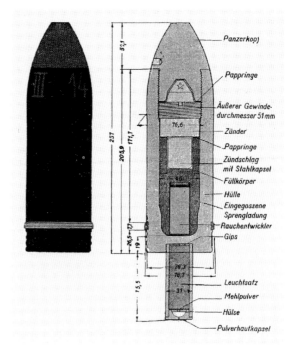

The 7.7-cm cannon shell 15 with armoured nose weighed 6.07 kgs. The best prospects for success in anti-tank gunnery was direct fire at below 700 metres range.
Key:
Armoured nose
Cardboard discs
Outer thread, diameter 51 mms
Detonator
Cardboard discs
Firing bolt with steel detonator cap
Filling material
Jacket
Poured-in explosive charge
Smoke developer
Plaster of Paris
Illuminant charge
Fine powder
Socket
Powder-membrane capsule

A tank commander of H Batallion, who attacked towards Ribecourt-Marcoing in his Mk-IV *Hadrian*, described it thus:

"A few minutes after the attack had begun, we heard behind us a loud rumbling. The tanks rolled at surprising speed past us into No-Man's Land. There were tanks everywhere. We counted twenty in our sector, and there were hundreds close by. We let them get somewhat ahead and then slouched along behind them, rifles slung around out necks, smoking happily. The Germans had wire entanglements twenty-five feet deep, but the tanks just rolled them down as if they were blades of tall grass and we followed in their tracks."

"On our way down the hill we had a good panorama of the battle in the dull, grey light. The enemy was totally surprised and the skies were ablaze with his coloured SOS lights. It was a magical and impressive sight. The whole corps with over 350 tanks took part. As far as the eye could see massive tanks, like prehistoric animals, each with an enormous bundle of fachines on the roof, proceeding forward mercilessly. The first two waves of tanks followed by infantry made good progress. Ahead of us was General (Elles) himself, watching

This Mk-IV "female" tank received a number of shell hits. Initially the German field artillery had only the 7.7.cm Kanonengranate 15 with long head-detonator 16m.V. In 1917 the special shell "Kanonengranate 15 mit Panzerkopf (armoured head)" which could penentrate 30 mms armoured steel arrived at the front. The 12-mm armour plates of the Mk-IV offered no protection against the latter shell.

The 7.7-cm Feldkanone 16 made its debut during the war. The poor traverse of only 4° was a disadvantage when engaging tanks. Rate of fire was over 15 rounds/min.

the attack with head and shoulders protruding through the upper hatch of his flag-tank Hilda.

The noise inside Hadrian was deafening, louder than the gunfire, and it was really impossible to make oneself heard. The rattling of the caterpillar tracks and the engine gave the impression of enormous speed, but we were only going at one mile per hour.

As we rattled across No-Man's Land, parallel to the Beaucamp-Ribecourt road, shells from an enemy field-gun hissed overhead and burst amongst the infantry, causing losses. Their Company commander was ripped apart by one of these shells. It was weird to see the dirt spray up 150 yards ahead and not hear the explosions. The noise inside the tank drowned out completely the explosions at that distance. Then an MG began to fire. The rain of bullets on the right side of the tank was like the tapping of innumerable small hammers.

On our way back (from Marcoing) we had the unpleasant experience of coming under fire from a field gun. Luckily the shells went too high and we escaped being hit by taking cover in a depression. On the other hand a low flying aircraft seemed to get an unlucky hit and crashed in flames a short distance away. Two of Gerard's three tanks were out of action and the third, Glauville's, got a hit from a light cannon which had also done for other tanks on the Flesquieres Ridge. It was probably the same gun, or one of the same battery, which fired at my tanks on the way back. It could have been the same gun which they say was manned alone by a German artillery officer (Corporal Krüger), whose great bravery was mentioned by Sir Douglas Haig in the Army Report about Cambrai."

The Course of the Battle on 20 November 1917

The German 54.Infantry Division, defending a kilometre long sector, suffered very heavy losses. The same applied to 20.Landwehr Division, involved in the fighting to the north whose units, principally Landwehr Infantry Regt.386, were attacked on the flanks. Towards the south was 9.Reserve Division. Units of these three formations were fully scattered in the fighting. Individual nests of resistance, such as that in the ruins of La Vacquerie, defended by 9.Comp/Reserve Inf.Regt 90/54.Inf.Div, had no lasting influence of the course of the battle on 20 November.

The battle around Flesquières developed in a different manner. Here the 51st Highland Division, which had fought in Flanders previously with especial distinction, was advancing. Contrary to other units, its divisional commanders had ordered their infantry to maintain a distance of 350 to 400 metres behind the tanks. Since the terrain was not swampy craterland as in Flanders the tanks had advanced rapidly and the infantry lost contact with them. Nevertheless the tanks kept rolling without infantry support towards the height of the Flesquières ridge held by the remnants of Reserve Inf.Regt 27/54.Inf.Div., reinforced by the two three-gun batteries of Field-Artillery Regt 202/20.Landwehr Div. and Field-Artillery Regt.108/54.Inf.Div. When the tanks surmounted the ridge they encountered the direct fire of both batteries. 16 of them were hit. The attack by the Highlanders, coming up from far behind, was broken up by the German machine-guns. Several attempts to occupy the village failed, even in the afternoon when seven tanks travelled through the village firing on the defenders.

In the early afternoon, tanks accompanied by cavalry and infantry headed for Marcoing. The Germans there were taken by surprise and since their pioneers had not destroyed the bridges, British tanks crossed the L'Escaut Canal. The attempt to cross the canal at Masnières failed after Tank F-22 of F.Batallion broke through the incompletely demolished bridge and fell into the canal.

Ribècourt was also taken: there was fighting only in the northern sector. Attacks by 1st Cavalry Division *The Kings*, which had received orders that morning to advance, petered out in the shooting from Cantaing: the flanking fire by German troops at Flesquières also prevented the deployment of cavalry. However, as the artillery ammunition at Flesquières began to run out, the German defenders saw the danger of their being encircled and cut off and they abandoned Flesquières during the battle.

Despite all setbacks the Tank Corps had forced its way through the Siegfried Line to a depth of nine kilometres along a twelve-kilometre broad front by the afternoon hours of 20 November. Between this attacking force and Cambrai three to four kilometres distant stood only a thin veil of German defenders. The British had taken 10,500 prisoners and captured 142 guns, a success never achieved

The Mk-IV "male" F-22 of F-Batallion/3rd Tank Brigade fell through the incompletely demolished bridge over the L'Escaut canal at Masnière around midday on 20 November 1917.

previously along other sectors of the front after months of bitter fighting with enormous material involvement. In London the church bells pealed news of the victory.

The Tank Corps losses by enemy action as at midday on 20 November could only be estimated roughly. It was thought that 59 tanks in all were out of action. 22 of these were attached to 3rd.Tank Brigade, which had supported with 146 tanks the attacks by 20th and 12th Infantry Divisions on the right flank. During the offensive the actual total of these 3rd Tank Brigade losses was 54 tanks. Besides the already mentioned 22 to artillery fire, 16 had stuck fast in trenches, one had sunk in the canal and 16 were immobilized with engine damage.

On the German side it was only during the course of the 20th that an impression was gained of the dimensions of the British attack. The QM-General at 3.Supreme Army Command, General von Ludendorff, wrote in his memoirs first published in 1919: "I did not obtain a clear picture of the size of the breach until midday: I was greatly concerned."

The Chief of the General Command Staff, XIII Army Corps, Infantry-General Freiherr von Watter, estimated in the forenoon of 21 November: "We must not avoid stating that, if

the enemy continues his tank attack before the arrival of our heavy artillery, we shall scarcely be able to prevent a further penetration and with it perhaps a real breakthrough. Even after this crisis (of 20 November – *the author*), the situation remained serious."

For the British not everything went according to plan. Because the cavalry attack had come to nought on the 20th, the chances of penetrating deeper into the German trench system had decreased. The cavalry had appeared on the battlefield too late and been halted in the machine-gun and artillery fire of the gradually strengthening defence.

On the second day of the attack the fighting in the area of German III.Army Corps had met with no success. An attack by 20th Infantry Division on Crèvecoeur failed. The attempt by 29th Infantry Division to capture the trenches east of the L'Escaut canal with the support of nine tanks from Marcoing was also repelled. At Noyelles sur Escaut the German counter-attacks were only warded off with great difficulty. These were launched by 3. and 4.Comps/Reserve Inf. Regt 232/107.Inf.Div. which had come from the Eastern Front in the expectation of rest and recuperation along the allegedly quiet section of the front near Cambrai.

The Course of the Battle on 21 November

On 21 November the concentration of effort of the battle transferred to the left wing, where IV Korps was established. No effort had been spared there to get the German artillery forward. For the British, Cambrai lay very near at hand: both sides had been ordered to the highest operational state of all their forces. 51st Highland Division and the 62nd (2nd West Riding Division) received orders to capture the Bourlon Massif, closely followed by the 1st Cavalry Division which would take control of the Nord Canal bridges. 36th Division was to proceed west of the canal.

After patrols had reported Flesquières free of enemy forces on the morning of 21 November, the attacking units occupied their readiness positions. 2nd Tank Brigade had been assigned. The day previously it had been with III.Army Corps on its right side and did not arrive until 12.30 hrs on account of the long journey. The attack on Containg succeeded nevertheless, the village being taken and several hundred German prisoners brought back. The rest of the German defenders pulled back towards La Folie Woods. In the fighting for Containg, the "male" tanks equipped with cannon had performed exceptionally well.

Towards 1600 hrs on the afternoon of the short November day, B-, C- and H-Batallions formed up together with infantry at Fontaine-Notre Dame. Between Bapaume and Cambrai lay a ruler-straight road barely three kilometres to the goal.

62nd (2nd West Riding-) Division attacked left of the 51st Highland Division. Its objective was the heights west of Bourlon Wood and the village of Bourlon. 1st Tank Brigade

A Mk-IV ("female") of J-Batallion in front of the first houses at Fontaine-Notre-Dame stuck in a ditch on 23 November 1917. The crew was taken prisoner.

was despatched in support but had a long drive from its technical base in the woods at Havrincourt and did not arrive until around midday. In the heavy fighting which followed around the village of Bourlon and the woods of the same name the tanks and infantry made continual advances. Some penetrated the woods but were not able to consolidate. Nevertheless the second day of the battle brought the attackers on the left wing considerable successes to which the Tank Corps contributed to a marked extent though suffering heavy losses. Once all fighting in this area terminated in December 1917, 36 damaged tanks, some totally broken apart, remained behind in the region between Anneux, Containg and Fontaine Notre-Dame, but mainly in Bourlon and its woods.

The End of the Battle

The tank battle ended on 21 November. The attempt to break through had failed. The British Commander-in-Chief had allowed a window of 48 hours to achieve it and time was up. German reserve forces were on their way to the area from all directions. Resistance stiffened appreciably and a continuation of the fighting promised little hope of success. Furthermore, the advance by IV Corps to the Bourlon Massif had created a dangerous situation for the fighting troops. The British commanders had two possibilities, either to retreat to Flesquières or fight on over the next few days. Haig decided for the latter. Therefore bitter fighting broke out between 23rd and 25 November around Moeuvrres, Bourlon and Bourlon Woods resulting in more gains of territory by the British.

On the night of 22 November 40th Infantry Division, especially experienced in fighting in forests, relieved the 62nd Infantry Division, but only stayed until 26th November during which time it lost 172 officers and over 3,000 men. The 62nd (2nd West Riding-) Division, whose troops had rested for a few days at Havrincourt, came forward to relieve them. The British had lost the village of Bourlon on 25 November, but they held the woods until the night of 4 December when they

The wreckage of the Mk-IV ("male") F 6 *The Dartifice* in Bourlon Woods after being hit by artillery. Photograph taken in December 1917.

Scarcely 500 metres from F 6 *The Dartifice* is the *Gurkha*, a "female" tank from G-Batallion/1. Tank Brigade. This unit attacked on 20 November with an authorized strength of 126 tanks (46 per batallion).

were forced to pull back by the weight of the German counter-attack.

A gunner of 1.Battery/Field Artillery Regt 44/16 (Bavarian) Infantry Division gave the following report on the anti-tank campaign of 27 November to an officer war correspondent at Army Group *Kronprinz Rupprecht*. The gunner had been a crew member of two 7.7-cm field guns brought forward as an anti-tank platoon to engage tanks by direct fire.

The "female" Mk-IV C-51 belonged to C-Batallion under Colonel Charrington which attacked in the German 12.Infantry Division sector towards Le Pavè. It was destroyed just north of the Gouzeaucourt-Le Pavè road. Because of its favourable location at the roadside it was one of the most popular sights for German soldiers' commemorative photographs.

"For some days the anti-tank platoon of our battery had lurked in various positions around Bourlon village awaiting its opportunity. On the evening of 26th it had moved into a position well forward about a kilometre south of the fiercely contested village and dug in. We had been informed that the enemy had two prepared fresh Divisions and 30 tanks for the attack, and we were at the highest state of alert.

At 0630 hrs the sentry reported lively dispersed fire at the village of Bourlon and the surrounding countryside and an hour later artillery fire fell on the forward trenches. This seemed the right moment and so: everybody out – to the guns!

It was still dawning and a light rain was falling. Enemy shells were exploding at regular intervals around the guns, there were two fresh craters with a whitish smoke billowing out about a metre from the right gun. A few minutes of great tension passed. Then at spot height 100 south of Bourlon Woods, sharply silhouetted against the horizon, there rose a hunchback constantly growing in size which then got smaller and smaller and beforre sliding down the slope on this side. The game repeated itself several times. They are coming! The shout came almost as a relief. The guns were aimed. The first tank was taken under fire at 1400, 1300 metres. Aha, he wants to cut and run to the right – another round! It flares up brightly, the smoke from the shell envelopes the dark shadow – a hit! The tank cannons ceased firing. Now for the next! Bring the tail of the chassis around! – it wouldn't budge. It had dug itself so deeply into the soft loam floor due to the recoil it couldn't be shifted. Everybody lend a hand! Dig out the chassis tail, drag the gun free!

Another heave, another effort by everybody and finally the gun was outside the emplacement and in the open field, but now free and mobile. Meanwhile the enemy tanks had come 200 metres nearer, close together offering us their full breast profile, five of them, heading for Bourlon, offering lively fire to all directions. Now followed round after round from our two guns at the monsters betraying themselves by their own fire. We were sprayed by their machine-guns, a distinctly perceptible whistling above our heads. Now it was them or us, no round to be fired which had not been deliberately aimed. The heat of the moment had gradually seized the crews, the commander had put himself in the first gunner's seat. The gun jammed! Another round! Out with the dud! Almost at the same instant the shout came from the mouths of several gunners, the joy of battle bright in their eyes. Is he still firing? One round, another, and then it all fell quiet. The next! Fire! Before the next, aim a bit higher – hit! The tank tried to turn, another couple of rounds, and then this one too lay still.

The battlefield at the western entrance to Bourlon. Nine tanks from F- and J-Batallions were hit and destroyed here. Tank left hand side is F 30 *Flaming Fire*.

To finally capture Fontaine-Notre Dame, the cornerstone of the German defence on the Bourlon ridge, 2nd Guards Division was made ready. They relieved the exhausted 51st Highland Division and probably succeeded in entering the village on 27 November, but their success was only temporary.

An important conference took place in 2.Army HQ on 27 November, those present including Infantry General Erich von Ludendorff and the Commander-in-Chief of the Army Group, Crown Prince Rupprecht of Bavaria. Main subject for discussion was the German counter-attack. This began at 0800 hrs on 30 November with an artillery bombardment enclosing the semi-circle of terrain west of Cambrai. At 1100 hrs the German infantry moved in and recaptured from the British most of the territory they had gained since 20 November, and more. The fighting ended on 8 December, and trench warfare regained its supremacy. The judgement of battle had been delivered.

Our other gun had meanwhile taken its toll, the two tanks it had hit burned with bright, licking flames, flaring up from time to time as the ammunition inside exploded. Nothing more stirred over there. Six enemy tanks in all, five of them strung close together, heavily damaged, others burning in the terrain. After we had looked over the guns and prepared them for possible further attacks, the crews went under cover after almost two hours exposed to enemy fire. Most fell asleep at once, only a few, nerves still tingling with the unusual tension, sat discussing the great success. On later inspection we saw that each of the tanks had received two or three direct hits, their crews either lay dead with horrible wounds below their tank or around it.

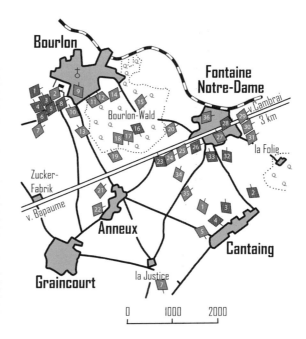

Map showing wrecked British tanks in Bourlon Woods.

Mk-IV "female" tank H 48 Hyaena after the attacks on Fontaine-Notre Dame on 23 November in which H Batallion/2nd Tank Brigade had participated with twelve tanks. H 48 was on the road between Bapaume and Cambrai, about 300 metres short of Fontaine, when it came to grief. A few weeks later the wreck was exhibited to the German public as a war trophy in the market place at Leipzig.

The Lessons of Cambrai

The concept, execution and results of the tank battle for Cambrai were evaluated intensively by both sides. Only the British drew the correct conclusions from it. As far as they were concerned, tanks as weapons of attack had proved themselves outstandingly. For this operation a concrete and limited task had been given to the Royal Tank Corps. It was to pave the way for the infantry through the obstacles in the field and German trenches. Previously, certain units of the 2nd and 3rd groupings had received further tasks: the capture of the bridges over L'Escaut Canal at Marcoing and Masnières and to hold them pending the arrival of the infantry. No further use of the tanks was envisaged. To complete the thrust into deeper territory had been the job of the cavalry units. As it turned out, this was beyond them for various

reasons and so the real objective of the operation was not achieved. What the Germans apparently overlooked in their analysis was the fact that the tanks had done what was required of them. The setbacks at Flesquières, Fontaine-Notre Dame and Bourlon, and the failure to cross the bridges, altered nothing.

After the Germans had warded off the attack on the left wing on the Bourlon Massif, the tanks set off in small groups – often in pairs, at the end alone – to fight a German defence increasing in strength. On 20 November, the British tank sector had 362 tanks at readiness. By 8 December 1917 the Germans had captured 71 of these, either put out of action by their troops or bogged down. Another 50 tanks lay within the British lines. The total of tanks lost was 121, one third of the force as at 20 November. The British casualties in tank crews dead, wounded and missing were put at 118 officers and 530

Mk-IV "male" tank B 28 *Black Arrow* (left) came to rest in the centre of Fontaine-Notre Dame village. Only lightly damaged, at the beginning of December it was towed away and used by the Commander of Motorized Troops/2.Army for evaluation and description of British Mk-IV tanks. Greater recognition was accorded to the "female" Mk-IV C 47 *Conqueror* (right) put out of action by foot soldiers of Infanterie-Regt *Graf Kirchbach* (1.Lower Silesian) No.46. They appreciated particularly the caricature of a diabolical German soldier on the hull rear right-side.

"Female" Mk-IV tank being loaded by German collection command troops at Cambrai railway station. The F 31 *Fearnought* of F-Batallion/3rd Tank Brigade was put out of action on 27 November during the fighting for Bourlon.

NCOs and men, in view of the successes not overly high.

On the other hand the anti-tank defences of the German side had not been especially effective. The resolution of the serious crisis situation, and the successful counter-attack of 30 November, strengthened the Supreme High Command in its estimation of the new weapon. Certainly they recognized a shortcoming in anti-tank gunnery and now put more emphasis on the development and supply of anti-tank weapons, but otherwise things returned to what they had been beforehand.

The Mk-IV tanks captured at Cambrai were passed to the Commander, Motorized Forces of the German Army for renovation and use in a Captured-Tank Battalions. By 11 March 1918 it was reckoned that of the wrecks towed away, 20 could be repaired. This estimate increased later. By 15 September 1918 five battalions had been so equipped.

Gruppe Caudry
Genkdo XIII. (K. W.) A. K.
Ia 529 op.

K. H. Qu., 27. 11. 1917.

Tankbekämpfung.

Erfahrungen einer Division aus den Kæmpfen bei Cambrai.

Die Division hat am 22. 11. in der Schlacht bei Cambrai eingegriffen und seit dieser Zeit wiederholt und immer erfolgreich gegen zahlreiche englische Tankangriffe gefochten. Die Erfahrungen werden ergaenzt durch mehrere Aussagen englischer Tankbesatzungen, darunter auch ein Hauptmann einer Tank-Kompagnie.

Taktik der Tanks. Gliederung in Tank-Bataillone zu 48—50 Tanks, jedes Bataillon 3 Kompagnien (16 Tanks) zu 4 sections (4 Tanks). Vorgehen moeglichst überraschend. Die Infanterie muss dichtauf folgen und schleudert noetigenfalls Nebelbomben, um die Tanks zu verhüllen. Jeder Tank (section) hat sein Zeichen, damit die Infanterie weiss, mit wem sie zu arbeiten hat (Pique-Ass, Kleeblatt, Granate usw.).

Der Tank faehrt gerade über den Schützengraben, schwenkt dann hinter dem Graben ein und soll die Besatzung abschneiden. Feuer wird im allgemeinen nur gegen Unterstützungen abgegeben, von hinten in unsere Truppen kann er schlecht schiessen, um die eigenen Truppen nicht zu gefaehrden. Einzelne Tanks gehen gerade aus weiter, um den Durchbruch zu vollenden.

Am 20. 11. haben etwa 300 Tanks angegriffen. Deutsche Gegenwehr und Gegenwirkung war schwach. Blutige Verluste auf beiden Seiten kaum nennenswert (Aussagen des am Angriff beteiligten englischen Kapitaens).

Bauart. Etwa 2,20 m hoch, 2 m breit, 8 m lang. Einteilung in „Maennchen" (male) mit 2 Geschützen und M.-G., und Weibchen (female) nur mit M.-G. ausgerüstet. Der wundeste Punkt: die Benzintanks. Sie befinden sich bei den neueren Tanks hinten.

Leistungsfæhigkeit: 5—6 km in der Stunde. Ueberwinden nahezu alle Hindernisse. Ein Tank in Fontaine stieg einen steilen Obstgarten hinan, brach die Baeume, überfuhr 2 feste, 1,50 m hohe Gartenmauern und nahm beim Wenden eine Hausecke mit. Sie koennen auf der Stelle durch Vor- und Zurückkehren wenden.

Ernste Hindernisse sind: Graeben von mindestens 4—5 m Breite und 3 m Tiefe; ferner sehr tiefer, modriger Boden. Gepflügter Acker wird leicht überwunden, desgleichen Barrikaden.

Bau von Hindernissen lohnt nicht, besser ist gründliche Bekämpfung.

Artillerie: Schon beim Anmarsch müssen die Tanks heftig beschossen werden, auch wenn keine Wahrscheinlichkeit besteht, sie wirklich zu treffen. Hauptsache ist, die

feindl. Infanterie zu verhindern, den Tanks zu folgen. **Sie** muss das Tankgebiet fürchten. Tatsaechlich blieb bald die engl. Infanterie 1—2 km hinter den Tanks zurück und folgte bei Fontaine fast überhaupt nicht. Zur eigentlichen **Bekämpfung** nur geeignet in **vorderster Kampfzone** aufgebaute **Geschütze**, welche mit direktem Schuss die Tanks sofort erledigen. Jeder Volltreffer toetet einen Teil der Bedienung und führt haeufig zu Tankbraenden. Rückwaerts aufgestellte Züge sind ohne Orientierung und kommen meist zu spaet.

Solche Geschütze müssen **grundsætzlich** vorne aufgestellt werden, dann gelingt dem Feind die Ueberraschung nicht.

Für Aufstellung der Tank-Geschütze muss der K. T. K. verantwortlich gemacht werden. Kraftwagengeschütze leisten bei guten Strassen ausgezeichnete Dienste.

Infanterie. Die Kampflinie darf nur zum Durchlassen der nicht erledigten Tanks geöffnet werden und Deckung nehmen, keinesfalls zurückgehen. Tanks müssen **hinter** der Front erledigt werden. Hauptsache ist **Abwehr der feindl. Infanterie.** Der Tank-Kapitaen sagte: „**Tanks koennen wohl Boden gewinnen, ihn aber nie allein behaupten".** Das ist der Leitsatz für ihre Beurteilung.

Einzelne rückwaertige Kommandos mit Tankbekampfung beauftragen.

Kampfmittel:
Wichtigstes: das **S. m. K. Geschoss.** Ist bei den Tanksbesatzungen gefürchtet, weil es glatt durchschlaegt, dabei eine lange Flamme hervorruft, die oft den Benzintank entzündet.

Am besten den Tank von hinten angreifen. Kann nach hinten schlecht schiessen, ist auch am wenigsten geschützt. Haeuserkampf mit Tanks ist für Infanterie sehr günstig. Die Mannschaften nehmen Deckung in den Haeusern, lassen den Tank vorbei und beschiessen ihn dann mit M.-G. und Gewehren auf kurze Entfernungen. Regt 46 hat in Fontaine innerhalb unserer Linien so 4 Tanks erledigt.

Handgranaten. Einzeln wirkungslos, Wirkung nur als geballte Ladung (mehrere Koepfe um eine Granate) moeglich, unter den Tank geworfen; ist aber schwierig.

Minenwerfer. Leichte Werfer koennen im Flachbahnschuss wirken. Vereinzelt gute Erfahrungen gemacht.

Der Kampf gegen Tanks muss besprochen und geübt werden, dann verlieren sie ihren Schrecken. Die Leute kaempften schliesslich mit Passion, waehrend 4 Stunden in Fontaine gegen 8 eingedrungene Tanks, von denen nur 2 zurückkehren konnten (4 durch Infanterie, 2 durch Artillerie erledigt) ausserdem liegen 11 tote Tanks unmittelbar vor unseren Linien.

V. s. d. G.
Der Chef des Gen.-Stabes
Müller-Loebnitz,
Major.

The following report was issued from the Kaiser's HQ on 27 November 1917 by Major Müller-Löbnitz, Chief of the General Staff, Gruppe Caudry, under the title: *"Fighting against Tanks. Experiences of a Division Fighting at Cambrai."*

"The Division was involved in the Battle of Cambrai on 22 November and as from then fought repeatedly and always successfully against numerous British tank attacks. The experiences gained were supplemented by a number of statements from British tank crew members including the captain of a tank Company.

<u>Tank tactics</u> Organized into tank Batallions of 48-50 tanks, every Batallion of 3 Companies (16 tanks) of 4 sections (4 tanks). Proceedings if possible by surprise. Infantry has to follow close behind and if necessary they fire smoke bombs to hide the tanks. Every tank (section) has its own insignia so that the infantry know with which to work (Ace of Spades, Three-Leafed Clover, Artillery Shell, etc).

The tank drives straight across our infantry trench and then veers behind it and disengages. In general the tank will fire only if support arrives; shooting at our troops from the rear can endanger their own infantry. Tanks can keep going individually in order to complete the breakthrough.

About 300 tanks attacked on 20 November. German defence and reaction was weak. Bloody losses on both sides hardly worth mentioning (statement by British captain involved in the attack.)

<u>Construction</u> About 2.2 metres high, 2 metres wide, 8 metres long. Divided into "male" with 2 cannon and MGs, and "female" only equipped with MGs. The most vulnerable spot – the petrol tanks. In the new tanks they are located at the stern.

<u>Efficiency</u> 5-6 kms/hr. They can overcome almost any obstacle. A tank at Fontaine climbed up steeply to an orchard, broke down the trees, went over two sturdy garden walls 1.5 m high and upon turning took off the corner of a house. They can move backwards and forwards on the spot.

The most difficult obstacles are: trenches at least 4-5 m wide and 3 m deep, also very soft ground. They cross ploughed agricultural land and barricades easily. The setting up of obstacles is not worth the effort, a good fighting technique is better.

<u>Artillery</u> When tanks are coming up we must give them heavy fire even if there is little liklihood of hitting. The main thing is to stop the infantry following the tanks. <u>They</u> must fear being in the tank surrounds. As it was, the British infantry remained 2 kms behind the tanks and were almost absent at Fontaine. For useful engagement, only purpose-built guns which can take out a tank at once with direct fire are suitable, and should be positioned in the most forward fighting zone. Every direct hit kills some of the crew and often results in the tank catching fire. Platoons set up to the rear lack information and mostly arrive too late.

In principle, such guns must be set up forward, for then the enemy is deprived of suprise.

The KTK (*probably Anti-tank Commander- Transl.*) must be made responsible for siting the anti-tank guns. Guns mounted on vehicles on good roads provide excellent results.

<u>Infantry</u> The battle line may only be **opened** to allow the passage of the undamaged tanks and take cover, never to go back to their own lines. Tanks must be destroyed **behind** the Front. The main objective is to **defend against the enemy infantry**. The British tank captain said: **Tanks can certainly win territory but never hold it alone**. That is the governing principle for our assessment.

Give individual fighting groups to the rear the task of engaging the tanks.

<u>Anti-tank weapons</u> The most important: **the SmK shell**. Is feared by the tank crews because it penetrates smoothly with a long flame which often ignites the petrol tank.

Best to attack the tank from the rear. Has poor shooting ability to the rear and its armour is weakest there.

Engaging tanks from houses is favourable for infantry. Our troops take cover in the houses, let the tank pass by and then fire on it with MGs and rifles at short range. At Fontaine, Regt.46 destroyed 4 tanks inside our lines in this way.

<u>Hand-grenades</u> By themselves ineffective. They have possibilities only as a balled charge (several heads around one shell) thrown under a tank, but this is difficult.

<u>Mortars</u> Light mortars can be effective with flat trajectory. Good experiences obtained using single mortar.

Warfare against tanks must be discussed and practised, then they lose their terror. Finally our people fought with passion, during 4 hours in Fontaine against 8 tanks which had got that far, only 2 were able to return (4 knocked-out by infantry, 2 by artillery), besides these, 11 wrecked tanks are lying immediately in front of our lines."

Apparently nobody in the General Staff gave a thought as to how a German attack after breaking through the enemy defence – a tactical victory – might be turned into a significant operational victory. The possibility which the use of massed German armour offered was recognized too late on the German side.

Achtung – Panzer!

The later Inspector-General of Panzer Troops of the German Army, Colonel-General H.Guderian, wrote in his book Achtung-Panzer in the 1930s:

"It is manifestly obvious that the use of massed tanks as at Cambrai should have been of decisive significance for the battle, especially since in 1918 the enemy could rely on having a far greater number and of improved types."

In the technical respect the tank battle at Cambrai showed the British primarily two things: the need for an improved heavy tank to break through the enemy defences, and a lighter and faster tank for the pursuit. In 1918 both were available to the Royal Tank Corps in large numbers. These were the Mk-V – in the photograph a "male" version, and the Mk-A Whippet.

Instructional Pamphlet for Engaging Tanks dated 24 December 1917 issued by the Commanding Officer, Fighting-Vehicle Troops 2):

(A) (Key, top tank, clockwise from left). "Male" tank, cannon armament – ammunition, double armour – fuel, double armour – Laufbänder=tank tracks.
(B) (Key, centre tank, rear view). Ammunition – balled charge with hand-grenades – very rewarding target for SmK ammunition, Betriebsstoff= fuel tank
Text:

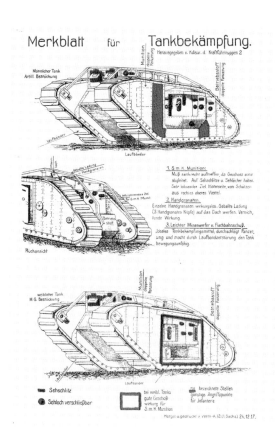

1. <u>SmK ammunition</u> Must strike vertically or the projectile slides off. Aim at viewing slits and viewing flaps. Very rewarding target at rear, from the guard rail outwards right upper quarter.
2. <u>Hand grenades</u> Single hand-grenades ineffective. Throw balled charges (three hand-grenade heads) on the roof. Devastating effect.
3. <u>Light mortars and flat trajectory rounds</u> Ideal anti-tank weapon, penetrates armour and immobilizes tank by destroying the tracks.

(C) (Key, bottom tank, read clockwise from the left) "Female" tank, MG armament – ammunition double armour – fuel, double armour – tracks.
(D) Key at foot: Sehschlitz=viewing slit, Sehloch=viewing hole with shutter. Symbol red square= on "female tanks" good shell effect for SmK ammunition. Places marked in <u>red</u> indicate favourable attacking points for our infantry.

Chapter Six

CHEMICAL WARFARE

The Science of Pure Annihilation

The chemical formula for Dichlorethylsulfide looks quite harmless $\begin{smallmatrix} Cl-CH_2-CH_2 \\ \quad\quad\quad\quad S \\ Cl-CH_2-CH_2 \end{smallmatrix}$ *but behind these innocent capitals and combination of numbers is concealed the most efficient chemical weapon of the First World War. And it proves in this case too that Death has many names: the Germans called it "Gelbkreuz" or "Lost"[1], the French "Yperite" and the British, "Mustard gas"[2].*

The science of chemistry, whose purpose is research into the structure and transformation of substances, made great strides from the beginning of the 19th century. These included the synthesis of urea (F.Wöhler, 1828), the use of electro-chemical procedures (M.Faraday, 1833/34), the fundamental ordering of chemical elements into a periodic system (D.I.Medeleyev and J.L.Meyer 1869) and the theoretical interpretation of chemical processes by physical chemistry, to mention just a few examples. The setting up of a chemical industry, in the sense of the application of natural laws for the industrial manufacture of high-value products through the conversion of inorganic and organic raw materials did not begin until the second half of the 19th century. On the basis of scientific knowledge gained, fast progress ensued in the production of fertilizers, dyes and medicaments. In 1909 the German chemist Fritz Haber demonstrated in his Karlsruhe laboratory how nitrogen in air combines with hydrogen in a high-pressure process. After years of experiments in collaboration with his colleague Carl Bosch of the Aniline and Sodium Carbonate Factory of Baden, he succeeded in making viable through the Haber-Bosch process the catalytic ammonia synthesis for industrial production. In the autumn of 1913 work was begun on the mass production of ammonia in a new major installation at Oppau (Pfalz). This development was of extraordinary significance for German

industry. Ammonia is a basic raw material for artificial fertilizers, but also for explosives. How important that would become for the German armaments industry in the First World War was not forseeable at that time.

Revealing in this respect is a letter of thanks from the Prussian Minister for War, H.Scheüch, dated 27 November 1918 to Professor Dr. Haber on the occasion of his departure from the Chemistry Division of the Prussian War Ministry. Haber was by then Government Privy Councillor, a Captain of the Landwehr and had meanwhile been appointed Director at the Kaiser Wilhelm Institute for Physical Chemistry and Electro-Chemistry: "It was not granted to Germany to emerge from the war victorious. The fact that we were not defeated after a few months by reason of shortages of powder, explosives and other chemical applications of nitrogen is thanks primarily to yourself." Haber's role in chemical warfare will be examined shortly.

History has many examples of the use of chemical weapons in warfare stretching back over the centuries. Mass killing with a scientific basis was a 19th century invention, however, and had its origins in fortress warfare. In this

British soldiers suffering the effects of battlefield gas. On 19 December 1915 at Wieltje on the outskirts of Ypres, the German Army attacked using a chlorine-phosgene mixture released through cylinders when the wind was favourable. Although the British had received prior knowledge of the preparations, 1069 men were affected by the gas and 120 died of its effects.

Prof.Dr.Haber as a Captain of the Landwehr with his service vehicle at the Front. The "Father of Gas Warfare" featured amongst the most controversial German scientists. The Swedish Nobel Prize committee honoured him with the Nobel Prize in Chemistry in 1918 for his resesarch into ammonia synthesis. He received it in 1919. At the same time he was named on the Entente list of war criminals.

context one can see that modern chemical warfare began there. Fortresses became increasingly resistant and more strongly defended. The transition to breech-loaded artillery with longer barrels, the introduction of the barrel recoil stop and new, more efficient propellants and explosives changed nothing. Besieging a fortification had become a wearisome affair. The attackers had now to think up new weapons to either force the defenders out of their bomb-proof bunkers and abandon their defence, prevent them manning their weapons or suffocating them. The advances in chemistry came at just the right time.

Initial Developments

The leaders in the field were the French. In 1912 the Laboratoire Municipale in Paris developed a 26-mm rifle grenade with a tear gas filling (*bromessigester*). It was tested in the same year by police in the Paris suburb of Choisyi-le-Roi against the *Bonnets rouges* (French, refers to the phyrigian cap worn by the Jacobins, nowadays the symbol of the Separatist Movement in Brittany). At the outbreak of the First World War, pioneer troops of the French Army took 30,000 of these gas grenades with them into the field, most of them filled with chloroacetone because of a shortage of bromine. Its use against even the very simply structured enemy positions was a failure: the

meagre contents were hardly noticed by the Germans.

In 1914 the chemist E.Justin-Mueller suggested to the French War Ministry the military use of chlorine and sulphur dioxide. The concept of using choking gases was not French. In Germany, scientists and industrialists had also put ideas forward. In a letter from the Hoechst Dye Works (previously Meister Luciuis & Brüning) to the General War Department at the Royal Prussian War Ministry dated 10 November 1915, the representative of this manufacturer protested that he had not only written on the subject since the outbreak of war, "…but several years before on the significance of lachrymator and poisonous substances as shell fillings, and had submitted examples of the material first to military centres, particularly the Reich Navy Office, for testing."

Such suggestions both in Germany and France found no approval – although not on the grounds of international law.[3] The Reich Navy Office rejected the proposal on the grounds of the special characteristics of naval shells which were not suitable for chemical munitions.

The outlook of the military changed with the introduction of trench warfare. On 27 October 1914 at Neuve Chapelle near Armentières the German Army carried out the first attempt at the Front by firing 3,000 10.5-cm fragmentation shells with a supplement of Dianisidins Salts[4] called "Ni-Stoff". The dust of the explosion was intended to irritate eyes and mucous membrane but had no noticeable effect. The next step was 15-cm 12-T shells for heavy howitzers. The explosive charge contained a T-substance, Xylylbromide, also classed as an irritant/lachrymator. It was first used in January 1915 on the Eastern Front near Lodz in Poland where it also proved a washout, the chemicals in the liquid state failing to evaporate on account of the low temperature. The grand première on the Western Front in March 1915 was more successful as described ahead. This was followed by 15-cm shells filled with "B-" or "Bn-Stoff" weighing between 43.7 and 45 kgs: a lead container inside weighing 2.8 kgs contained a 1.4 kg solution of potassium bromide. These were tried out in the West for the first time in July and August 1915.

All shells filled with liquid substances created ballistic problems both inside and outside the shell. The lead-, later iron, containers used until 1916 tended to compress under the stresses of firing. This had an adverse effect on their stability in flight and led to shells overshooting and a high incidence of scatter. Improvements were obtained by binding with magnesia sealing cement. This was only one of the many problems to be overcome which had little to do with the area of developing new irritant substances and battlefield gases. New substances were developed quickly and cheaply in huge quantities: the problem was the artillery and the new shells filled with a liquid, for there was no previous experience to fall back on. Both the use of single shells and their deployment *en masse* to gas a territory had to be examined scientifically. The Artillery Testing Commission often found it necessary to redirect the testing from the Kummersdorf range to more suitable troop training locations such as the Wahn firing range near Cologne.

In addition the Entente was monitoring and analyzing battlefield gases, which meanwhile their troops were eager to deploy. In order to do justice to the ever more complex demands of chemical warfare, organisational changes were required. For these reasons, Division 10

The Kaiser Wilhelm Institute for Physical Chemistry and Electro-Chemisty at Dahlem, then a high-class suburb of Berlin, after being taken over and expanded by the Royal Prussian War Ministry. At the end of 1918, 1,450 staff here were engaged on the development of battlefield gases and anti-gas protection.

An area of the laboratory for phosgene testing.

(Gas Warfare) was set up at the Royal Prussian War Ministry and Prof.Dr.F.Haber was chosen to head the project. Large laboratories for the testing and manufacture of battlefield substances were also set up.

The individual stages in the spiralling development of chemical warfare until 1918 as described herein make no claim to being in any way comprehensive.

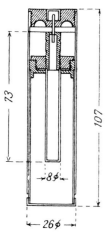

Sectional diagram of the French gas-rifle-grenade. It weighed 115 grams and took a 35 gram charge of tear gas, later the same quantity of chlorine. Its main purpose was to smoke out protected structures and MG nests, but had little success.

A Deadly Competition

A competition developed in which the opposing belligerents used the most recent knowledge and experiences of chemistry, technology and tactics to overcome deeply arrayed enemy trench systems and so achieve breakthroughs into the depths of enemy defences in the hope of bringing the war to a conclusion.

In the course of the First World War in the area of chemical weapons the Germans had three significant procedures: artillery gas-shells, which from the summer of 1915 included mortars,[5] the so-called *Blasverfahren* in which gas was released through aimed cylinders and borne on a favourable wind to the enemy lines, and electrically launched gas-mines.

The infantry also had gas-hand grenades and gas rifle-grenades. Aerial attacks using gas munitions are only known for certain in a few cases.

a. **Artillery Gas Shells** The procedure was first used in January 1915 and remained under constant further development for chemical weapons during the remainder of the war. That fact alone accounts for the quantities of 7.7-cm to 21-cm ammunition for field guns, and 7.6-cm and 17-cm calibre for mortars. A further stage was battlefield gas ammunition which had a combined weakly poisonous and lachrymator effect and arrived at the Front in August 1915.

From May 1916 the German side had "Green Cross" shells filled with Di-Phosgene, legitimized by the phosgene shells first used by the French in February 1916. These shells were purely gas carriers without splinter effect. According to British reports the limit of tolerability after exposure for a few seconds to phosgene was 1:200,000. Lasting or fatal damage to the respiratory organs occurred in a ratio of 1:50,000 (proportion gas/air) after one to two minutes. In the following months the opposing sides filled their arsenals with lachrymator-, poisonous- and battlefield gas munitions; the French in July 1916 with Vicenite and Manganite, Austro-Hungary with a bromium/cyanide preparation and then in January 1917 the Germans again with Green Cross (phosgene) and in July the first Yellow Cross shells (dichlorethylene sulphide or Lost, i.e. mustard gas). The latter substance spread over the entire body surface of the affected subject. It was used by the Germans to bombard whole areas of terrain in the field ahead of the defensive position to render it impassable. The operation required at least 100 rounds of 7.7-cm calibre per hectare within one hour (30 litres Dichlorethylene sulphide/Green Cross 1).

In 1918 the British and French introduced the gas Yperite (mustard gas) in artillery shells and various other containers: Lasting or fatal damage resulted to the respiratory organs from the ratio 1:1,000,000 (gas/air) after one hour. Up to September 1918 Germany deployed Yellow Cross 1 and Blue Cross shells, also used in gas/explosive filling in a ratio 3:1 which combined the gas with a minor splinter effect, and later Green Cross 3.

The following table shows the intended guns and mortars, and quantities of munitions intended by the Germans for gas warfare.

Examples of German Guns Intended for Use in Gas Warfare

Type of Gun	Calibre	Shell weight	Gas Content (l)	Weight of explosive	Range
Field Cannon 16	7.7-cm	7 kg	0.3–0.7	0.03–0.1 kg	8200–10700 m
Light howitzer 16	10.5 cm	16 kg	1 litre	0.06 kg	7000 m
10-cm cannon 17	10.5 cm	16 kg	1 litre	0.06 kg	12000 m
Long heavy howitzer/13	15 cm	42 kg	2.5 litre	1.0 kg	8500 m
Long 21-cm mortar	21 cm	118 kg	8 litre	4.0 kg	10000 m
Light mortar	7.6 cm	4.2 kg	0.8 litre	0.03 kg	1300 m
Medium mortar	17 cm	38 kg	8 litre	0.06 kg	1160 m
Heavy mortar	25 cm	65 kg	15 litre	0.06 kg	900 m

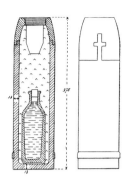

Sectional diagram of the light field-howitzer Blue Cross shell without howitzer-shell detonator 16. The sensitive howitzer-shell detonator 17 could be used in its place.

Amongst the first guns the Germans used to fire gas munitions was this 10.5-cm light field howitzer 98/09 from the howitzer batallions of the field artillery regiments.

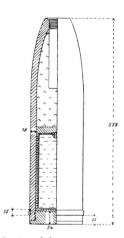

Sectional diagram of a 15-cm shell 12. The gas/explosive shell was filled with Green Cross 1 and 2 (phosgene/ di-phosgene) or with Yellow Cross (mustard gas).

The long-barrel 15-cm heavy field howitzer proved very suitable for firing gas shells.

Gas Release

The Germans differentiated the different ways of releasing battlefield gas as follows:

In Attacks:
- *Gas bombardment or small scale artillery shelling*
- *Creation of medium or large swathes of gas clouds, a gas barrier or long-term release of gas, – gas/explosive shelling.*

In Defence:
- *Ground Saturation*

The first service regulations concerning the tactics of firing gas shells appeared in 1917. During the course of the war, gas ammunition had been created which could do more than the original intention of keeping the enemy at bay. Thanks to new shells, even a well-protected enemy soldier with good respirator and excellent anti-gas discipline could be seriously harmed or killed if the following principles were followed:

- A gas bombardment using so great a quantity that a sufficient concentration of gas was created in the target area to render the gas mask less effective.
- Incessant firing of gas shells for a day in order at some point to render the wearing of a gas mask intolerable.
- To deceive the enemy as what gas was being used. This was achieved by gas/explosive ammunition, or by saturating an entire battle sector with Yellow Cross (mustard gas).

Lachrymators, Battlefield- and Poison Gases of the German Army and Their Effect

Military Designation	German Chemical Term	Common Term
White Cross	Benzylbromide, bromacetone, chloroacetone, xylylbromide	A tear gas. Irritation of nose and eyes.
Green Cross	Phosgene, di-phosgene. "Per" Stoff, chlorpikrin, ethyldichlorarsine (Green Cross 3).	Deadly, damages respiratory organs.
Blue Cross6	Diphenylchloroarsine, diphenylcyonoarsine, phenarsazinchloride (Adamsit)	Irritation of nose and eyes – the "Gas-Mask breaker".
Yellow Cross	Dichlorethylsulphide.	Mustard gas. Attacks skin surfaces. Used to saturate terrain.

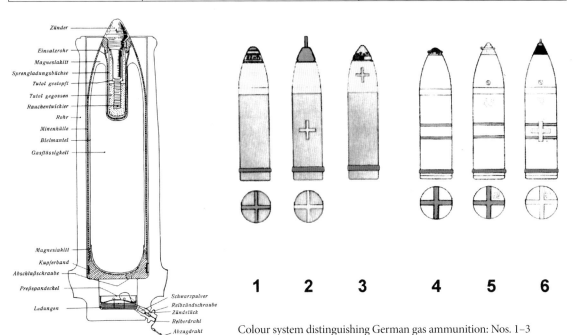

Sectional diagram of the barrel of a 25-cm heavy mortar with a gas-mine weighing around 60 kgs. The gas filling would be between 12 and 14 litres.

Colour system distinguishing German gas ammunition: Nos. 1–3 10.5-cm light field howitzer, Nos. 4-6 15-cm heavy field howitzer.

- Mixed delivery of Green-, Yellow- or Blue Cross munition combined with explosive- or smoke-munition. The Blue Cross shells were so-called "mask-breakers", forcing the wearer to remove the mask, exposing him to other lachrymators being used. This was known as "Buntkreuz" or Variegated Cross.

b. The *Blasverfahren (Wind-blown Process)*

Using this procedure at Ypres on 22 April 1915, the Germans secured their first substantial success in chemical warfare. A test was carried out first by Professor Dr. Fritz Haber and Colonel Bauer at the Beverloo military depot in Belgium. Bauer was attached to the Supreme Army Command and was very impressed by this test, as were all observers. Haber had come out in favour of chlorine, not suitable as a shell filling, for this method of attack aimed at the No Man's Land ahead of the German lines. Pioneer Regt 35 was given the task of making the preparations and was known from the spring onwards as "The Gas Regiment". A six kilometre long section of the Front north-east of Ypres between Bixschoote and Zillebeke had been selected which projected like a balcony into the German 4.Army Front. About half of all the carbonic acid flasks in current use in Germany were collected up, 1,600 of them being modified to take 40 kgs of chlorine. Later, smaller flasks weighing 38 kgs were made to take 20 kgs chlorine; 4130 of these were made available. The modification work was terminated on 10 March 1915, but changes had to be introduced two weeks later because of unfavourable weather conditions. The weather was also the reason for the numerous postponements of the attack until 22 April by when at last all flasks could be turned off and on.

After the war Major (ret'd) Lichnock, formerly of Reserve-Pioneer Comp 46/46. Reserve-Division, wrote of the gas attack:

"On 22 April at 1740 hrs the order came for the attack. At 1800 the flasks in the battery were aligned, opened and the gas was directed through a lead tube over the trench parapet towards the enemy. It looked wonderful: since the sun was fairly low in the West, it lent the gas a yellow-ochre colour in the evening light. Heavy clouds of gas rolled slowly and gradually expanding in the direction of the enemy infantry trenches: a splendid, unendingly fantastic sight!"

148.6 tonnes of chlorine was wafted westwards. It caused great confusion in the French defences amongst the members of the 45th Colonial and 37th Veteran Reserve-Territorial Division. The troops fled their positions leaving two great unmanned gaps in the Front. 2,000 prisoners were taken, 51 guns and 70 MGs captured. Various estimates are provided by the literature as to the casualties: they vary from 1,200 to 5,000 dead and 3,000 to 15,000 harmed by gas poisoning. Illuminating for the losses in the framework of chemical warfare are the following figures: In the area of the German 4.Army, 200 French and British soldiers were captured suffering from the effects of gas poisoning, and of these twelve died.

From the German point of view this first *Blasverfahren* gas attack was a complete success, the aim of the operation, to straighten the Front near Ypres, having been achieved. Nothing more, however, for the German leadership forbade any further use of poison gas. Presumably for both sides the scale of the success came as a surprise.

The Allies now turned to the *Blasverfahren* themselves, and on 25 September 1915 at Loos, facing a 28-kilometre length of Front, the British assembled 5,500 gas flasks with a total of 150 tonnes of chlorine, 1,100 smoke candles and 25,000 phosphorus hand grenades. The British attacked regularly using chlorine until 1918.

The effects of the attack was reported by the British news service as follows:

"...The physical effect on the Germans was very much less than that on their morale. Although the German anti-gas preparations were neither technically nor psychologically of the best, nevertheless the greater part of the German troops had been equipped with respirators and protective goggles."

The first of a total of 20 wind-borne attacks by the French Army took place in February 1916. A chlorine-phosgene mixture was used and later – as emulated by the British – sulphureted hydrogen. This method was also known to the Austro-Hungarian and Russian Armies. The attacks of the latter in February 1917 against the Germans, and in March against the Austro-Hungarians, made little impression.

The preparations for a wind-borne attack have been completed. Each of twenty heavy gas flasks 1.5 metres long and weighing 81.5 kgs were then closed up into a battery. The flasks were filled in Germany. Later, every gas regiment was given forty tankers for this purpose. The tactics of the attack were also modified, the gas being released in two to three waves. On a two-wave attack on 31 January 1917 in the Champagne region, the high concentration of gas caused 527 deaths and 1433 French soldiers and civilians harmed by gas poisoning.

The Ypres Bend. The German Front (thick line) before (and dotted line) after the wind-borne attack of 22 April 1915.

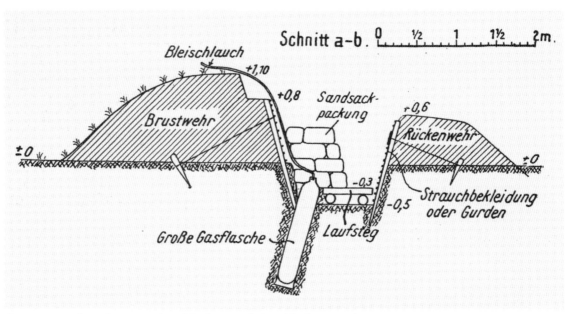

Cross-section of an infantry trench with built-in gas flask and lead pipe on the parapet.
Sadsackpackung = sandbags, Laufsteg = gangway, Rückenwehr = back protection, Strauchbekleidung = shrubby covering.

"Enemy attack on an infantry trench with poisonous gases," a print from a graphic representation by Ost-Petersen, 1915.

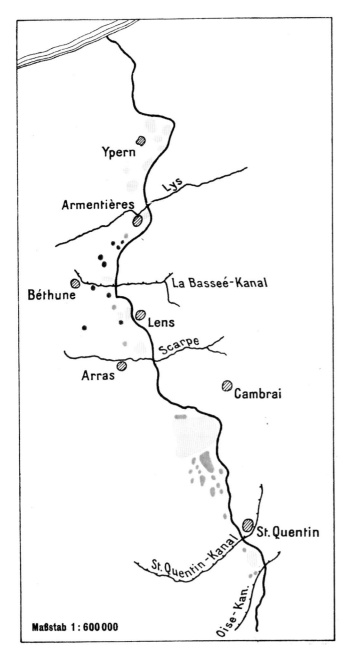
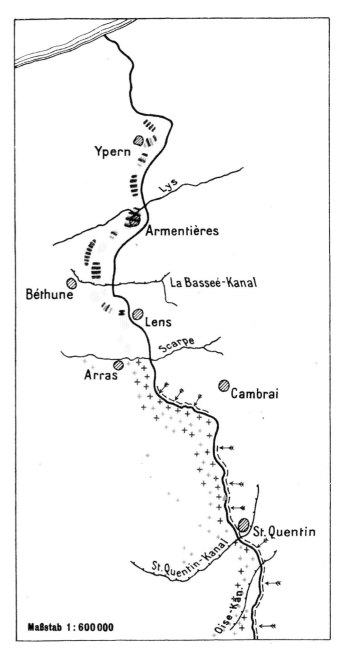

The German gas tactics in preparation for the Spring Offensive 1918 in the Ypres-Armentière-St Quentin sector (9–21 March 1918).

(1) The Germans made comprehensive preparations for the use of chemical weapons for their major Spring Offensive of 1918. The tactics were for the account of the artillery: in the framework of the planned laying of gas, the territory in the attack sector was saturated with about 250,000 Yellow Cross (mustard gas) shells between 9th and 15 March. For the purpose, 1,705 batteries (100 guns on a single kilometre of Front!) had been closed up. The artilleristic effect rested on the effect of the gas. Two days before the beginning of the offensive the third enemy line was barriered off from the forward terrain by huge quantities of Green Cross (phosgene) and Yellow Cross 1 (mustard gas) munitions, and known nests of resistance were then neutralised.

(2) On the early morning of 21 March, the artillery battle began with an enormous barrage on a breadth of Front of 70 kilometres length aimed at the enemy batteries and lasting two hours while enemy infantry trenches were also attacked. Mortars and 4,000 gas-launchers were thrown into the fray. The forward enemy lines were now the priority target of the Variegated-Cross artillery fire, but German assault troops wearing gas masks were seriously impaired by their own Blue Cross "mask breakers".

Artillery fire in connection with saturation gassing of a terrain.

Warning notice of Yellow Cross saturation at Armentières. The sign reads: "Attention! Gas Danger! Armentières saturated by mustard gas! Do not enter houses and bunkers! March through without stopping! Do not use water for drinking or washing!"

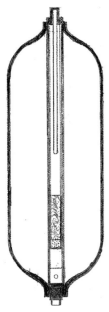

Sectional diagram of a gas-mine for the "Livens" mortar. It took 13.6 kg gas and a small explosive charge of 65 to 100 grams of TNT. The British preferred to make their gas attacks by night. They considered a wind blowing towards the enemy at 1.5 to 5 metres/ sec to be especially advantageous.

At first the Germans believed that in the *Blasverfahren* they had found the hoped-for means for penetrating the enemy defensive Front. By April 1917 they had launched fifty such attacks. The importance of the process was declining, however. Much depended on the weather and circumstances of the terrain. Both created an intolerable burden for the organisation and planning of an attack, to which had to be added the enormous time taken in preparation. A regiment needed three to five nights to set up 12,000 gas flasks.

c. Laying Gas by Gas-Mortars

The German Army replaced wind-borne gas attacks by specially designed gas-mortars. These were really a British invention occasionally mentioned in contemporary German publications. In October 1916 the British had used 17-kg mines with a 9.6 kg phosgene-tin tetrachloride mixture. The later 20.3-cm "Livens" projector was the response to the original requirement for a means to lob incendiaries into the German positions.

After the British gas-mortar had inflicted heavy losses on German troops, Supreme Army Command decided to copy it. The duplicated mortars entered service in the shape of a smooth bore 18-cm gas mortar in batteries of twenty tubes, a total of 900 units, to be dug into the ground. The propellant charges were ignited

The Livens Mortar

Its components were a tube 825 to 1220 mm in length with hemispherical floors and steel baseplate. The mortars were arrayed in rows elevated less than 45°, and loaded with two self-contained hemispherical mines weighing 30 kgs. The gas load weighed about 14 kgs with a small explosive charge and a primitive time fuze soon replaced by an impact fuze. The ignition of the several-part propellant was electrical, and a range of 1,600 metres was possible. The British used the Livens mortar on the grand scale for the first time on 4 April 1917 at the Battle of Arras with a bombardment of 2,340 mortar mines. In the last two years of the war, there were 300 gas attacks using this new mortar.

electrically. Range was 1,600 metres using gas-mines weighing 28–30 kgs. Before assembly a small explosive charge was placed through the axis and set off by a time fuze upon impact with the ground to release the 6.3 kgs of phosgene, 7.5 kgs of di-phosgene or 5.24 kgs Blue Cross "mask breaker" into the surroundings. German gas-mortars were first used on 24 October 1917 against Italian positions at Flitsch; on the Western Front at the beginning of December 1917 and in April 1918. The Germans also developed another 16-cm gas mortar with a long barrel. This had a range of 3,300 metres and was used for the first time in the Vosges on 21 August 1918.

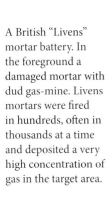

A British "Livens" mortar battery. In the foreground a damaged mortar with dud gas-mine. Livens mortars were fired in hundreds, often in thousands at a time and deposited a very high concentration of gas in the target area.

Streng geheim! **Nicht in die vordere Linie mitnehmen.**

Anweisung

für die Verwendung der Grünkreuz-Geschosse.

1. Grünkreuzgeschosse sind mit einer chemischen Flüssigkeit gefüllt, die sich beim Zerspringen des Geschosses nebelförmig verteilt. Das Gas wirkt tödlich.
   Das Geschoß zerlegt sich beim Zerspringen nur in wenige Teile. Auf Splitterwirkung ist daher nicht zu rechnen.
2. Bedingungen für den Erfolg sind
   a) ruhige Luft,
   b) Masseneinsatz der Geschosse.
3. Bei Windstille ist die Wirkung am größten. Sonnenschein und Bodenwind von mehr als 2 Sekundenmeter Stärke bewirken eine zu rasche Verflüchtigung des Gases, **starker** Regen drückt es zu Boden und macht es unwirksam.
   Die beste Zeit zum Gasschießen ist die Nacht. Bei Tage ist die Wirkung nur bei bedecktem Himmel erheblich. Die Abhängigkeit der Wirkung von der Witterung zwingt dazu, zu den Vorbereitungen einen Fachmeteorologen als Berater heranzuziehen.
4. Um Wirkung zu erzielen, ist es notwendig, auf den zu vergasenden Raum längere Zeit hindurch eine große Menge Gaskampfstoff zu verschießen. Selbst die beste feindliche Maske schützt immer nur eine beschränkte Zeit lang. Es ist zweckmäßig in der einem Grünkreuzschießen folgenden Nacht dieselben Räume erneut zu vergasen, da in der Zwischenzeit der Austausch verbrauchter Masken im allgemeinen nicht möglich sein wird.
   Je größer der Raum ist, der unter entsprechendem Einsatz von Munition vergast wird, desto schwieriger ist es für den darin befindlichen Feind, sich der Wirkung des Gases zu entziehen.
   Es empfiehlt sich Grünkreuzmunition nur in sehr großen Massen (mindestens 50000 kg Gaskampfstoff) einzusetzen. Schießen einzelner Batterien hat wenig Wert.
5. Die mit Gaskampfstoff beladene Luft fließt in stark durchschnittenem, schluchtenreichem Gelände, selbst wenn die allgemeine Windströmung eine andere Richtung hat, in den ersten Nachtstunden stark, in den späteren langsam von den Höhen nach den Tiefen ab. Deshalb genügt in solchem Gelände unter Umständen, die Höhenlinien und die Hänge zu beschießen.
   In ebenem Gelände sind solche örtlichen Luftbewegungen nicht zu erwarten. Hier ist die Windrichtung maßgebend.
   In Wäldern herrscht Windstille selbst dann, wenn der Wind im Felde merkliche Stärke hat. Grünkreuzschießen gegen Waldungen kann daher auch bei windigem Wetter erfolgreich sein. Hier, wie bei Windstille in ebenem Gelände, muß das Feuer auf den ganzen zu vergasenden Raum verteilt werden, wobei gegen bekannte Ziele in diesen Räumen das Feuer besonders zu verdichten ist. Bei bewegter Luft ist die Windrichtung in Rechnung zu stellen.
6. Grünkreuzmunition wird gefertigt für:
   a) die Feldkanone 96 n/A. (Gr. 15),
   b) die l. F. H. 98.09 (L. F. H. Gr.),
   c) die s. F. H. (15 cm Gr. 12),
   d) die 10 cm Kanone (L. F. H. Gr. und 10 cm Gr. 12),
   e) die lg. 15 cm Kanone (15 cm Gr. 12).
7. Auf eine Fläche von 2 ha (100 × 200 m) müssen unter entsprechender Verteilung auf den Raum in je 1/2 Stunde mindestens 250 kg Gaskampfstoff verschossen, d. h. Schußgruppen von
   etwa 500 Schuß der Feldkanone,
   125 Schuß der l. F. H. oder 10 cm Kanone,
   60*) Schuß der s. F. H. oder lg. 15 cm Kanone
   abgegeben werden.
8. Zum wirksamen Vergasen eines Raumes von 1 Quadratkilometer braucht man
   rund 24000 Schuß der Feldkanone,
   6000 „ der l. F. H. oder 10 cm Kanone,
   3000 „ der s. F. H. oder 15 cm Kanone.
9. Durch das schnelle Feuern auf meist große Entfernungen wird das Gerät stark in Anspruch genommen. Es empfiehlt sich im allgemeinen
   einer Feldkanonen-Batterie nicht mehr als 2000 Schuß,
   „ l. F. H.- „ „ „ „ 1200 „
   „ 10 cm Kanonen- „ „ „ „ 800 „
   „ s. F. H.- „ „ „ „ 600 „
   „ lg. 15 cm Kanonen- „ „ „ „ 500 „
   für ein Schießen von etwa 6-stündiger Dauer zuzuweisen. Zum Vergasen eines Raumes von einem Quadratkilometer innerhalb von 6 Stunden sind daher erforderlich
   12 Feldkanonen-Batterien oder
   5 l. F. H.- „ oder
   7–8–10 cm Kanonen- „ oder
   5 s. F. H.- „ oder
   6 lg. 15 cm Kanonen- „
10. Zur Schonung des Geräts sind die Feuerstellungen, wenn möglich, so zu wählen, daß
    die Feldkanone nicht auf Entfernungen über 7000,
    die l. F. H. „ „ „ „ 6000,
    die 10 cm Kanone „ „ „ „ 9000,
    die s. F. H. „ „ „ „ 7000
    zu schießen brauchen. Zwischen den einzelnen Schußgruppen sind nach Bedarf Feuerpausen einzulegen, deren Zahl und Dauer so zu bemessen ist, daß das ganze Schießen mindestens 6 Stunden dauert.
11. Jede zum Grünkreuzschießen bestimmte Batterie erhält eine Karte oder eine Planpause im Maßstab 1 : 25000, worauf der von ihr zu beschießende Geländeraum genau bezeichnet ist. Bei Verteilung der Zielräume ist anzustreben, daß deren Längsachse möglichst in der Schußrichtung der betr. Batterie liegt.
12. In ebenem Gelände wird das Zielfeld zweckmäßig in Rechtecke von 100 bis 150 m Breite und 200 m Tiefe eingeteilt und jeder Batterie mehrere solcher Rechtecke zur Bekämpfung überwiesen. Die einzelnen Rechtecke werden nacheinander derart unter Feuer genommen, daß die Batterie mit gleichmäßig auf die ganze Breite (100—150 m) verteiltem Feuer auf der nach der Mitte des Rechtecks ermittelten Entfernung eine Schußgruppe abgibt (vergl. Ziffer 7). Bei Bestimmung der Reihenfolge, in der die Rechtecke beschossen werden sollen, ist auch die Windrichtung zu berücksichtigen. Grundsatz ist, den Gasgehalt der Luft nach und nach zu verdichten. Deshalb sind die Rechtecke in der Windrichtung nach einander zu beschießen, wo nicht taktische Rücksichten eine Abweichung erforderlich machen. Nach Maßgabe der vorhandenen Munition werden auf die einzelnen Rechtecke mehrere Schußgruppen abgegeben.
    Die zu vergasenden Räume müssen mindestens 2 km von den vordersten eigenen Linien entfernt sein, damit bei ungünstigem Wind für diese keine Gefahr besteht.
13. In durchschnittenem oder bergigem Gelände sind die Zielstreifen für die einzelnen Batterien der Geländegestaltung entsprechend auf die Höhen zu legen, und jeder Batterie eine Zielbreite von höchstens 150 m zuzuweisen. Bei Bestimmung der Zielstreifen ist besonders darauf zu achten, daß das Gas nicht durch Talströmungen auf die eigenen Truppen geführt werden kann. Am günstigsten ist es, wenn Höhenzüge der Länge nach bestrichen werden können.
14. Die Entfernungen sind, wenn irgend möglich, durch Einschießen und zwar mit Brisanzmunition zu ermitteln:
    bei der Feldkanone mit Gr. 15 oder Gr. 14,
    bei der l. F. H. mit Langgranaten,
    bei der 10 cm Kan. mit 10 cm Gr. 15,
    bei der s. F. H. mit 15 cm Gr. 12,
    bei der lg. 15 cm Kan. mit 15 cm Gr. 12.
    Bei allen Geschützarten mit Ausnahme der l. F. H. und der 10 cm Kan. bei Anwendung von L. F. H. Gr. stimmen die Flugbahnen der genannten Brisanzgeschoßarten mit denen der betr. Grünkreuzgeschosse annähernd überein, sodaß die ermittelten Entfernungen auch für die Grünkreuzgeschosse zutreffen. Dagegen müssen für das Wirkungsschießen die ermittelten Entfernungen vergrößert werden:
    a) bei der l. F. H. auf 4000 m um etwa 100 m,
    „ 6000 m „ „ 150 m,
    b) bei der 10 cm Kan. auf 7000 m „ „ 250 m,
    10 cm Kan. 04 mit „ 8000 m „ „ 320 m,
    L. F. H. Gr. „ 9000 m „ „ 470 m,
    c) bei der 10 cm Kan. 14 „ 7000 m „ „ 220 m,
    mit L. F. H. Gr. „ 8000 m „ „ 300 m,
    „ 9000 m „ „ 660 m.
    Batterien, die sich nicht einschießen und auch die Entfernung nicht von einer Nachbarbatterie übernehmen können, sind auf Abgreifen von der Karte angewiesen. Ermittelung des richtigen Geländewinkels und wenn irgend möglich des „Entfernungsunterschieds“ ist für diese Batterien besonders wichtig.
15. Besondere Sicherheitsmaßregeln sind beim Gebrauch der Grünkreuzmunition für die eigenen Truppen nicht erforderlich. Die Geschützbedienung trägt die Gasschutzmasken im Bereitschaftsbehälter, ebenso die Teile der eigenen Linie, bei denen eine Belästigung durch das Gas immerhin im Bereich der Möglichkeit liegt.
    Jede Batterie und jede beteiligte Kolonne erhält rechtzeitig vor dem Schießen ein Merkblatt über die Behandlung der Grünkreuzgeschosse zur Unterweisung der Offiziere und Mannschaften.
16. Anforderungen auf Grünkreuzmunition sind an die oberste Heeresleitung zu richten.
17. Wenn Schießen in größerem Maßstabe geplant sind, empfiehlt es sich, für die Leitung sachverständige Offiziere bei der obersten Heeresleitung anzufordern.
18. Die Erfahrungen bei Grünkreuzschießen werden von Zeit zu Zeit bekannt gegeben.

*) Die Gasmenge muß hier größer sein, weil die Verteilung infolge der geringen Schußzahl schlechter ist.

This unsigned and undated "Instructions for the use of the Green Cross shell" was circulated to artillery officers. Recipients were "not to take it with them to the front line." Phosgene is described as a chemical liquid which when released upon the shell hitting the ground forms a lethal mist. The conditions for success are "calm air". The effects are greatest when no wind is present. Sunshine and a ground wind in excess of 2 metres/sec cause the gas to disperse too quickly, heavy rain forces the gas down and makes it ineffective. The best time to fire the munition is at night, by day the sky must be overcast for effect. Since the weather is important, the presence of a specialist meteorologist is required.

The new gas-mortars were decidedly weapons of attack, the gas attack was a bombardment. Setting up the batteries was comparatively easy, making all preparations, including the timing of the attack, relatively simple. The cloud of gas engendered lay far beyond the German lines limiting any danger to German troops who were equipped in any case with reliable anti-gas protection. The changeover from wind-borne gas attacks to artillery brought about a growth in size of the gas troop and its reorganization. Supreme Army Command strove for smaller, flexible units able to respond quickly at locations where fighting was fiercest.

As from the summer of 1918 the German Army suffered from a lack of battlefield gases.

Dug-in German 18-cm gas-mortar battery. It was composed of twenty barrels aligned either in a row or one behind the other. Ignition was electical by means of a self-ignition screw in the tube bottom.

Contemporary German field postcard, 1916.

German officer wearing gas mask, 1915. Initially various medical centres made gas masks and distributed them to the troops. The German Army gas mask with single filter insert Mod 21/8 was introduced in August 1915.

A. O. K. Süd   A.-H.-Qu., 30. Sept. 1916
G. S. O. Ib Nr. 4700

Schützengraben-Merkblatt.

Beachte für den Gaskampf:

1. Deine Maske schützt Dich, wenn sie in Ordnung ist und Du sie **sicher und rasch** zu gebrauchen verstehst. Ein Einsatz hält mit Sicherheit auch den längsten Gasangriff aus.

2. Trenne Dich nicht von ihr. Musst Du sie ablegen, halte sie in **greifbarer** Nähe bereit.

3. Schone sie wie Deine Waffe. Schütze Maske und Einsätze vor Nässe. Deine Gesundheit hängt von ihr im Gaskampf ab.

4. Achte auf die Gummidichtung im Mundstück und befolge genauestens die Gebrauchsanweisung der Maskenschachtel.

5. Vergiss bei Gasangriffen nicht zu alarmieren; **die Gase sind schnell da.**

6. Vertraue Deiner Maske; atme möglichst ruhig und langsam.

7. Bediene Deine Waffe ruhig wie sonst.

8. Der Unterstand schützt Dich nicht vor Gasen, wenn Du keine Maske hast. Ein Zurücklaufen wäre töricht, da die Gaswolke mit Dir zieht.

9. Nimm, wenn die Maske beschädigt, das Gewinde des Einsatzes in den Mund und halte die Nase zu.

10. Nimm die Maske nicht zu früh ab.

11. Entfette Deine Waffe, wenn sie im Gas war, und fette sie frisch ein.

12. Sorge nach einem Gasangriff für Lüftung von Graben und Unterstand.

13. Wische nach Gebrauch die Maske sorgfältig innen und aussen trocken.

14. Ergänze Deine Gasschutzmittel für den nächsten Gaskampf.   **A. O. K. Süd.**

Druckerei der Et.-Kdtr. 4|III

Circular issued on 30 September 1916 from AOK South "*Instructional Pamphlet for the Infantry Trenches*":

Take Note for Gas Warfare:

1. Your mask protects you if it is in good order and you understand how to use it quickly and surely. One filter cartridge will certainly last you for the longest gas attack

2. Do not become separated from your gas mask. If you have to put it aside, then keep it **within reach**.

3. Care for it as for your weapon. Protect mask and filters against damp. Your health depends on it in gas warfare.

4. Inspect the rubber seal in the mouthpiece and follow the instructions for use in the mask box precisely.

5. Don't forget to raise the alarm in gas attacks: the gases arrive quickly.

6. Trust in your mask; if possible breathe calmly and slowly

7. Use your weapon calmly as always.

8. The bunker will not protect you against gas if you have no mask. Running to the rear is senseless, for the gas cloud accompanies you there.

9. If the mask becomes damaged, take the thread of the filter in your mouth and hold your nose.

10. Do not take off your gas mask prematurely.

11. Clean your weapon if it was exposed to the gas, and re-oil it afresh.

12. After a gas attack ventilate trench and protective housing

13. After use wipe the mask dry carefully inside and out.

14. Ensure your gas protection equipment is complete for the next gas battle.

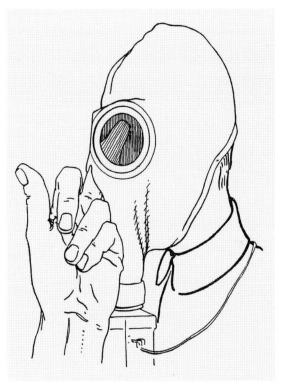

Left: A German soldier wearing a captured British gas-helmet with small filter-can from the year 1916. It was the immediate fore-runner of the can-respirator.

Right: The Russian Zelinski-Kummandt gas mask from the year 1916. Because of substantial defects the filter was replaced by a filter-can designed by the Russian chemist Josef Prince Avaloff.

This was caused by the difficult situation in the raw material situation and labour markets and the high expenditure of the gases. 30 percent of all artillery shells (in 1918 the monthly production was on average 11,000,000 shells) were for gas warfare. The Allies took the lead in this field, and with that Germany lost the chemical war.

The document states that there is little point in a single battery firing shells. The operation requires at least 50,000 kgs of the munition to be fired. The greater the area covered by such a bombardment, the more difficult it is for the enemy to withdraw from the gas.

Since even the best enemy gas masks give protection only for a limited period, the target area must receive saturation fire over a long period, and it is expedient to repeat the operation the following night for the enemy would not have had time to replace the masks by then.

Comparison of gas masks (left to right): US gas mask BOS-type respirator – French gas mask M 2 (L.T.N.) – British P.H. helmet from 1915 – German gas mask 15 with ready-change can.

Wind direction over the plain is decisive, but woodlands remain calm within even when the wind in the field is strong, and therefore Green Cross gas can be used against woodlands which should be saturated more densely when known targets are inside it. Even when the wind has a different direction, airborne gases flow down a terrain rich with gullies and ravines…. Comprehensive instructions for the artillery follow.

The Horror of Gas Warfare

What gas warfare was like is depicted in the following eye-witness report by Staff Medical Officer Dr. Legahn, in October 1917 Regimental Medical Officer attached to Reserve Inf.Regt 201/43 Reserve-Div. As such he experienced the heavy fighting south west of the Ailette. The French were in final stages of preparing an attack and had thoroughly gassed the Ailette area and the Pinon Wood. I.Batallion of the regiment had set out wearing gas masks and had spent the whole night making their way to Vaudesson and Chavignon.

"After a long march we approached the canal. It was enveloped in a thick fog whose nature soon became clear to us for suddenly there was a general coughing and sneezing and wiping of tears throughout our ranks: we had entered into a gas battle zone. The whole valley was filled with it. The smell of ether became more intense, a gas-fog. More and more shells fell; many of them detonating with a thud: gas shells! Then we kept going through the ruins of Bruyères. Putting on our gas masks was never considered, it would not have been possible to march wearing them. The gas-fog hung before us like a curtain: if a man stretched out his hand into it, he would lose sight of it. One of our two officers entered the fog. He stumbled and fell into a shell crater. He made it back with some effort. His hands glowed like fire, but he did not have the slightest burning sensation. He wiped them down his trousers; his trousers glowed without burning. Phosporus! Poison gas! Every step here meant wandering astray and a death from gassing. Captain Zaehle therefore gave the order to go back over the bridge to behind the railway underpass. There the batallion waited in a light gas-mist until daybreak. Then we went back over the dangerous

bridge and through malignant Bruyères. On the outskirts of the village a shell hissed down exactly on the spot occupied by our officer. It seemed that he was ripped into such shreds that there was nothing left of him to see. Then we came to the location of a catastrophe which must have occurred a short time before. A gigantic shell crater in the middle of the street, an ammunition waggon half sunken down in it; of the four horses one was dead, the second fell as we watched, blood was spurting from the carotid artery of the third, the fourth was hale and hearty. Near the second horse lay a medical corporal: the animal had fallen on top of him. His leg had been torn off from the middle of the upper thigh. I did what I could for him. The firing get ever more unpleasant and the gas thicker. Combined with the physical exertion, gradually it began to affect one's breathing. Towards 11 of the morning after following various false trails I finally arrived at Baudesson gorge where I met III.Batallion under Lt. von Enckevort with Batallion Medical officer Dr.Wild. There was good accommodation in the roomy gorge for the many wounded and gassed soldiers whom the doctors attended without rest."

The Consequences of Gas Warfare

It is a difficult matter to provide the figure for the quantity of battlefield gas deployed and its victims. An idea can be gained from the following: Between March and 11 November 1918, 1,967 tonnes of Yperite tear gas was manufactured in France to fill 2,393,000 artillery shells. Between 1914 and 1918 the German chemical industry supplied 111,600 tonnes of battlefield gases, of which 44,800 tonnes was mustard gas.

The total number of those who suffered permanant injury from gas, and those who died from it, remains disputed to the present day. It is fair to assume that one million men were gassed, and of these about 65,000 died, some of them not until years or decades later from the effects. The Russian losses put at 250,000 persons gassed and 38,599 dead, and these are the highest casualty figures by far. The cause lay in defective gas masks. The capability of the Russian military authorities to keep up with the rapid further development of chemical weapons was limited. When the Zelinski-Kummandt gas mask was introduced in 1916, Russian soldiers said, "If the German poison gases don't kill us, the Russian gas mask definitely will."

At the outbreak of war none of the belligerent nations had anti-gas equipment for its troops. The gaps at the Front had to be closed with makeshift solutions. An example was the so-called "Breathing Protector", pads soaked in an alkaline sodium-thio-sulphate solution distributed to the troops at the Ypres Bend in April 1915. Only the pioneer troops and auxiliaries given the task of setting up and carrying out the *Blasverfahren* received Dräger-Tübben oxygen equipment. Gas masks became the most important personal protection. Various versions were introduced amongst all armies participating in the war and were being continuously improved. The introduction of German mustard gas and its harmful effects on the body called for a rubberized protective suit. Collective anti-gas measures included earth filters laid in infantry trenches and caverns, and gas-proof protected housing and bunkers.

The psychological effect continues to be discussed in connection with the evaluation of gas warfare experiences. Its use was not only pursued with the aim of harming and poisoning the body, but of causing mental distress, particularly when soldiers lacked trust in the anti-gas measures of their Army or when they feared unforseeable consequences from encountering new alien substances. Chemical weapons make the highest demands on morale and intelligence of soldiers. In 1957, Colonel W.Volkart, an instructor in the Swiss Federal Army wrote: "In the long run, only very good, very disciplined troops can withstand the manifold threats inherent in gas warfare."

German NCO with leather gas mask 1917 and filter with three layer cartridge, Model 11/11. The Supreme Army Command had information concerning an imminent phosgene attack by the French and at the end of 1915 ordered more effective gas masks. The conversion to impregnated leather was caused by the lack of raw rubber and the short warehouse life of regenerated rubber.

Notes

1. "Lost" was made up from the names of the German chemists <u>Lo</u>mmel and <u>St</u>einkopf.
2. On account of the acrid, mustard-like smell.
3. Hague Declaration of 29 July 1899 regarding the prohibition of the use of shells with asphyxiating gases, published in the *Reichsgesetzblatt*, year 1901, p.474ff, and the Treaty Concerning the Laws and Usages of Land Warfare of 18 October 1907 – the Hague Land Warfare Ordinance. Therein it was expressly forbidden to use weapons, shells and substances made to cause unnecessary suffering.
4. Important base for the production of cotton-azo dyes, aniline dyes containing the chromophores of the azo-groups which provide the colour. The first azo-colouring was aniline-yellow in 1863.

Medical corps soldier of Inf.Regt 369/10. Reserve-Div. during the fighting in September /October 1917 in Flanders. From a sketch by Döberich-Steglitz.

5. In May 1915 the Germans formed Gas-Mortar Batallion 1 with 24 long barrel heavy mortars. After the development of the wind-borne release of gas from cylinders and later the gas-mine launcher, mortars lost significance in gas warfare.
6. Blue Cross (diphenylchloroarsine) was a particulate. A solid, when the shell exploded, it created an asphyxiant dust which could penetrate a respirator causing intolerable irritation to sinuses, forcing the wearer to remove the mask and so expose himself to the other gases.

Chapter Seven

FROM THE CATAPULT TO THE MORTAR

The Lessons of Port Arthur

In the German Army, mortars were considered pioneer equipment, and not weapons. In the event of war, and therefore if the need arose, they could be requested from one of the eight Pioneer Siege Trains (Nos. 18–20, 23–25, 29 and 30) made up of Pioneer- and Pioneer-Park Companies. This complicated procedure had its origins, as did the mortar itself, in the Russo-Japanese War of 1904/1905; it was a result of the evaluation of experiences gained from the forces involved in the fighting in East Asia.

Port Arthur was a Russian-held naval base on the Liaodong Penininsula (38°51'N 121° 15'E). The purpose of the fighting there was to control its excellent natural harbour. Especially in the six-month siege of the fortress at Port Arthur, the opposing armies were in fortified positions only a short distance from each other. "One of the most striking facts of the whole war is the quite unusual extent which the field fortification takes on both sides. In south-east Asia it celibrates a true triumph" commented a Major Löffler of the Royal Saxon General Staff in the second edition of the 1905 military officers' quarterly journal *Vierteljahreshefte für Truppenführung und Heereskunde.* This complicated tactical situation had shown that the heavy artillery was unable to destroy the obstacles in front of the enemy positions without endangering its own troops. It was one of the tasks of the pioneers to create alleys through which assault troops could approach the enemy using wire cutters, drive lanes through the minefield or bring up explosive charges, 50 kgs being considered the minimum for achieving anything worthwhile. These projects took much time, were extremely difficult to carry through and had little chance of success. To make things easier, consideration was given to the old idea of launching explosive charges by means of machines into the obstacles in front of the enemy positions. The Japanese found a different method. In front of Port Arthur they used bamboo tubes through which small charges of powder up to two kgs could be fired, the forerunner of the mortar.

German Considerations

From the point of view of the German General Staff, fighting against fortresses had a high priority. In the event of war with France, the operations of the German Army to its east would come up against numerous fortifications which would have to be captured within a short time. This explains the lively interest in the mortar question. In the quest for a solution a number of pioneer batallions built and tested mechanical catapults and muzzle-loading mortars of the simplest kind. Mechanical devices were considered preferable because in contrast to mortars using powder, the fire, smoke and detonation did not betray their position. The pioneers built the most diverse range of catapults. Some copied Roman and Greek ballistae, machines based on the crossbow design, similar to those which existed in replica in the Saalburg, a Roman fort on the Limes in the Taunus. However, there were problems. In tests it had been found that shells with a least charge of 50 kgs were required to destroy wire entanglements, iron gates, Spanish riders and hedge-type obstacles of trees and branches. Furthermore a range of 400 to 500 metres was needed. Catapult machines able to achieve this distance were too big, heavy and unmanageable, and their accuracy was poor.

A heavy mortar embedded on a turntable providing a traverse of 360º. It was developed by Rheinische Metallwaren und Maschinen factory ("Ehrhardt") although the manufacture was declared to be by, amongst others, "The Lepelmann Brothers' Workshops for Iron Constructions" of Düsseldorf.

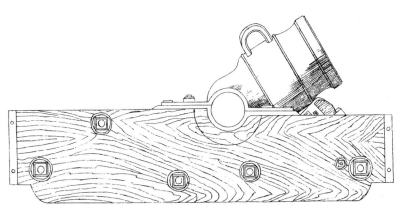

In the early days of trench warfare earth-mortars were a makeshift solution. They consisted of an iron pot with attached guide rails to give the 24 kg bomb its direction. The bomb was place in the pot and fired by explosive propellant.

Technical Development and Organisation of the Mortar Arm

In 1905 the Royal Prussian War Ministry contracted with the firms of Krupp and Ehrhardt for the development of a gun able to fire a mine or bomb of at least 50 kgs weight a short distance in a high trajectory, the purpose being to take out fully concealed obstacles in trenches. The gun was to have the greatest possible accuracy so that without any follow-up work a lane could be opened for passage through extensive obstacles and without endangering one's own troops. Finally the weapon was to be as light as possible so that it could be carried assembled or dismantled over the most difficult terrain up to the front lines.

Obstacle Destroyers

Short range mortars capable of firing an explosive charge of at least 50 kg at a steep angle for effect even against fully protected obstacles in trenches. They provided the greatest possible accuracy for creating passageways through extensive obstacles, without the need for the follow-up work which was hazardous for assault troops. The mortars were lightweight for assembly and could be dismantled for portage over the roughest battle ground to the foremost positions at the front.

Early examples of mine launchers were the mechanical devices of the Greeks and Romans such as this balliste for hurling rocks, later incendiary balls (above). The lower diagram shows a 25-pounder mortar on a wooden chassis as used by the Prussian fortress and siege artillery until the introduction of long-barrelled artillery.

The tests with powder-propellant mortars were no better. The pioneer batallions tried old cannon-ball mortars, and earth mortars with a firing ramp of wooden staves. These were dug into the earth at an angle one metre deep and fired using a container of explosive or powder. To ignite the propellant a time fuze was used.

These were not satisfactory solutions. F.Krupp AG at Essen suggested firing round-mines on a haft from small cannons, but again, accuracy was poor.

Finally it became clear that the search for a mortar could not be based on ideas some of which dated from the Roman period 2,000 years ago, or 700 years back, the first powder-propellant guns. Only when it had been shown that the desired results could not be achieved with these ancient technologies did the Germans turn to the newest developments in artillery armament, to which long barrels, barrel recoil and nitro-cellulose powder belonged.

Lt-Colonel Koch from the Engineering Committee of the pioneers' technical testing authority took on responsibility for the technological development. What was being asked for was a design carefully thought through and corresponding to the military requirements. It was no easy task to design an "obstacle destroyer", the effect of whose bombs would be comparable to those fired by the foot-artillery, but only one-third of the weight of the 7.7-cm light field cannon n/A. That was what the following years were to show.

From the winter of 1908 the Engineering Committee worked closely with the firm Rheinische Metallwaren und Maschinenfabrik (Ehrhardt) at Düsseldorf, which in the first instance proposed a a muzzle-loader with a smooth bore on a fixed chassis. There were various reasons for muzzle-loading. It would be easier to drop the bomb into the barrel from the confines of a narrow trench, it did away with the technically difficult breech mechanism (which moreover added to the weight) and also in this manner met the requirement for the height trajectory.

Exhaustive trials were necessary to meet all the military specifications. As these went on, it became clear that the accuracy demanded could not be achieved with a smooth bore and fixed chassis. This forced the changeover to a long barrel and chassis with barrel recoil, finished by the autumn of 1910: testing was concluded by the end of 1911.

The heavy mortar of 25-cm calibre with a range of 450 metres proved suitable to substitute for the heavy guns in attacks on fortresses. The stability in flight of the 990-mm long (barrel length of mortar L/3.45 = 862 mm) bomb weighing 95 kgs was considered no more than satisfactory whereas the accuracy of the heavy calibre was significantly greater as compared to artillery. There was minimal dispersal long or wide at such short range. The effect of the projectile itself lay not in the force of impact but its blast – at least 50 kgs nitro-explosive or 45 kgs ammonium nitrate.

In the winter of 1911 the War Ministry approved the supply of 80 heavy 25-cm mortars to equip four Companies in the eight pioneer siege trains. Since this was a totally new weapon, adjustments were being made to it continually. Thus at the outbreak of the First World War, the requirement had only been partially met. What had been made available was sufficient for training purposes.

The heavy 25-cm mortar provided the pioneers with an effective weapon for attack. Obviously this technique could be made useful

Technical and tactical details of German long-barrelled mortars with barrel recoil (State as at 1914/1915)

Mortar:	7.6-cm	17-cm	25-cm	38-cm[1]
Calibre	75.85 mm	170 mm	250 mm	380 mm
Muzzle velocity (metres/sec)	77–110	75–90	50–65	not known
Rate of fire (rounds/minute)	20	1	1	not known
Range	160–1050 m[2]	105–920 m[2]	150–470 m[3]	400–1500 m
Elevation	+45 +75°	+45 +75°	+45 +75°	not known
Traverse	70–170 (3600)	200	200	3600
Barrel length	L/5.2 = 400 mm	L/4.42 = 752 mm	L3.45 = 862 mm	not known
Weight, transportation	180 kg	635 kg	730 kg	not known
Weight, firing position	140 kg[4]	482 kg	570 kg	2000 kg
Weight bomb	4.6-4.75 kg	10–12 kg	95 kg[5]	400 kg[6]
Weight explosive charge	0.56 kg	0.56 kg	45–50 kg	200 kg
Propellant, number charges	I.-V.	I.-VI	I.-IV	not known

Heavy mortar manufactured by Rheinische Metallwaren und Maschinenfabrik (Ehrhardt) at Düsseldorf. The barrel had a reinforced baseplate, the bedding was wood and for transport it needed only a drawbar and two wheels. It remained at the prototype stage.

The "heavy mortar" with barrel recoil and 95 kg explosive bomb received by the fighting troops.

The "medium mortar" was built on the principle of the heavy mortar. On testing problems arose. The bomb oscillated too strongly on the descent path. The solution was to increase its weight to 50 kg, and in order to make the range the propellant charge had also to be increased to a maximum of 155 grams.

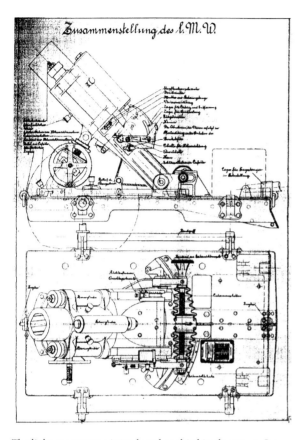

The light mortar was introduced as third in the group. Its characteristics were a high rate of fire and mobility. For that reason it was especially suitable for engaging living targets. On the other hand the effect of a round against targets with any resistant strength was slight.

The light mortar in firing position. The high rate of fire (20 rounds/min) made great demands on the crew in preparing and loading the munition, and also for ammunition supply.

The three mortars for comparison. The medium and large mortars were Modell 16b. The photograph was taken in March 1918 of Mortar Company 230/30 Reserve-Division at Upper Alsace.

Only a single "very heavy mortar" prototype was built and tested. This photograph of the loading procedure provides an idea of the effort required to fire the weapon.

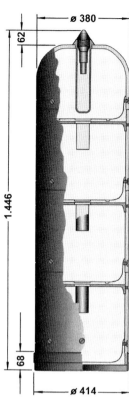

Sectional diagram of the 400 kg bomb for the 38-cm mortar.

for the defence of one's own fortifications, as for example to interrupt the expected heavy mortar attacks by the enemy.

From the experience of the Russo-Japanese War it was known that the attackers' protected housing had thick beams with one metre of earth on top. Building materials, a labour force and time were limited. For that reason a medium mortar with 50 kg bombs (containing ten to twelve kgs high explosive) was considered sufficient, although the range would be double that of the 100-kg bombs of the heavy mortar. Accordingly the Engineering Committee made its proposals to the War Ministry for a light mortar with a 4.5 kg bomb (1 kg HE), and the very heavy 38-cm mortar with bombs weighing 400 kgs (200 kgs HE), The Ministry turned them both down. The troops found the makeshift design for a light mortar to be acceptable, later a prototype of the very heavy mortar was ordered and tested.

Medium and Light Mortars

Only after repeated urging by the Engineering Committee did the War Ministry finally agree to allow Ehrhardt to build the medium mortar, but at the firm's expense. Construction and testing of the new design was concluded at the end of 1912. Over the next two years manufacture and equipping of the fortifications was begun. In some fortresses the medium mortar was built into the rear of casemates so that it could be brought out, fired and then returned to full cover.

As with the medium mortar, the War Ministry was not able to force through its concept with the light mortar. Its development and construction was considered necessary by the Engineering Committee for fortress and field fortification warfare to combat infantry and workers in trenches and under light cover. Since it was to be suitable for defence and attack equally, the properties of great mobility, rate of fire and accuracy had to be included in the design. Development and testing were so time-consuming that the light mortar with long barrel and barrel recoil were not declared ready for the Front until shortly before the outbreak of war.

The mortar barrel being of 7.6-mm calibre, the weight of the light explosive bomb was

4.75 kgs. Using all propellant charges its maximum range was 1050 metres. The very high rate of fire, 20 rounds/min, was achieved by use of a tension spring trigger in the barrel. The light mortar could be quickly intergrated almost anywhere: it needed very little space, no more than 2 square metres.

Mortars in Warfare

The existence of the mortar was for the most part a well-kept secret until the outbreak of war. 2nd Lt.(R) M.Kilian coming from the field artillery reported:

"...I had pesisted in my attempts to serve nearer the Front. Then on 14 November, Captain von Kuhlmann our Staff 1a summoned me and with a grin showed me a very interesting order stamped "Highly Secret". Medium mortars, of which we had never previously heard, were to be fetched out of the fortress at Istein and made mobile. They wanted to form special small units and were looking for suitable officers. If these things are of modern construction I shall think it over (…) some days later two riders came trotting at a fast pace (…) crossed the Rhine to the Istein eyesore (…) up there on the crag I was shown for the first time in the casemates the mortars kept so very secret up until now. (…) The things are impressive as close-combat mortars. In skilful and bold operations one ought to be able to obtain extraordinary results, those were my thoughts. Thereupon I made my decision to serve with the mortars."

The mortars had had their baptism of fire three months earlier, on 13 August 1914 at the siege of Fort Flèron (one of the ring of forts around Liège). After the war Major (ret'd) Thorner of 4.(Mortar) Company/Pioneer-Batallion 24 recalled:

"On 12 August at 1400 hrs 4./Pi.24 at Liège received orders to proceed in lorries through the front line to Battice to fetch mortars and ammunition and then take Fort Flèron as part of 18. Infantry Division.(…) We received our mortars and got back to Liège at midnight. At 0700 hrs on 13 August we were taken by lorry to Fort Flèron. (…) I had four heavy mortars brought up across the rails at the railway station under cover of a train standing there and positioned them, two in the gulley and two on the right flank.(…)

The mortars were quickly but carefully embedded, exactly as the pioneers had learnt to do it at their training grounds in Cologne. It was the first time that live ammunition was to be fired, in peacetime only practice ammunition had ever been used. Everybody waited excitedly for the first round to be fired and its effect, but instead we had an unexpected and really unpleasant problem which delayed the start of our attack by several hours. We discovered that the bomb, which had to be muzzle-loaded into the short barrel of the mortar, would not fit because of the barrel grooves. (…) On all bombs it was found that the guide rings had been bent out of shape by the loading and unloading. On these first mortar bombs, the copper guide rings projected beyond the base and created a cavity at the end. Their purpose was to disperse the powder gases from the relatively thin walls of the cavity and force them against the grooves. As the result of this experience at Liège the projecting part of the guide rings were later removed and this did not really adversely affect the bomb in the barrel or the accuracy.

On 13 August, however, this memorable day of the first mortar operation, we had to sort out the problem by ourselves. From a blacksmith we obtained rasps and other tools and laboured to remove all the dents and other edges.(…) By 1200 hrs we were ready to fire the first mortar bomb of the Great War. Everybody watched its flight until it disappeared into the surrounding ditch where it impacted and the detonation followed (…) which made everything tremble. A huge black cloud of smoke, mixed with earth, rose to the heavens. Now we fired round after round. The pioneers hauled up the bombs weighing well over a hundredweight without much thought for the whizzing splinters which came our way on account of the close range.

We had got as close to the fort as the last bit of cover allowed. We were attacking the Kehle, that is to say the rear side of the fortification least exposed to attack. Meanwhile the range had shortened to the middle of the surrounding ditch and the covered exit to the Kehl-wall(…). The fort replied with heavy fire from all armoured turrets. Although it sounded as though all hell had broken loose, the enemy could not reach us because he had no steep trajectory fire to get at us behind cover.

The enemy seemed to be holding out, or at least that was what we believed. On 14 August (…) his resistance crumbled and the fort surrendered.[7] (…) At Fort Flèron one could distinguish the difference between mortar bombs and artillery rounds. Our range was limited but our accuracy perfect, since the dispersal of fire was only 3 metres but the radius of the explosive effect much wider. None of the armoured turrets had been within our range, but our artillery had not managed to take any of *them out. Instead our mortars had churned up the moat surrounds metres high, shattered the windows of the massif barracks, completely caved in a parapet and knocked down large concrete blocks.(…) The remaining mortars were brought back on 15 August and handed over to the pioneers' siege train."*

The 25-cm heavy muzzle-loader "Ehrhardt" was of simple contruction. It could fire explosive bombs of 232 and 38 kgs with detonator, the so-called "coal bucket", or in the 20-, 30- and 40 kilo range with time fuze. Because of their characteristic shape they were nicknamed "Pickelhauben" after the early war issue of German protective helmet with spike.

In 1915 several mortar companies received the 490-kilo smooth-bore heavy mortar as a substitute for the long barrelled mortar with barrel recoil. The 18-cm calibre bombs weighed between 27.5 and 30 kilos. The maximum rnage was 730 metres.

Thorner's report describes the use of mortars for fortress warfare, the purpose for which they had been developed. When the war on the Western Front solidified into trench warfare in the autumn of 1914, the entire German Army saw itself confronted with tasks for which this kind of warfare was typical. Now the pioneers with their weaponry, apparatus and equipment came to the fore, in the use of which the infantry at this time had no experience. This included hand-grenades, balled and pole charges as well as mortars from storage.

At the outbreak of war there were 70 heavy and 116 medium mortars available, and some smooth-bore light mortars as prototypes for future mass production. Although only to hand in small numbers, they had great success under the new conditions. Up to the spring of 1915 the pioneers formed independent mortar sections but armed with only two mortars each.

The Supreme Army Command and the War Ministry ordered the accelerated production of mortars and their ammunition. Rheinmetall could not deliver it all and so other undertakings, amongst them the Zimmermann-Werke Maschinen- und Werkzeugfabrik A.G. of Chemnitz, had to be co-opted. Despite that, it was some time before the ordered quantities reached the front lines. Meanwhile the troops helped out themselves with a variety of catapult machines, some of them really adventurous. For example *Ausbläser* (artillery shells whose explosive gases had escaped without the intended effect of shattering the shell casing) or large sections of barrel through which tin boxes filled with explosive were fired. The tried and tested "earth mortar" was seen again, and various smooth-bore prototype mortars. 4.Army pioneer park at Ghent made an explosive-charge launcher to a design by Captain Magener. Very soon industry took up the challenge of smooth-bore mortars, such as Heinrich Lanz oHG of Mannheim and the Mauser weapons factory at Oberndorf/Neckar. As a substitute for the heavy mortar, Rheinmetall manufactured the 25-cm mortar, also turned out in other factories, amongst others at Heidenheim.

In Part 7 of the regulations for trench warfare *Vorschriften für den Stellungskrieg für alle Waffen* of 1916, dedicated to mortars, their disadvantages are expressly laid bare. "Because of its limited range, the mortar must be set up very far forward.(…) It is very difficult to hide its fire from enemy observers. Known mortars under cover will soon be wiped out." Based on such experiences came the idea of using compressed air as propellant, and a 10.5-cm compressed air mortar was developed in combination with the firm of Kanzler & Söhne, Neustadt/Weinstrasse, which fired winged-bombs.

For the 15-cm mortar the bombs were egg-shaped. The Marine Corps in Flanders had a 26-cm compressed air mortar. Despite their advantages (no muzzle fire, no smoke and no report when fired) compressed air mortars had so many more disadvantages that their use was abandoned by the Germans.

Germany's enemies reacted to the German mortar with their own developments. In September 1915 in the fighting in the Artois and Champagne when the French 240 mm fin stabilized-mortar bombs appeared, the German front troops wanted a copy, and

contracts were awarded to Maschinenfabrik Germania at Chemnitz and the Oberschlesische Eisenbahn-Bedarfs A.G., a railway parts firm at Friedenshütte, Gleiwitz and Zawadski. Of the two kinds of finned-bomb mortars, "Iko" (short for Engineering Committee) and "Albrecht"

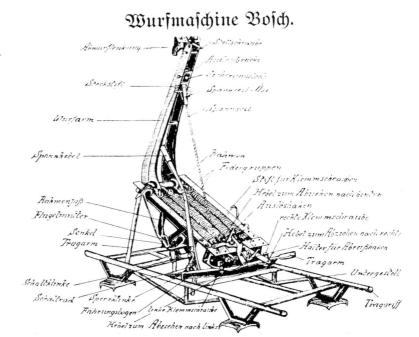

Mechanical catapults and bomb launchers fulfilled the same purpose in trench warfare as the mortar. Depicted here is a "Bosch" spring-catapult which could hurl simultaneously over a distance of 125 to 155 metres, up to three discus- or two round hand-grenades, or hand gas-bombs.

The mortars "15" and "16" were also used by the infantry. They appeared for the first time at the Front in the spring of 1916. The various kinds of heavy fin-stabilized bombs weighing about two kilos could be fired 500 metres.

Because the light mortar with barrel recoil was not available in sufficient numbers until well into the war, mortar units were supplied with smooth-bore light mortar "H.L." (9-cm mortar Lanz), It weighed 65 kilos on the firing position and fired two kinds of projectile.

The 10.5-cm compressed air mortar with a maximum pressure of 100 atüs (atmospheric plus pressure). The fin-stabilised bombs weighed 6.5 kg. A compressed air bottle was sufficient to fire ten of these. The maximum range was 800 metres.

(name of the inventor)700 were turned out up to the end of the First World War. They were assessed as valuable additions to the long barrelled mortars, being moreover cheaper and more quickly produced.

Further Developments in the Course of the War

The increasing extent of the entrenched positions rearwards led to the need for greater range, and modified ammunition. Larger propellant charges and the introduction of lighter bombs, as for example for the heavy mortar, did not result in any notable improvement. The only recourse was to elongate the barrels as was done to model 16a and 16b mortars at the end of 1916. Model 16a was given a smooth-bore barrel extension, and on the models 16b approaching completion the calibre rings were not cut away contrary to the usual practice. The maximum ranges were now respectively 1160 and 960 metres. The range of the light mortar n.A. was now 1312 metres, by the late summer it had increased to 1730 metres, that of the medium mortar to 1600 metres.

Another requirement was to widen the angle of traverse, too small for the trenches due to constructional peculiarities of the mortar. For that reason the light mortar was given a turntable bedplate in the summer of 1915 allowing lateral movement through 360º.

The medium and heavy mortars were fitted with a turntable for trench warfare, but neither

had a removeable turntable bedplate until shortly before the war's end in 1918.

The appearance of British tanks in 1916 was the motive for the introduction of a makeshift mounting for flat trajectory fire to enable light mortars to engage in anti-tank work. This resulted in a chassis with tail and earth anchor, and large wooden wheels, the so-called "flat trajectory chassis" for use in mobile warfare. Armoured targets were engaged at distances below 500 metres using the light mortar bomb which could go through 15 mm thick armour plate at an impact ange of between 60° and 90°. Thus the light mortar had become a light infantry gun. It was also used in mountain warfare, transported by mules.

Light mortar n.A.on firing turntable with light explosive bomb.

Types of Ammunition

In August 1914, parties from the 4.(Mortar-) Companies on the pioneer siege trains had gone into action with a few hundred explosive bombs. In the course of the war the number of various types of mortar bomb rose to not less than 300. The changes to munitions can only be roughly indicated in this connection. In 1915, gas-bombs for long-barrelled mortars were introduced. When the use of gas by the first mortar batallions failed to achieved the desired density over selected sectors of terrain, gas bombs were gradually withdrawn, and the task was taken over by special gas-mortar squads.

The light mortar n.A weighed 180 kg for transport. Its main components were the barrel with tension trigger, barrel cradle, braking device, chassis with elevating gear, turntable bed with wheels and crossbar, and aiming equipment.

Stocks of Mortars in the German Army between 1914 and 1918[8]

Type of Mortar:	7.6-cm light	17-cm medium	25-cm heavy	Winged-bomb
August 1914	prototype only	116	70	0
September 1916	1345	674	465	0
August 1917	12247	2331	1355	0
January 1918	13329	2476	1322	n/A
November 1918	12400	2400	1200	700

The multitude of types of ammunition shows how indispensable mortars, and especially light mortars, had become for the infantry. Besides the already mentioned explosive- and gas-bombs, there were smoke-bombs, light anti-tank bombs, incendiary bombs (also used by the medium mortars), light signals-bombs, light newspaper-bombs for propaganda purposes, flare bombs, practice bombs and training bombs.

The constantly increasing requirement, the continual improvements to existing types of bomb and the introduction of new kinds of mortar bomb caused ever greater problems as the war went on. There was a lack of suitable manufacturers, trained workers and the necessary materials and explosives. Suitable substitutes for TNT, all of which had been commandeered by the artillery, had to be used. Weeks passed. There was a general lack of time for thorough testing and acceptance, a deficiency for which the fighting troops had to pay. In the second half of 1915 the number of bombs exploding in the mortar barrel increased. The monthly requirement of mortar munitions in 1918 was for 1.4 million light-, 120,000 medium- and 20,000 heavy explosive bombs, and 15,000 winged mortar bombs.

In 1915 there was a shortage of new mortars coming to the Front. Of the 4,700 new mortars ordered by the end of 1915, only 1,400 were delivered. That fact and the relatively high requirement at the Front had a disadvantageous effect on the enlargement of the mortar branch wanted by Supreme Army Command. Even the transfer-out of the makeshift mortars and explosive-charge launchers remaining with the pioneer companies was made possible to help make up the numbers. In August 1916 a total of 1,500 was achieved and the output up to 1917 increased to about 4,000 per month.

The Expansion of the Mortar Branch

The mortar successes at the beginning of the war were attributed to the pioneer companies of the pioneer siege trains. These companies had only been assigned the mortars for the duration of the operations, there was no proper mortar branch as such. In the autumn of 1914 the need was recognised to set up independent mortar detachments,[9] and these came about in the second half of December.

These detachments, some horse-drawn, others motorized, received between two and six mortars from fortress stocks. The detachments would serve with Armies or sections thereof, and be placed temporarily with Divisions for the duration of a particular operation.

By now the light mortar was being series produced. On 22 September 1915 it had been ordered that every Division should have one mortar company with two heavy, four medium and six light mortars. On account of the shortage of mortars this requirement had not been met by the end of 1915: the training of mortar branch troops was proceeding, and

The munitions for the light mortar in 1916 (from left to right): (light explosive bombs 16) L Lotte, E Ernaliese; (light explosive bomb) A Annaliese: (light smoke-bombs) Flora and N: light anti-armour bomb Ida and G gas bomb. A characteristic of the munition was the placing of the propellant on the bomb floor which, in combination with the spring trigger, made a high rate of fire possible.

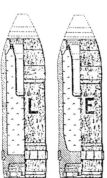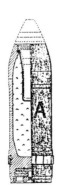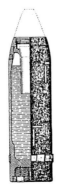

firing and range-measuring techniques refined.

On 16 January 1916 it was decreed that every pioneer company could be given six light mortars. At the beginning of February 1916, Supreme Army Command placed two heavy mortar detachments, each with two mortars, and a medium mortar detachment with six mortars, at the disposal of every Army Corps and Reserve Corps.

In April 1916 the first mortar batallions were formed. The authorized allocation initially was ten light and twenty medium mortars. In 1916 the number of mortar companies rose to 217, and of mortar batallions to six.

By 1917 seven mountain-mortar companies had been formed, and the assault and rifle batallions received their own mortar companies with eight light mortars. The pioneer reserve levels were insufficient for further transfers into the mortar branch, and by the order of 16 November 1916 the light mortars were placed with the infantry while the existing pioneer mortar companies and batallions were reorganised into batallions, each with four companies, each company having eight medium and four heavy mortars. Ultimately the medium mortars also went to the infantry.

In August 1918 the mortar companies at divisional level were disbanded and their mortars re-allocated to the three infantry regiments of the division, each of which then had a 13th (mortar-)company.[10] The heavy mortars went into the Army reserve. By the time when the Armistice came into effect in November 1918, the restructuring had not been completed. In any case, the mortar was no longer emblematic of the pioneers: it had become an infantry weapon.

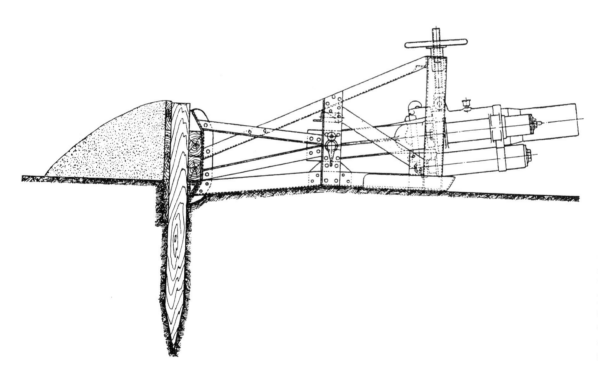

Locating a light mortar in a flat trajectory frame provided a temporary solution for shooting at an elevation of 20° over 900 metres as an anti-tank gun.

The preparations for the attack in the spring included fitting the light mortar n/A with a chassis tail and spade-anchor, and a projection for the eye-connection of the limber. When the mortar was fired at this flat trajectory, the anchor resisted the recoil.

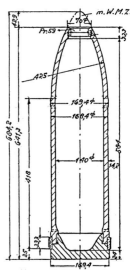

A medium mortar 16b No. 4568 manufactured in 1918, in transport mode. The sectional diagram is of the medium explosive mortar bomb 16 ("Marga"). It was of seamless steel; the pre-cut guide rings were of zinc alloy or brass. It weighed 53 kgs of which 12.5 kgs was the explosive charge.

Heavy mortar 16b
ready to fire.

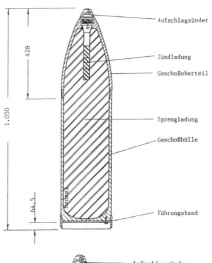

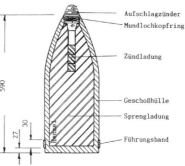

Sectional diagram of a heavy mortar bomb. It weighed 95 kgs and was made of cast steel. About 42 kgs of the weight was the explosive. In order to increase the range of he heavy mortar the "half-heavy mortar bomb" was introduced. It was of cast steel, weighed 63 kgs and took between 25 and 26 kgs of explosive. It could reach targets up to 840 metres distant but the accuracy was poorer than with the original.

Three men were needed to load a 95 kg mortar bomb. A special device was used for the operation, another served to place the propellant charge in the floor chamber of the barrel.

Key: Aufschlagzünder = impact detonator
Zündladung = ignition charge
Geschossoberteil = upper part of bomb
Sprengladung = explosive
Geschosshülle = bomb casing
Führungsband = guide ring
Mundlochkopfring = Removable ring for fitting special lifting device into bomb head (see photo top left, also p.150, top).

Repairs to a heavy mortar 16b by the armourer of Mortar Company 230.

Supplying the
ammunition for
the heavy mortar
was hard labour.
Commemorative
photo of a loading
party with whole and
half mortar bombs.
These were delivered
in shaped wicker
baskets. In wartime
the vulnerable guide
rings were given
special protective
caps.

The Strasbourg firm
of Wolf Netter and
Jacobi manufactured
the fin-stabilized
mortar bomb
"Albrecht". It weighted
98 kgs and could be
fired 1550 metres.

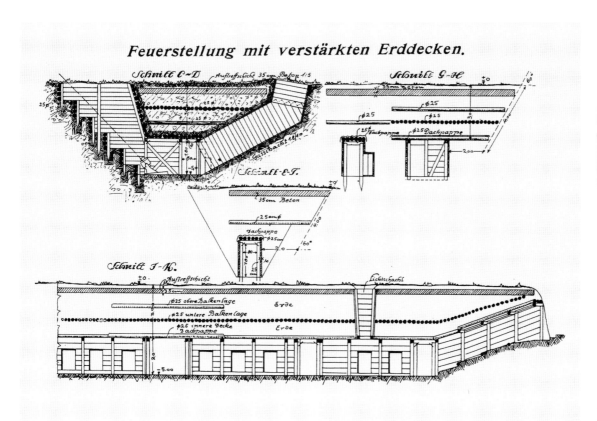

Feuerstellung mit verstärkten Erddecken.

Firing position with reinforced earth roofing.

The medium mortar 16b with equipment weighed about 650 kg for transportation. In construction it was similar to the heavy mortar (730 kg) but had a few minor differences (chassis walls lacked triangular recesses and the 90° traverse gear.)

Mortar Developments of Other Nations

After the British had failed to score any success in the summer battle with flame-throwers, the engineer Livens came upon the idea of mixing cotton waste with oil, placing it in simple iron containers with a small explosive, lining up the containers as earth mortars and then firing them in quick succession. Upon impact the bombs would explode spreading incendiaries, smoke, explosives and battlefield gases into the enemy trenches. The first trial of twenty of these primitive "oil projectors" took place on 23 June 1915 near Pozières, not far from the northern French town of Albert. It led to the Livens' gas mortar.

The invention by the Briton Stokes, who had developed a simple three-inch mortar consisting of a steel barrel and a bipod stand, was designed to fire an explosive. The weapon was turned down at a demonstration on 25 June 1915 for too short a range at 320 metres although it appeared to be very suitable for firing gas munitions. For a frontline experiment by troops, 29 mortars with the large calibre of 105 mm were constructed. Because the gas munitions for it did not become available until September 1916, the troops made their own incendiary and smoke munitions meanwhile. These produced such good results that that infantry wanted the Stokes mortar

for explosive ammunition. Comparable to the German 7.6 mm light mortar in effect, it became the infantry mortar of choice. Each brigade received an eight-mortar battery. 240 mm winged bombs were introduced. The mortar could fire 68 kg torpedo-shaped bombs a distance of 1050 metres. They were used in the divisional "trench mortar batteries". The American expeditionary corps in France availed itself of the British development.

In 1912 the French had made their first cautious experiments to develop special trench mortars. By the outbreak of war nothing had been completed. Therefore after the transition to trench warfare, the French infantry was faced by the same problems as the Germans, but were worse prepared; they had no mortars at all. This breach had to be filled quickly, and so the French had recourse to curious antiques stored in their fortresses: 150 mm bronze mortar "Model 1838", and the 220 mm and 270 mm "Model 1839". In October 1914 there were 102 of the 150 mm mortars at the front. They were known as "Crapouilotts", saluting guns.

The following year was also characterised by improvisation. A new arrival was the 58 mm mortar "T No 1", which could fire a fin-stabilized bomb weighing 16 kgs a distance of 300 metres. It was used in action of the first time in January 1915 and during the war underwent continual

The British 3-inch (7.62 mm) "Stokes" mortar impressed by its simple but very practical construction. It was the forerunner for the modern mortar.

The 155-mm mortar model 1838 could fire a bomb weighing 7.5 kgs a distance of 600 metres, and a 25 kg-bomb 200 metres. It weight 150 kgs, the rate of fire was one round every two minutes.

180 "Mortier de 58 T No 1" were delivered between December 1914 and February 1915. Its weight was said to be 114 kgs.

improvements ("T No 1 bis" and "T No 2"). The stock on 1 March 1917 was 1066. Other weapons appearing for the first time were the 75 mm light mortar built by the firm Schneider/Le Creusot and the 150 mm fin-stabilized mortar. The Germans were particularly impressed by the 240 mm mortar "Model CT 1915" which made its debut in the Artois and Champagne. This one, and its successor "LT 1917", fired bombs weighing between 50 and 85 kgs over a range of 2850 metres. They were fin-stabilised, held steady in flight and with the delay fuse were able to break ground into shallow underground refuges. The mortars were so effective that the Germans copied them.

The 340 mm mortar "T" with its 195 kg bombs appeared much more rarely. It had to be dismantledled into three parts for transport. The prototype was tried out by the French at the end of 1915 at Hartmannsweiler Kopf in the Vosges.

As the word "mortar" implies, in France the weapon was considered to be part of the artillery, and was spoken of as "trench artillery". The mortars were organised into batteries, of which each Division had two to three; there were further batteries at Army Corps level.

Austria also lacked mortars at the outbreak of war even though the firm of Skoda had offered prototypes in 1909. At first – as everywhere – improvisation plugged the gaps. Subsequently there were 17 models of smooth-bore and long-barrelled mortars with a calibre between 80 and 260 mm. The Austrians imported from Germany mortars of the Lanz trade mark and compressed-air types designated as "air-mortars" in Austria. Their diversity was especially striking. Amongst the imported types of 105 mm and 150 mm calibre, the firms of Skoda and Austria manufactured their own 200 mm types. Mortars belonged with the pioneers initially but as the war went on were turned over to the infantry and artillery.

Italy entered the war on the side of the Entente on 26 April 1915 and benefited from the war experience of its partners. The lack of mortars, known as "bombardes", led to a series of local developments including the 150 mm bombarde "Maggiora", but it was more commonly the practice to seek recourse to foreign, especially French, constructions.

The Russian Army already had experience of steep-fire weapons in the war against Japan and

From February 1915 the French artillery in the trenches received a much improved mortar in the Mortier de 58 T No 2. Its range was 1450 metres, as against the 1150 metres of its predecessor.

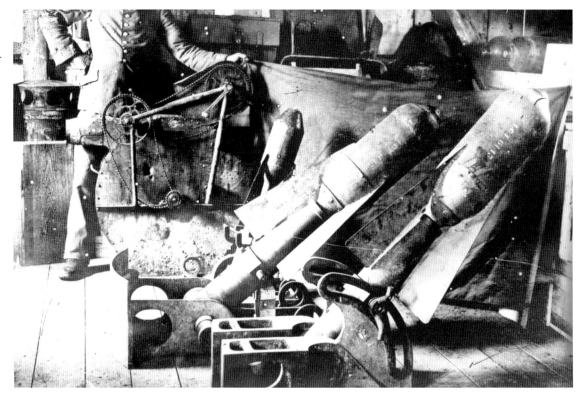

The 240 mm mortar model 1916 weighed 3.6 tonnes in firing position and proved very effective. It was dismantled into three parts for transportation and took 20 hours to re-assemble. Rate of fire was one round every six minutes.

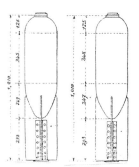

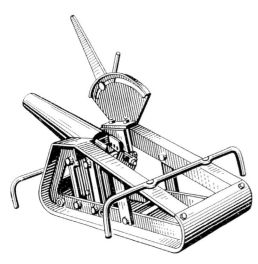

Russian 47 mm Lichonin system mortar.

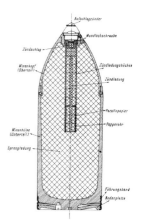

The Austrian 26 mm M.17 mortar was developed by Skoda Werke. Between 36 and 40 of them were delivered monthly from March 1918. The long-barrelled muzzle loader weighed 1.6 tonnes and fired bomnbs weighing between 60 and 83 kgs over a range of from 2200 to 2400 metres.

Bringing up and digging in the medium and heavy mortars with barrel recoil, as they were deployed operationally by German mortar units, could be heavy going.

its fortifications. In their defence of Port Arthur they had used 11.5 kg bombs fired from over-large calibre guns achieving ranges between 50 and 400 metres. By the outbreak of the First World War, however, they had only prototypes of the "minomets". Their own designs during the war lacked any significance apart from the 47 mm Lichonin System mortar and an 89 mm mortar from the Ishorsk Ironworks. In order to close the gaps, French 58 "T No 1" and "1 bis" were imported in large numbers.

The Battle for Hartmannsweilerkopf

The Hartmannsweiler Kopf is a mountain 956 metres in height on the western side of the Upper Rhine lowlands in the Vosges.[11] It was the location of bitter fighting for three years, for whoever controlled the mountain had a commanding view over the southern plain of the Rhine. Mortars played an important role in the fighting. It is true that there were battles in which a considerably larger number of mortars were used, for example in the spring of 1916 when the first mortar battalions with 202 mortars become involved in fighting which had raged for months. Also in the German Michael-Offensive in March 1918, when 3534 mortars were in readiness. In comparison the numbers used at Hartmannsweiler Kopf were very few; in October 1915 about twenty, the highest number being 47 at the beginning of January 1917.

As has already been mentioned, mortars were intended for use in fortress warfare, and little value was placed on mobility, but more on accuracy and bomb-effect. The effect they had in mountain operations was reported upon by 2nd Lt.(R) H. Kilian, a volunteer for mortar duty from Field Artillery Regiment 76. Mortar Detachment IV set up by him was attached to Army Section *Gaede* in December 1914. At that time it had two medium mortars and 120 rounds. At the request of the artillery, Army High Command ordered its transfer to Hartmannsweiler Kopf.

Two German attacks, the first beginning on 4 January 1915, against the peak of the mountain had failed because it was very difficult for the artillery to hit the Felsenberg where the

French were established. Kilian reported on the difficulty of transporting one mortar and its ammunition. Although he had six strong horses and over 70 men, the movement took all night on the 20 January 1915 to complete.

> "...Long, heavy hawsers were bound to the mortar, then the men began to haul it upwards metre by metre along the narrow path.(…) After some short pauses to recuperate, towards 0700 hrs we had heaved the mortar up close below the Oberrehfelsen. Then we could go no farther.(…) There was nothing for it but to dismantle the mortar and drag up the individual parts the last few hundred metres to Aussichtsfelsen. While doing this we received bad news: On the way we had become unsettled by the non-appearance of the beasts of burden with the ammunition. Now we learned the reason. The mules lent by Mountain Howitzer Battery (Baden) No 1 refused to budge with 17-cm bombs (their carrying frames were for 10.5-cm shells). (…) Therefore all the ammunition had to be brought up individually by our men."

At 1400 hrs they began firing the mortar.

> "..."Fire!"--a loud report. It sounded like a distant metallic crack.[12] Then the bomb hissed steeply away skywards above the tall fir trees and headed for the crest. We could not see it, only follow its flight by the whizzing. Reluctantly we ducked down in the trench and listened upwards intently. The whistling grew louder, the bomb was falling, it was approaching our observation point with increasing speed, howled close above the tree-tops, dived down towards us – my heart missed a beat – but no, it passed us by, thank God, and was going to hit the Felsenberg on the north side not far away. (…) "Take cover!" I roared.
>   We pressed ourselves against the trench wall. The detonation was enormous, the mountain trembled down to its foundations. A hail of splinters flew away over us. Yellow smoke drifted through the timber forest on the crest. The echo of the heavy explosion rolled down to the valleys and gradually resounded. I lay forward on the snowbound slope in order to see exactly where the first bomb hit.(…) Apart from us few, nobody on the mountain knew what was happening. Our infantry, frightened by the enormity of the explosion, clung against the rockface. A strange, deathly silence reigned on the entire mountain, nobody fired.
>   The smoke had drifted away. Now I could see precisely: the first round was well aimed. I adjusted the mortar's fire nearer so as to hit the

Two views of the
Hartmannsweiler
Kopf from the time of
the First World War.

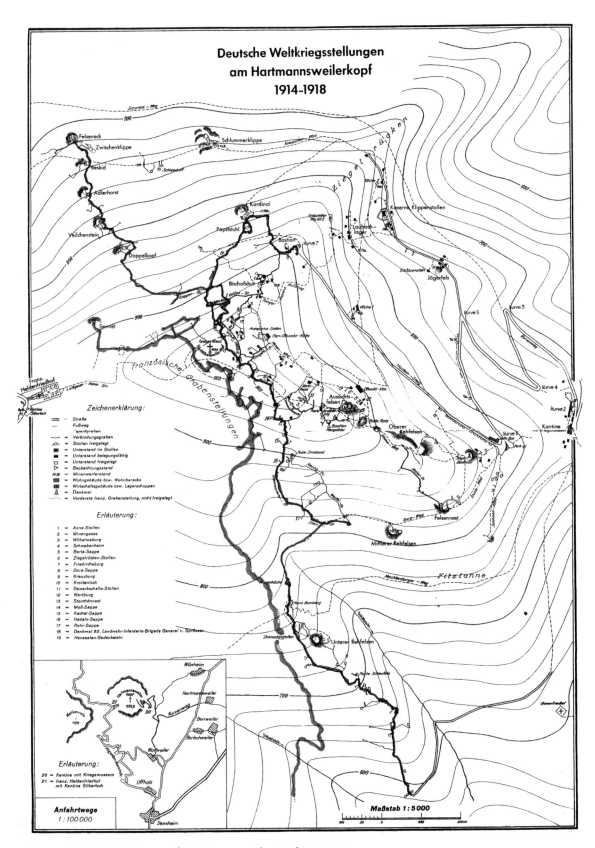

German Great War Positions on the Hartmannsweiler Kopf 1914–1918.
(This is a postwar tourist map. The inset bottom left shows the geographical position of the mountain with regard to local villages. The important part of the map for Lt. Kilian's account is (1) *Grosses Kreuz* on the peak of the mountain within the 950 metre contour where the French were established (Felsenburg, not marked) (2) *Aussichtsfelsen*, 300 metres SE where Kilian had his spotter post and from where his mortar fired and (3) *Oberrehfels* (actually Oberer Rehfelsen) another 200 metres SE down the mountain from where he hauled up the dismantled gun. He does not mention any other location prior to reaching this point. The respective trench positions did not run either side of the mountain peak in December 1915. Transl.)

The concrete bunker "Dora" behind Aussichtsfelsen on the Hartmannsweiler Kopf. Photograph taken in June 2011.

centre of the Felsenberg. Despite the danger for ourselves, I wanted to keep reducing the range in order to demolish the blockhouse about 60 metres distant.(…) "Fire!" The bomb hissed away high above us, fell and burst in the Ringburg. It flamed up, a gigantic tree burst apart and burned. Heavy branches of fir trees fell into the snow with a crack. Bomb splinters and blocks of rock were flying around. According to plan the whole area of the enemy-occupied Ringburg would now be subjected to indiscriminate bombardment. To our astonishment there were duds. Two bombs fell at an angle and broke apart against the rocks. The yellow TNT filling coloured the snow a poisonous greenish-yellow. On the other side the bugles of the French alpine infantry fell silent.

The end: after twenty rounds Lt. von Düring came forward to us in the trench. He was unarmed, and wearing his grey officer's cloak with the collar up. We saluted and exchanged a few words. His adjutant accompanied him, in greatcoat without a belt, carrying a white flag. During the last few rounds a thick mist had gathered. Visibility in the wood was now so bad that we could hardly make out any part of the blockhouse.(…) 9 minutes 50 seconds, 51 seconds – there – from below on the right we heard a shout from within the mist. It was von Düring's voice. "Hallo, hallo, over here!" I shouted. He had lost his bearings in the mist. We heard his voice again: "It's all ours!"

We broke out into shouts of jubilation, tumbled from the trench and ran towards the alpine infantry fortification. Now we also saw von Düring, he had gone too far towards the northern slope. As he approached we waved, wading through the deep snow. I got forward quicker than the others and was first to reach the ruins of the blockhouse and a trench buried under rubble full of rifles, sidearms, ammunition, uniform belts, cartridge pouches, tins of preserves and much else. Huge trees had fallen across the trench. Blocks of rock had bored down into the snow. The terrain was churned up and of a yellowish colour, spattered here and there with blood, an indescribable sight. All around wherever one looked were strewn splinters of rock, burnt gigantic firs and fallen branches, dead and wounded. Amongst it all intrepid French alpine infantry. (…) Strange fellows. In the middle of the Ringburg suddenly I came across a giant crater in front of me, almost eight metres in diameter. We had never seen anything like it before. Surprised, I shouted over to the nearest alpine soldier in French: "Comrade," I asked him, "what caused this giant crater?"

"That was the officers' protected shelter," he replied, "A bomb hit it.""

Photograph taken from within the the interior of a reinforced mortar shelter with heavy mortar 16b. The crew have the mortar on its baseplate bedded within a wooden box on account of the heavy weight of the bomb and the force of the recoil.

On 22 January 1915 the Hartmannsweiler Kopf was in German hands, but after numerous French attacks the peak was lost on 23 March. The eastern slopes remained the starting point for German assaults, however, so that between then and 25 May the higher positions changed hands repeatedly. The Germans then held them until late in 1915.

Mortar Detachment 151 – previously IV – was reinforced on 23 May by two heavy and a little later by two light mortars and transferred at the end of the month to another sector of the Vosges Front. Kilian was ordered to to take over Mortar Detachment 150 and in September 1915 combined it with one heavy and two light *Abteilungen* to form Mortar Company 312 of 12.Landwehr-Division. Also attached was a horse-drawn *Abteilung* and the column of mules which had been with Mortar Detachment 151 for portage of the munitions. In the autumn several bombs exploded in the barrels of medium mortars as the result of defective ammuntion.

After an intense artillery bombardment, on 21 December 1915 the French recaptured the peak of the Hartmannsweiler Kopf but lost it the following day to counter-attacks by Landwehr-Brigade 82 and three infantry batallions – except

for the Hirzstein, where the French held out until ejected by Infantry Regiment 189 on 8 January 1916. There was repeated heavy fighting up to the summer of 1917, but this brought no permanent change in the situation. The trench systems were fortified so that the French occupied the western slopes of Hartmannsweiler Kopf and the Germans the eastern slopes.

The firepower of mortars for defence as well as attack was looked at very closely. Transport and assembly at the firing point naturally involved toil by the supply of ammunition was amongst the worst problems. Therefore Part 7 of the regulations for trench warfare *Vorschriften für den Stellungskrieg* of 15 November 1916 stipulated: "The supply of ammunition is the most difficult problem for mortar activity. The difficulty is that munitions often have to be brought forward long distances while under enemy fire. Mortars are not to open fire(…) until the full requirement of munitions for a specified task has been assembled forward." Hartmannsweiler Kopf, 700 metres above the Rhine plain, caused indescribable problems. Firing the mortar in the steep mountainside, often in high winds, was a further complication.

The trajectory of the bombs was very steep in order to destroy from above targets hidden from horizontal sight. The sharp curve in the flight path so as to fit the character of the target was brought about by numerous partial propellants. Characteristic of all mortars was the low altitude required, which made deployment possible in immediate proximity to the enemy.

It was almost impossible for the French artillery – whether cannons or mortars – to engage the mortar emplacements on the steep eastern and north-eastern slopes of the Hartmannsweiler Kopf. Kilian reported on this in connection with the fighting on the Untere Rehfelsen at the end of December 1915:

"…Their 22-cm batteries fired at our mortar positions in the porphyritic rock daily. The salvoes hit the ridge breaking off great blocks of rock which then fell into the abyss. Some heavy shells exploded very close to our position. I was distant artillery spotter and could see where they were hitting: it was enough to frighten the life out of you. After every artillery barrage our mortar emplacements had to be dug out of countless porphyritic lumps of rock, but our positions proved so first-rate that the enemy never succeeded in destroying our hated mortars with a direct hit. We also had no casualties: the men waited in rock galleries until the artillery barrage was over and then immediately afterwards fired off a few rounds in order to show the Frenchies what a waste of time their efforts had been."

French 155 mm cannon model 1877 "de Bange" in the Vosges. Cannon like these with a flat trajectory had little prospect of success against the German mortar positions on the Hartmannsweiler Kopf.

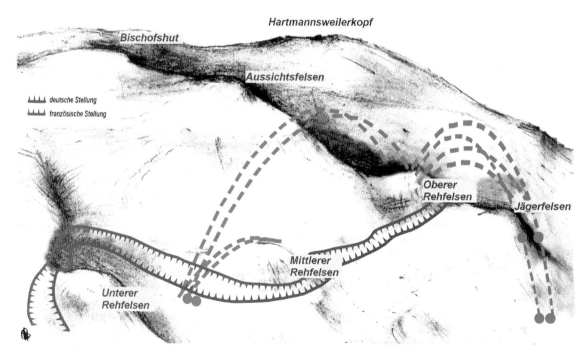

Sketch of the engagement of mortars on the south and north-east slope during the fighting on 22 December 1915.

In the Vosges the mortars developed into close combat artillery competent to operate in mountainous terrain. In 1917 there was still fierce fighting on the Hartmannsweiler Kopf: it gradually died down as the year went on.

By 1918 it was considered a quiet sector of the Front. On 15 November after the Armistice the last German troops left the formerly bitterly contested mountain.

Archaeological find on the Hartmannsweiler Kopf , the upper part of a mortar turntable bedding. Photograph taken in June 2011.

Notes:

1. Only one prototype was built.
2. During the war range extended to 1312 metres and 1160 metres respectively.
3. With the half-heavy explosive bomb 840 metres, with the quarter-heavy explosive bomb 1300 metres.
4. With the chassis tail introduced towards the end of the war, 215 kg.
5. The half-heavy explosive bomb weighed 60 kg (weight of HE, 20–25 kg).
6. Other bombs weighing 100, 200 and 300 kg were also tested.
7. Fort Flèron was made of unreinforced concrete instead of masonry. Its surface area was the shape of an isosceles triangle 300 metres at the base with sides 235 metres long. Around the perimeter was a ditch 6 metres deep and 8 metres wide exposed to covering fire from guns in casemates and heavy artillery in four armoured rotating turrets grouped around a central massif. Inside the ditch were the ramparts. The fort company was 387 men. It would appear from the literature that the Belgian defenders refused to parley with German artillery officers at midday on 13 August, and Thorsten's mortars were involved after the German offer was rejected. The fort surrendered at 0945 hr on the morning of 14 August because the shell hoists had been destroyed and the massif was full of suffocating smoke.
8. Not including smooth-bore, compressed air and explosive-charge mortars.
9. The word used in the German text is *Abteilung*, a common German artillery term used for convenience to mean any unit grouping of guns, mortars or batteries with no indication of its actual size.
10. Four companies=one battalion; three battalions=one regiment.
11. The Vosges mountain range in the province of Alsace-Lorraine was a province of the German Reich during the First World War since the Franco-Prussian War.
12. Lt Kilian was dug in well forward as spotter on the slope facing the mountain peak, the mortar was hidden behind the Aussichtsfelsen ridge. The range was a maximum of 300 metres.

Chapter Eight

FLAMETHROWERS IN PLACE OF FIRE-EXTINGUISHERS

Mass Killing with a Civilian Background

Very rarely has the ambivalence of usefulness and destructiveness in human creative activity been shown more clearly than in the development of the flamethrower: fire brigade equipment become the inspiration for a fearsome close combat weapon.

The idea of spraying streams of flame to achieve a military effect was not new. During the Peloponnese War in 424 B.C., flamethrowers were used during the siege of the town of Deleon. Also fire-sprays – portable machines to spray water on burning objects to extinguish fire – existed long before. Development did not stop there however. In 1864 two Frenchmen, C.Charlier and the engineer A.Vigon, invented a gas-based spray. It consisted of a barrel containing sodium-enriched water which was converted to carbonic acid by the addition of chemicals. This created a sufficiently high pressure to expel a powerful stream of water to dowse fire. In 1893 the Glasgow firm of Dick & Co. improved this "extinguisher" apparatus. On 27 July 1876, Herr C.Bach took out a patent in Saxony for a steam-driven extinguisher. In 1880 a certain Herr Raydt of Hanover patented a simplified gas-based extinguisher which directed liquid carbonic acid at 0ºC and 36 atm. of pressure into the container of extinguisher water. This was to become the principle behind the flamethrower 35 years later. The only difference was that the latter container was filled with a flammable liquid.

The German Developments

The development of the flamethrower is associated with two names: the Berlin engineer R.Fiedler, a former pioneer corps man, and the chief of the Leipzig Fire Brigade, Fire-Director Dr.B.Reddemann. Fiedler had gone to the Berlin-Weissensee carnival to display the so-called "Burning Lake". He poured an inflammable liquid on the waters, lit it and fascinated the public with the floating flames. In 1901 Fiedler offered the discovery for military evaluation to the Royal Prussian Engineering Committee for Pioneers and Fortifications who agreed to look in to the idea. Over the ensuing years until 1908, work was done on flamethrower design and testing. The first were specially built hand sprays which syphoned up and sprayed a lightly inflammable liquid from iron containers. By 1908 there were already two other kinds of apparatus. One was smaller, carried on the back like a field pack and intended to be used against shooting embrasures during attacks on fortresses. The other apparatus was larger and resembled a barrel on a special cart.

It was intended to be used in the defence of fortifications. In a fort at Küstrin in 1909 a major exercise using flamethrowers under simulated conditions was held, the new weapon making a great impression.

As a result of these successes, several pioneer batallions were formed, and in 1912 small flamethrowers were delivered to the pioneer siege trains where – as with the mortars – they could be called upon if necessary.

Initially, Reddemann had no knowledge of Fiedler's work. In 1907 as a reserve officer and commander of a Landwehr-pioneer company, he was directed to attend a major fortress

Assault troop attacking using the small flamethrower "KleiF".

Mobile steam fire extinguished consisting of steam boiler and pump on a wheeled trailer. This was the idea of C.Bach patented in Saxony on 27 July 1876.

warfare exercise at Posen. He reported later that he had been given the order to think up a new weapon to defend Fort Glowno to the north-east of the city. He recalled the idea of "Greek Fire" which the Byzantines had used successfully to defend their city in the 7th century. Supported by the Posen fire brigade, he used a fire extinguisher filled with benzine and petroleum which self-ignited in air. After this success a fire brigade platoon was transferred to the fort where it set up a steam-powered spraying machine using wall pipes to project a stream of fire with water. That concluded the display.

Reserve officer Reddemann was later called up for the Front and remembered at the end of 1914, once the mobile Front had become frozen in trench warfare, how it was thought that streams of flame ought to be a viable weapon against enemy troops in trenches such a short distance away. Renewed attempts were made with fire spraying equipment and the results performed for the Royal Prussian Engineering Committee for Pioneers and Fortifications. At this time the two inventors became personally acquainted. A small number of the devices had been distributed to pioneer units in August 1914 and brought to the Western Front, but since nobody knew how they worked, they were sent back. The need for men who worked

with fire was obvious, and Reddemann formed a special unit recruited mainly from the corps of the professional brigade at Leipzig which then became known as the 48-man strong "Flammenwerfer-Abteilung *Reddemann*". His firefighters were given the opportunity to familiarise themselves with the Fiedler flamethrower. Reddemann doubted at first that the 100-litre supply of flammable oil for the large flamethrower developed for the defence of fortifications would be sufficient for the intended tactical purpose.

At the beginning of 1915 his 48-man squad, very mobile with ten automobiles and thirty single-axis trailers for weapons and equipment, arrived at the Western Front. The equipment was no longer small and portable but consisted of fifteen large flamethrowers operated by specially designed hand-pumps which could spray burning liquid up to 35 metres. In Malancourt Wood north of Verdun, twelve of these, including two gas-pressure sprays, were located fifteen to thirty metres from the French lines in "Sappen" trenches burrowed forward ahead of the most advanced German positions. The squad went into action for the first time on 26 February 1915. One minute before the infantry attack the flamethrower teams began to "comb" a 50-metre broad section of enemy tranch, subjecting it to a thorough dowsing

The large flamethrower "GroF" mobile on a GroF cart.

with flaming oil. Reddemann himself described it later:

> *"The fiery serpents, rising from the ground, roaring and hissing to the enemy trenches, had not only a great success against the enemy physically, but also on his morale. From them furthermore there rose thickly balled, coal-black clouds of smoke which heightened considerably the fear of this weapon even amongst the enemy in his rearmost positions. Yes, even left and right of the 700-metre long stretch of Front attacked, the impression was so great that the enemy abandoned the trenches and ran."*

The lesson to be drawn from this first operation was of a technical and tactical nature. Flamethrowers were a success after just thirty seconds of sprayed fire. That meant that in place of the archaic hand-pumped sprays, modern gas pressure sprays copied from fire brigade equipment could be used which, with the use of nitrogen, would eject flaming oil up to 45 metres. A 45-second long spray was now considered sufficient. Of great value was the introduction of self-closing valves to regulate the period of a spray. Moreover, the importance of small portable apparatus was recognised for follow-up effect after deploying the large, fixed-position flamethrower. It was therefore necessary to develop further the small flamethrowers currently available and adapt them to conditions at the Front.

The Development of German Flamethrower Squads

After the first successes, in March 1915 Reddemann receive the order to form immediately a flamethrower batallion whose officers would be drawn preferably from amongst the ranks of professional firemen. Two months later Staff III./Garde-Pioneer Batallion made up of three Companies (9–12) appeared in the field. Once again great value had been placed on mobility, and instead of the automobiles every company now had 4-tonne "subsidy" lorries (see Chapter 9), Flamethrowers proved their worth as close-combat weapons in their first operations, and also proved how – once tactical skill had been achieved – they could be used successfully against especially resistant targets. These included flanking installations, concrete bunkers with MGs, blockhouses, bases etc. The requests for flamethrower deployment was correspondingly so high that the currently existing flamethrower companies were insufficient. Therefore in Octtober 1915, 13. and 14., and in December 1915, 15. and 16.Companies were formed, followed in February 1916 by Staff IV./Garde-Pioneer Batallion with two more companies. In April 1916 the flamethrower pioneer units were reorganised. The Staff/Garde-Reserve-Pioneer Regiment was given an experimental section, recruit depot, workshop section and three batallions each of four companies (1–12). The workshop later became a flamethrower factory at Regimental Staff in France which handled repairs to damaged equipment as well as final assembly and improvements.

Each flamethrower pioneer company was mobile with lorries and had from thirty to forty small, and twelve to fifteen large, flamethrowers. The total strength of the corps rose in sixteen months from 48 to over 3,000 men. They were directly subordinated to Supreme Army Command for use at priority points. When assault detachments, later assault batallions, were formed in the armies, each was given a flamethrower platoon with personnel and equipment from the Garde-Reserve-Pioneer Regiment.

The first major flamethrower actions in which the new tactic was tried took place during the attack on Verdun in February 1916. Eight flamethrower pioneer companies with 400 small flamethrowers (about half the stock from December 1915) were assembled and distributed amongst twelve and a half assault divisions of 5.Army. They were particularly

important at the beginning of March when many small attacks were made in the attempt to approach the goal of Verdun.

Flamethrower Tactics

The first attack in February 1915 was a so-called "standing attack" (see illustration). The arrival of small flamethrowers at the Front allowed the "leaping attack" or a combination of both. Attacks were made from underground in which the assault squad used a tunnel to reach the centre of the enemy positions to suddenly rise up from the ground and hose the trenches with fire. There were also assault-squad and pincer tactics in which squads with twelve small flamethrowers would work closely with hand-grenade and infantry groups. Flamethrowers also played an important defensive role, as for example against tanks.

The basic principle of the flamethrower was to spray through a tube from a container a light flammable oil using gas pressure. An igniter lit up when a tap on the steel tube was opened and set the oil afire as it passed the muzzle. Originally carbonic acid was used for the

Demonstration of a "standing attack" with a battery of seveal large flamethrowers.

Demonstration of the Small Flamethrower to accustom its users to the peculiarities of the new weapon.

gas pressure, but when the man carrying the equipment ran with it a foam developed which acted disadvantageously on the fire stream. Experiments with oxygen led to an explosion due to oxyhydrogen gas developing. Finally recourse was had to nitrogen which proved satisfactory.

The Garde-Reserve-Pioneer Regiment used three models during the First World War:

1. Medium Flamethrower, originally known as the Small Flamethrower with the official designation "KleiF" (Kleine Flammenwerfer). It was available from the outbreak of war as such until 1917 when the "Wex" came into service,. The characteristic of the apparatus was the bottle containing six litres of gas welded above the cylindrical oil containers. These held sixteen litres of oil, sufficient for about 23 jets of flame.
2. Large Flamethrower, officially designated "GroF" (Grosser Flammenwerfer). The stationary large flamethrower containers stood ready in the siege parks at the outbreak of war for use if needed in defence of

fortifications. At that time hand-pressure pumps were favoured for spraying the oil. There were also models with nitrogen flasks; Flammenwerfer-Abteilung *Reddemann* used at least two of the twelve large flamethrowers in this way during the first operation in February 1915. The oil containers of the "GroF" series held 100 litres. The usual nitrogen gas bottles were used in conjunction with the oil containers giving a total weight of 135 kgs ready for use thus requiring a specially constructed GroF-cart for transport.

The tongue of fire of the "GroF" was significantly more powerful, it was possible to fire one jet per second or a jet of long duration lasting up to forty seconds. The range was between thirty and forty metres: used together positioned fifty to sixty metres apart several ("Double-GroF" or "Numerous GroF") could build up entire fire-fronts. It was also possible using longer tubing so that the battery commander could direct fire at the enemy position while thirty metres distant from the battery.

Pioneer troops
of the Garde-
Reserve-Pioneer
Regiment with the
small flamethrower
"KleiF", redesignated
as the medium
flamethrower after
the introduction of
the "Wex" apparatus.
Notice the Death's
Head badge on the
lower left sleeve
authorised on 27 July
1916.

Sketch of a Totenkopf (Death's Head) pioneer with the
changeover apparatus (Wcchselapparat) hence the official
designation "Wex" introduced in 1917 as the new small
flamethrower.

Training with
the medium
flamethrower
"KleiF" originally
introduced as the
small flamethrower.
Clearly seen are the
cylindrical 16-litre oil
containers with the
rounded container on
top for three litres of
nitrogen.

3. Small Flamethrower, official designation "Wex".

When the "Wex" was introduced in 1917, the small flamethrower "KleiF" was rescheduled as a medium flamethrower but kept the abbreviation. "Wex" was a contraction of "Wechselapparat" (changeover apparatus). The change was brought about by the "KleiF" having three oil containers and three pressure bottles all connected up to only one firing line which meant that during an action each empty container or bottle had to be exchanged. Since this process was too unsatisfactory, the idea behind the Wex was a single combination with its own firing line.

The Wex consisted of a carrying frame to which the oil container shaped like a ship's lifebelt containing eleven litres of oil was attached. A bottle with three litres of gas was screwed into the centre of the ring. When full the Wex weighed 21.5 kgs and could be carried comfortably by one man wearing it in the manner of a backpack. To fire the apparatus the tap on the tube was opened to light the igniter, the gas forced the oil to the igniter to light the stream into flame. Range was about 25 metres; the equipment could deliver about 18 fiery jets or a pulse of fire lasting 20 seconds.

The commonest operational use of both Wex and KleiF was using short bursts. In 1917 consideration was given to arming armoured fighting vehicles with flamethrowers. As a result the "Überland- (Sturm-) Panzerwagen Bremer" (the non-armoured version of the A7V tank) was conceived with 2-cm machine-cannons, 4 MGs and a flamethrower.

The Flammable Oil

Flamethrowers operated with a compromise of light fuel with high volatility but heavy enough to carry the farthest distance possible. The mixture was one of tar products with added light and heavy hydrocarbons, tar oil and carbon disulphide. German flamethrower pioneers used four kinds of flammable oil:

1. Blue oil – the most commonly used at the Front. This was a thick liquid which burned brightly giving off heavy smoke and fumes said to have a demoralizing effect on the enemy. In low temperatures the liquid thickened which was not desirable and it was therefore replaced by:
2. Yellow oil. A thick liquid which developed little smoke and had a fire stream which was very hot and burned quickly. Blue and yellow oil mixed together produced:

German Flamethrower Attacks

Year	1914	1915	1916	1917	1918	Total
Total of Attacks by year	0	32	160	165	296	653

Comparison of Technical/tactical Details of German Flamethrowers (as at 1918)

Designation	KleiF	GroF	Wex
Year of introduction	1914	1914[1]	1917
Team	1–2 men	2 men	1–2 men
Weight (ready to fire)	30 kgs	135 kgs	21.5 kgs
Flammable oil content	16 litres	100 litres	11 litres
Gas content	6 litres	not known	3 litres
Working pressure (atüs)	23	15	23
Number of jets of flame (max.)	23	30	18
Time longest single jet of flame	25 secs	40 secs	20 secs
Weight empty	14 kgs	35 kgs	10.5 kgs
Range	22 metres[2]	35–40 metres	25 metres

3. Green oil which developed only moderate smoke.
4. Red oil was used only for training purposes, never at the front.

During the war the flamethrower-pioneers mounted 653 attacks of which 525 (82%) went off successfully. On 28 July 1916 memebers of the Garde-Reserve-Pioneer Regiment were authorized to wear the *Totenkopf* (Death's Head) badge on the lower left sleeve. During the war the flamethrower proved to be a very effective close-range weapon and was eventually to be found in the arsenal of all armies.

Allied Developments

Germany's enemies had quickly become aware of the new close-combat weapon and had begun the development of their own designs, many makeshift. The first use of a flamethrower by the British was on the Somme and came from engineer Livens' idea of cotton waste, oil and an explosive charge in a metal container fired from an earth mortar. During the war the British had two heavy apparatus and a portable flamethrower of 28 kgs.

Initially the French used makeshift devices of various designs. Two light and one heavy flamethrower were accepted into service. Italy (two-man DLF) turned to the French; the United States produced its own light flamethrower. The Allies added phosphorus to the oil they used.

France produced three designs each requiring a two-man team: No.1 bis (operational weight 23 kgs, working pressure 50 atm, range 18–30 metres), No.1–3 bis (operational weight 30 kgs, no further details known) and No.1 (operational weight 125 kgs, pressure 140 atm, range 30 metres.)

Great Britain also produced three designs, the Vincent was operated by a two-man team, the information is not available for the other two. Lorenz (operational weight 28 kgs, pressure 15 atm, range 30–35 metres), Vincent (operational weight 1500 kgs, pressure 15–81 atm, range 60–80 metres) and the Fortress-Livens (operational weight 3700 kgs, pressure 24 atm, range 200 metres).

Men of Pioneer Company 285 showing off a French flamethrower captured in the Argonnes, photograph taken in September 1916.

The Flamethrower Attack in the Caillette Woods near Verdun, 1 June 1916.

This attack by 10.Flamethrower Comp./Garde-Reserve-Pioneer Regt. on 1 June 1916 in the Caillette Woods was described in a field-post letter by the Company Commander, 1st Lt. Theune:

"…The enemy had undoubtedly recognized that we were planning a big attack. His artillery bombarded the few assembly areas still available to the German infantry, the narrow attack strip of 6.Inf.Div. about 1 kilometre broad with all the abundance of its heavy ammunition.(…) During the night I had visited the batallion staffs in the most forward lines and once again held forth to the assembled infantry company commanders on how the attack would proceed. The hurricane of shells howling overhead depressed our mood, however. How would the reserves get through an artillery barrage of that kind? What had become of my company?(…) It was 0700 hrs and nobody had arrived for an attack scheduled to start at 0930 hrs. Finally at 0730 hrs some of the people from my company turned up with a section of the infantry who would be accompanying us. I did not recognize my own people! A corporal, one of the best, reported to me, "They are all dead!" There was a terrible look in his eyes. They called it "panic"!

Now we had to act! I felt the full responsibility on my shoulders for this attack. There was only one thing for it, to have a look for myself and gather up the men individually!

Possessed by doubts whether the attack was possible or not, I returned with haste to the graveyard. I was deaf to the enemy artillery, blind to the dead and wounded, I had only one thought – "the Company". I found it! In the dreadful gulley behind Casemate Gorge (Kasemattenschlucht), in the graveyard, my people were mixed in with sections of the infantry. Five large flamethrowers had been destroyed, the black oil was flowing over corpses and the wounded, some nitrogen bottles had been hit by shell splinters and exploded. All the same, the report which the corporal had made to me was exaggerated. All was not yet lost. But all lacked the Will, the energy, to advance!(…)

I decided not to spread the five remaining large flamethrowers across the divisional sector but concentrate them on the left sector of Regt.66.

The position there offered good prospects. The undamaged concrete bunkers of the enemy infantry which would be very difficult for our infantry assault could be favourable targets for the small flamethrowers.

The five large flamethrowers were set up 50 to 60 metres apart in the foremost tline of Inf. Regt.66 sector, and I distributed the twelve small flamethrowers between them building a flamethrower front of 450 metres breadth. Now I had my people in the palm of my hand again.

The infantry companies who would be making the assault alongside us had arrived forward under the energetic urging of their officers and had assembled closely bunched on the southern slope of Casemate Gorge. They had also suffered heavy losses. Their losses were so high that they had had to call up reserves.(…).

Then something incredible happened! Our own heavy calibre guns fired too short into the crowded mass of troops in the narrow assembly area! As every heavy shell landed the troops there cried out like crazy: they were no longer soldiers, but just people in wild despair. Then came the shout, "Gas masks on!" The gas from our own artillery's gas shells had also fallen too short.

The reason for this regrettable occurrence with our artillery was the worn-down gun barrels. They had been in ceaseless action for several months and the scatter of fire enormously exceeded the acceptable dispersal. My own company escaped this catastrophe in Casemate Gorge because I had set them up beforehand in the foremost trenches. As was so often the case, the most advanced trenches were the safest retreat. The time for our attack was fast approaching but the first wave of infantry, which was to form up behind the flamethrowers, had not yet put in an appearance. I went to my people and impressed upon them that the attack must begin at 0930 hrs with or without the infantry. I was sure of my people!

How was the enemy faring? Our artillery had driven them forward out of the Vaux Gorge and they were clinging to its northern slope. They had also found protection to some extent in their own forward trench line, and here they were grouped together with no intention other than to do nothing.

Our artillery now began to fire full out. The barrage reached its maximum, would it ebb away as had happened so often in the past and expire unused?

The time had come! 0930 hrs struck!

"Close-combat will bring the decision!" A short word which we did not know in this sense. A basic principle for the future.

The cataclysm of fire broke over the Frenchmen, a roaring sea of flame rolled towards them as they waited thickly grouped together in the foremost trenches. The enemy saw flaming, licking tongues of flame coming for them from within gigantic billows of black smoke, they saw no troops nor weapons, only what seemed an event of Nature of

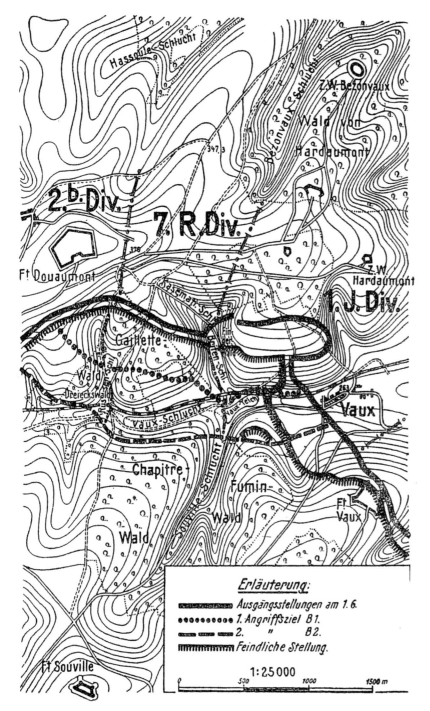

Map showing the flamethrower attack by 10.Flamethrower Comp./Garde-Reserve-Pioneer Regt, 1. June 1916 in the Caillette Wood near Verdun.
Key: Black line = Departure points on 1 June; Dotted line = 1st attack target B1; Pecked line = 2nd attack target B2; Combed line = enemy trenches.

enormous dimensions, too much for the nerves to withstand!

At first the French stood grouped close together, hands raised, in the foremost trenches. No shot was fired and then they flocked together and ran for it as the small flamethrowers advanced with the shock troops.

Surprise reigned within our ranks! An excited expectation lit up all faces! Something unknown, totally new, was in the air! Every man had the impression that something huge, uncommon, had occurred.

At a stroke the mood in our lines was transformed. Our troops had seen the flames roar over to the enemy, saw the flames engulf him without his being able to fire a round in reply. The fearsome rage of this new weapon was a unique experience, it swept the hearts behind the hissing flames forwards, ahead, away from the torment of hell which was Casemate Gorge.

The fiery flames from the five large and twelve small flamethrowers was the signal for the 66th to attack. With the help of the small flamethrowers and the dashing shock troops of Sturmbatallion Rohr[3] who formed the first decisive wave of attackers we had complete success.

Behind our artillery barrage our objectives were attained without great losses, we advanced as far as Chapitre Wood. The stubbornly defended concrete bunkers of the French infantry, undamaged by the hellish artillery fire from our largest calibres, were quickly taken as our small flamethrowers smoked out the occupants. A short burst of flame broke all resistance. Private Brodersen of my company distinguished himself particularly in this respect.

66 officers and 1851 men were delivered to the assembly point for prisoners, amongst them a regimental commander. We also captured 3 artillery pieces and 33 MGs."

Notes:

1. The first GroF were still fitted with hand pumps.
2. Two KleiF coupled up could reach 35–40 metres.
3. A Sturmbatallion (assault batallion) was a unit formed during the First World War and divided up into shock troops for especially difficult attacks. In peacetime they were military instructors. The organisation of such a batallion was: Staff, two assault companies, one MG company, one mortar company, one infantry-gun battery and a flamethrower platoon.

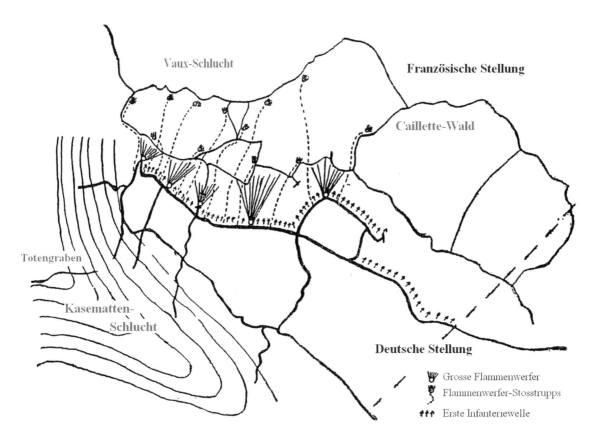

The cooperation between the "standing attack" by the large flamethrowers and the "leaping attack" with small flamethrowers during the fighting on 1 June 1916 is an example of the German combined-assault tactic.

Key: Grosse Flammenwerfer = large flamethrowers; Flammenwerfer-Stosstrupps = assault troops carrying flamethrowers; Erste Infanteriewelle = first wave of infantry. Schlucht = gorge, ravine etc, Wald = wood, Totengraben = graves/cemetery, Kasematte = casemate; Stellung = position, lines.

Two man team with Wex flamethrower during the General Strike in Berlin, photograph taken at the beginning of March 1919.

Chapter Nine

MOTOR VEHICLES IN FIELD-GREY

(From Gee-up! to Motorized)

Carl Benz and Gottlieb Daimler would certainly have had no military objective in mind when they created what would become the automobile. On the other hand, the development of the automobile began in antiquity with the invention of the wheel and the use of the animal-drawn cart. From there it was only a small step to the chariot of the Assyrians. In the centuries which followed, the numerous ideas of inventors and scientists, ingenious tinkerers and puzzle solvers contributed finally to the triumphal procession of self-propelled vehicles – including those of the military.

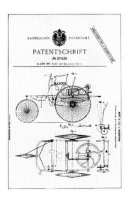

Patent No. 37435 for a wheeled vehicle with gas-motor propulsion was granted by the Kaiser's Patents Office on 2 November 1886.

Over fifty inventions contributed to the construction in 1885 of the first three-wheel motor vehicle by the German engineer Carl Benz, in respect of which he applied to the Patents Office for a patent on 29 February 1886.

The investigation of new technological achievements has been a component of military thinking since time immemorial. The massed use of motor vehicles was more complicated than usual for it required clear concepts of usage and deployment, corresponding industrial efficiency and far-seeing personalities in a position to recognize the connections. This was something at first lacking in the area of Army motorisation in the German Kaiserreich.

On the Road to Unified Military Vehicles

Research into the military use of methods of communication led to the setting up of the "Inspectorate of Communications Troops" on 25 March 1899. Under its roof the telegraphy-, railway- and airship troops found their point of convergence, and also the experimental sections of transport troops. In the course of experiments with steam-driven lorries, owner-driver goods trains and heavy Army road trains, the petrol-engine lorry – considered initially as a fragile toy prone to breakdowns – won acceptance. The German Army administration, in collaboration with industry,

began research work in 1898. Barely ten years of intensive trials later, viable and reliable military transports and tractors had been developed which were not bound to railway lines. Moreover they were faster and endowed with greater endurance than the countless and endless horse-drawn columns of transports required to bring up supplies – the best conditions for the comprehensive supply for an Army of millions such as that being built up at the beginning of the 20th century. Nevertheless the military use of lorries still caused the Army administration a host of problems, not least of which was that a motor vehicle had different requirements to make it go than a horse.

Additionally the great need of the Army for supply lorries in the event of war could not be met by purchases, for the firms did not have the capacity, and the setting up of large depots in peacetime lay beyond the bounds of the military budget.

The Enormous Variety as an Obstruction

In the period between 1896 and 1918 within the borders of the Reich, 103 firms and establishments (in 1909 there were 54) were known to be involved in the development and production of lorries and special vehicles. The multifarious types and lack of standardisation militated against military use.

Men of a signals
unit unloading
equipment. Staff-
signals *Abteilungen*
with the newly
formed telephone
twin-platoons were
partly motorized.

It was seen that the explosive further development of automobile technology would soon render obsolete the vehicles purchased by the Army administration. Accordingly another solution was found: in the case of mobilization, the Army administration could sequester any vehicle whether from business, trade and industry of privately owned by virtue of an emergency powers act[1] (on the statute books since 1873 and continually amended in the decades following**.**) Such an aggregation of vehicles would differ as between themselves in construction, dimensions and performance but have one thing in common, namely wheels.

The next step was to define the technical and tactical specifications for lorries able to fulfill military transport tasks. The new generation of vehicles of 1908 were known as "Subsidy Lorries" (the State subsidised their production and maintenance and would requisition them in the event of war); with trailers known as "Subsidy Road Trains". The technical parameters were modified again in 1913. For a Subsidy Army Road Train certain parts were standardized such as the chain drive, brake drums, journal shafts, compressor valves, trailer couplings and the starter motor. The prototype was supplied by the firm of "H.Büssing, Special Factory for Motor Lorries, Motor Omnibuses and Motors" at Braunschweig. An additional Subsidy Lorry introduced immediately before the outbreak of the First World War was the three-tonne "Fast Lorry" which could make 30 kms/hr maximum (then considered very fast) and placed in the lorry columns of the eleven cavalry divisions to become known as "cavalry lorries".

Vehicle Classifications

1. Passenger cars. These were six- or seven-seaters of typical commercial structure built as limousines, landaus and Mercedes Doppelphaeton. They were used at the higher command levels and by the commanding officers of railway-, telegraph-, radio-telegraph and vehicle formations. With a 40-hp engine they had a top speed of 60–70 kms/hr and it was expected of them that they should be capable of travelling at least 300 kilometres per day.

2. Small cars. Under this heading came four-wheeled automobiles with up to four seats, a 6 to 15-hp engine and a speed of 50 kms/hr. Their use was foreseen for transmitting orders and signals.

3. Omnibuses. Had seating for between 15 and 40 persons and speeds of between 18 and 27 kms/hr. They were seen primarily as transport for the larger military Staffs (Staff buses).

4. Heavy lorries. Their carrying capacity lay between 3 and 5 tonnes. They could make 20 kms/hr with a 40-hp engine and were planned to operate in the lorry and lorried ammunition columns.

5. Road trains (Army road trains). These were made up of lorry and trailer and could take a load of between six and ten tonnes. With a 40-hp engine their speed was 16 kms/hr. Their primary purpose was the transport of supplies.

6. Heavy road trains. Vehicles with petrol-electric drive and five trailers could transport 30 tonnes. They were still under development at the outbreak of war.

7. Motor-cycles. Used in Staff service, first seen in the Kaiser manoeuvres at Mecklenburg in 1904. In 1912 military trial runs held with improved motor-cycles concluded satisfactorily, NSU and also Wanderer developed an "Army model" for despatch riders.

8. Three-wheelers. From the military point of view these lacked interest being too small, light, prone to breakdown and had poor carrying capacity.

The three-tonner Horch 25/40 corresponded to the subsidy lorry specifications and were manufactured during the war at Zwickau.

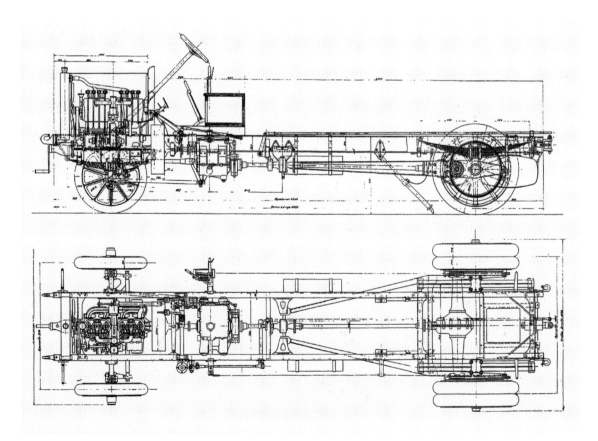

1912 technical drawing of a Daimler subsidy lorry for the Experimental Division of Communication Troops.

When the First
World War broke
out in 1914, private
cars had reached a
high technical stage
even without Army
support, but now
the development
came to an abrupt
halt, available motor
cars being converted
to military use and
frequently later
mothballed.

A closed ambulance
with single-axled
trailer leaving the
field hospital at
Juniville south of
Rethel. Seriously
wounded or epidemic
victims were usually
transported in these
light vehicles. Of
similar design were
open ambulances,
field-pharmacy
vehicles and field-
ambulance trains.

Subsidy Lorries and Other Military Driver-Owners at War

At the outbreak of war on 1 August 1914 the German Army and Navy had over 500 motor cars at their disposal. The number of subsidy lorries was well under the aim of 800 by the end of 1914 – only about 500 had been passed as fit for war use. The need for motor vehicles on mobilisation was covered by the emergency powers act enabling the Army to fall back on 7,085 motor cars, 20,235 motor cycles and about 10,000 lorries. Of the lorries including subsidy lorries (stock as at 1 January 1913), the Army administration classified only 3,500 three- and four-tonners as usable. However, in order to fill the vehicle parks of the Great HQ, the 95 vehicle and ammunition vehicle columns and 17 vehicle depots, the Army administration needed a total of at least 5,000 vehicles including motor cars. Besides these, the airship-, aviation-, railway-, medical and other special troops required vehicles and a large shortfall of vehicles could be envisaged. Although the members of the "German

Type of Vehicle: Carrying capacity:	Lorry 4,000 kgs	Lorry 3,000 kgs
1. Provisions		
Bread	4480 portions[2]	2670 portions
Thin bacon	20,000 portions	10,000 portions
Dried vegetables	45,833 portions	20,833 portions
2. Fodder		
Compressed hay	65 balls = 1800 rations	32 balls = 880 rations
3. Munitions		
3.1 Infantry Ammunition		
Bullets	112 cases = 3998.4 kgs	56 cases = 1999.2 kgs
per road train[3]	189,000 bullets	189,000 bullets
per rearward vehicle column	1,701,000 bullets	1,701,000 bullets
3.2 Field artillery Ammunition		
Field-basket for 3 x 7.7-cm shells	144 baskets = 4032 kgs	72 baskets = 2016 kgs
per road train[4]	648 7.7-cm shells	648 7.7-cm shells
per rearward vehicle column	5832 7.7-cm shells	5832 7.7-cm shells
3.3 Foot artillery Ammunition		
Baskets with 15-cm long shells	84 baskets	42 baskets
per road train[5]	126 shells/cartridge cases	126 shells/cartridge cases
per rearward vehicle column	1134 shells/cartridge cases	1134 shells/cartridge cases
4. Personnel Transports		
per road train	50–55 men[6]	50–55 men[6]
per rearward vehicle column	450–495 men[7]	450–495 men[7]

Lorries were used operationally for Army supply. This included the bringing up of munitions, provisions and equipment, the transport of war materials of all kinds, or raw materials; and the bringing back of captured material and men from the front.

Volunteer Automobile Corps" and their motor cars were attached to the higher Staffs and had volunteered for war service this did not help much.

The first weeks of the war proved the importance of transport vehicles. The requirement for subsidy lorries in particular rose constantly, and by the war's end a further 12,000 had been procured. They were used in all theatres of war. Broken down into individual manufacturers the number of lorries delivered was comparatively small. VOMAG for example

had provided only about one thousand by 1918. Opel managed 4,000 in the same time frame.

One column carried the volume of a horse-drawn transport park column or two provisions- or two infantry or artillery ammunition columns. The motorised columns moving across rearward territory behind the lines were three times quicker than the horse-drawn columns. The table on the previous page shows some loading variations of an Army road train in a nine-vehicle column crossing such territory.

An unnamed eye-witness wrote this account in the 1 October 1928 edition of the journal *Der Kraftzug in Wirtschaft und Heer* regarding the deployment of a rearward motorized vehicular column used as a troop transport during the fighting for Verdun in the spring of 1916:

"Fighting was raging at the Front. Hell spat death and injury to thousands, whipped the air, churned the earth. Our fighting troops needed reinforcements urgently.

Far to the rear the columns of lorries droned along the French roads. It was baking hot. In his box forward at the wheel it was not easy for the driver. Haste was being called for.

The Companies were already standing divided into groups at the roadside. The column leader had gone on ahead to ensure that there would be no delays in loading up.

While the infantry stowed their gear and packs as instructed, each driver checked over his vehicle, lubricated engine and chains, tightened a loose screw here and there.

Then a whistle and a command, a wave – and the convoy set off. Clouds of dust marked the way. The fine dust penetrated pores, nose, mouth and eyes, making the already-dry throat intolerably rough. But this must be disregarded. What mattered was to bring help to our comrades under pressure at the Front.

Hours went by. The windows of one village after another trembled as the columns rattled through. Men in field-grey hailed their singing comrades with shouts. Scouting ahead, the column leader searched out the best route to pass the villages by so as to avoid any waste of time.

The motorized columns bearing reserves streamed from all sides to the location where the enemy was preparing a breakthrough with an artillery barrage. If he succeeded in overwhelming the most forward lines, he would find fresh reserves behind them brought to the endangered spot in fast motorized transport.

Then the columns of vehicles returned in haste to fetch more fresh reserves. That went on in the great battle day and night, hardly allowing time for a meal. One hardly ever thought of rest."

Tractors and Other Special Vehicles

The multitude of special vehicles delivered between 1914 and 1918 is striking. They include ambulances and ambulance-trains, field-pharmacy-, post, X-ray-, bathing-, field-telegraphy and radio-, tank- and workshop vehicles, and vehicles with mounted guns. By the end of the war there were 156 of the latter.

5-tonne Büssing Type V lorries with Special Command 500 in Turkey. At the beginning of 1916 German columns of vehicles with selected personnel and equipment were fitted out and sent to the Taurus mountains. Here they undertook assignments in the vicinity of the Baghdad highway which still had gaps along stretches.

New developments artillery tugs, cross-country vehicles, street-armoured cars and the first panzers.

Also urgently required were towing machines to haul heavy guns. No vehicle of this type existed, until 1914 the artillery was exclusively horse-drawn. By way of example, the 21-cm mortar weighing 11.9 tonnes and dismantled for transport into three sections required 18 heavy Army horses to move it. Other methods were planned for guns of the heaviest calibre (28, 30.5 and 42 cms). Nothing had materialised by the outbreak of war and had to be ordered with haste. While waiting, consideration was given principally to steam-plough locomotives and similar vehicles: tugs and platform waggons were even requisitioned from the Sarrasani Circus. Steam ploughs and street locomotives proved unsatisfactory. The motorized ploughs of Daimler, Lanz and Podeus were rated more favourably while Büssing, Dürkopp, Lanz and Pöhl developed completely new lines of heavy duty tugs. Horch produced at Zwickau a rather lighter tractor ZU capable of towing an 88-mm flak gun. For the Army's heavy guns a Daimler 100-hp towing machine was found acceptable. It was being planned to move lighter field artillery by so-called "motorized limbers". Various well-known names in the vehicle manufacturing industry were involved and pursued a number of technological concepts: all-wheel drive as well as half-track and full caterpillar track tugs. For heavier artillery there were now tugs such as the von Dürkopp with 2 x 80-hp engines, and the A.7.V (non-armoured version of the assault oanzer A.7.V.) of which 75 units designated "cross-country vehicles" were delivered to the Army's full-track columns.

Large, heavy motor cars especially those of Daimler, Wanderer and Horch proved their worth and 20,000 were delivered during the war. Against a background of economic shortage, small cars of the Dixie and Wanderer types gained in significance. The value of luxurious fittings faded into the background in an era when reliability was the by-word. The vehicles received a livery of field-grey paint, halters for rifles, entrenching tools and hoes. Very bright searchlights were important and acetylene (a colourless gas smelling of ether in the pure state) proved better than electric.

As a result of excessive use, many of the heavy lorries sequestered under the emergency powers legislation were soon in poor repair, some being no longer serviceable for lack of spare parts or war damage while others

The heaviest batteries of the foot artillery had no towing machines, these had to be developed first. The choice fell on the motorized tractor Lanz ZF weighing 18 tonnes and equipped with a 120-hp petrol engine. 269 of these heavy-load tractors were built.

The cross-country waggon, or "overland waggon" or "ammunition tank" had the same chassis as the assault armoured vehicle A.7.V. It was used to transport a load of up to ten tonnes of supplies. 79 were built and used operationally in Army motorized convoys.

failed towing trailers. The original carrying capacity of a convoy laden with 54 tonnes (corresponding to an infantry division's rations for one day of operations) was therefore reduced to 30 tonnes or less. Motor-pool troops were not able to make any decisive contribution to solving the enormous problems of supply during the continued fighting, and the available vehicles remained below requirements. German industry supplied around 75,000 vehicles to the German Army of which 40,000 were still serviceable at the war's end though

In 1918 there were 156 examples of the 7.7-cm flak gun M.1914 L/27 on the "Gun waggon 14" manufactured by Krupp/Rheinmetall operational. The self-propelled chassis won increasing significance not only against aerial targets but also in anti-tank work.

The end of a convoy of German fighting vehicles in a scrapyard at Le Poré in France.

handicapped increasingly by shortages of fuel, tyres and spare parts.

The Allies on the other hand had 240,000 vehicles. Britain and France also led in the development of tractors for heavy artillery.

The Lifeline of the French Defenders at Verdun

New lorries after delivery to a depot on the Western front. They amounted to four rearward base lorry convoys. During the war the number of medium and heavy lorries delivered rose from 6,597 in 1915 to 9,272 in 1917.

For the Allies their superior motorization at Verdun proved decisive. The city with its outlying forts formed the northern corner-stone of the French Front between the borders of Luxemburg and Switzerland and jutted in a semi-circle into the German Front. On 21 February 1916 the German attack began here. The French defence would stand or fall depending on adequate supplies, and reliefs organized in rotation for the troops in the most advanced front line. Supplies had to be routed on a stretch of narrow gauge railway via Amblaincourt and along the dual carriageway from St.Dizier, Bar-le-Duc, Souilly to Nixéville. Other roads lay too close to the German Front or were insufficiently developed for substantial burden. Therefore vehicles played a vital role in the French defence of Verdun, and by June 1916 the number of vehicles in this sector had risen to 12,000. For the first time in the war an entire Army – the 2nd French – was supplied principally by motorized convoys.

In 1928, no less a personality than the later General and Inspector General of Panzer Troops, Heinz Guderian, wrote in the magazine *Der Kraftzug in Wirtschaft und Heer*:

"The driving force in the area of the French motorization during the war was apparently Major Doumenc, who set out his experiences in a book well worth reading entitled Les transports automobiles sur le front français 1914–1918. *The statistics for this article are taken largely from Doumenc's work.*

Major Doumenc guaranteed the French Command the supply each day of 2,000 tonnes of material and 12,000 men if his motor-pool men were given sole right to use the highway.(…) The military commanders met the demand of their technical adviser and did not regret it.

The highway from Bar-le-Duc to Verdun was a dual carriageway of light surfacing material. It was decided to have vehicles proceeding in both directions while horse-drawn traffic and pedestrians were diverted to parallel roads. Essential road repairs seen as likely to occur with such heavy road usage were not to be allowed to interrupt the flow of traffic. Accordingly it was decided to open a number of stone quarries and lay the limestone gravel extracted along the sections of track without further ado. Traffic sentries were posted at crossroads: with their permission a road could be crossed but never used. This single two-lane lifeline to the fortifications was a copy of the railway block system. The carriageway was kept open ruthlessly, immobile vehicles were given short shrift and pushed into roadside ditches.

Relief troop transports went by train to the three unloading stations at Barrois, Bar-le-Duc and Revigny, and from there the infantry was taken by lorry to Verdun while horse-drawn sections were directed to by-roads for the two-day haul.

Ammunition stations were set up at Bar-le-Duc and Vaudonvillers (on the St.Dizier-Revigny stretch). From here munitions were brought to Verdun by lorry. Only the provisions went all the way by train, being loaded on the narrow-gauge railway at Revigny.

The integrated vehicle traffic could only be controlled if the traffic plan of the columns coincided with the railways. At the moment

when the trains arrived, the columns had to be waiting ready at the station. That required a close cooperation of the motor-pool officers with the railway authorities. For this purpose, Bar-le-Duc was made seat of the first Commission régulatriée routière (Lorry-routing commission) set up on 1700 hrs on 19 February 1916. As is known, the German attack began at 0700 hrs on 21 February.

The locations of the ammunition parks had to be adapted to suit the course of road traffic, and those parks formerly at Heippes, Lemmes and Verdun were shifted to Nixéville and Fort de Regret.

On 19 February the Commission began its duties, and on 22 February the new regulations for traffic came into force. The size of the traffic can be seen clearly from the following data:

On average, 8,000 vehicles made transit of the dual highway daily (on 25 February 3,500 lorries, on the 13th about 9,000, in June 1916 about 12,000.) In the period from 22 February to 4 March 1916, 132 batallions, 20,700 tonnes of munitions and 1,300 tons of various materials were transported.

From March onwards the monthly movement of men varied between 400,000 and 426,000 men and 220,000 to 260,000 wounded. Furthermore in March 587,000 tonnes of material was shipped of which 140,000 tonnes was gravel and road-making ballast; in April, of 560,000 tonnes, 60,000 tonnes was gravel and ballast, and in May of 660,000 tonnes of material, 186,000 tonnes was gravel and ballast.

A French ambulance being loaded with wounded men. The best known makes of ambulance were the Peugeot 502, Renault and later Citröen.

French convoys of lorries roll endlessly on the dual carriageway from Bar-le-Duc to Verdun, others left the besieged fortifications with the wounded. Photo taken in the spring of 1916.

These huge quantities of gravel and ballast show the care which the French gave the highway: it was due to this that it withstood for long months the enormous demands made of it. In mid-June captured French officers expressed their astonishment quite openly about the pitiful condition of the roads behind the German Verdun-Front which bore no comparison with those of the French. The lack of labour and the iron tyres of our lorries were the main cause of the deterioration of the roads in our sector, but also the lack of experience in fighting a major battle on the Western Front, which had resulted in our making insufficient preparation in this respect.

Some idea can be gained of the density of vehicle traffic if one visualises that over a 24-hour period in March 1916 at any given point on the highway 6,000 lorries passed, on average one lorry every 14 seconds. The daily consumption of fuel has been estimated at 200,000 litres petrol, 20,000 litres of oil and 2,000 kgs of grease.

The nature of the traffic made extraordinary demands on drivers such that the crews might alternate at the wheel for several days without a break.

The supply to the Verdun Front during the months when the battle raged arrived almost exclusively on the single highway Baudonvillers-Bar le Duc-Verdun. Not only the material supply, but the reliefs for all the infantry and the shipping out of the wounded. The Germans must have known of this situation. Just a glance at a map was sufficient to recognise it. Moreover, we knew the way in which the reliefs were being made by various methods of reconnaissance. It would not be an exaggeration to state that the defence of Verdun stood or fell with the maintenance or not

of the lorry traffic on the voie sacrée *("the sacred road"-Guderian) or, as per Major Doumenc puts it, "C'est la route qui mène à la bataille" ("That is the road which led to the battle"-Guderian). Any disruption of this traffic would have occasioned the greatest problems for the defenders. From French sources known to the author to date, it does not appear that any interruption of the traffic worth mentioning occurred on the road. They might have been inflicted at least temporarily by long-range flat trajectory artillery fire and bomber squadrons."*

Notes

1. Kriegsleistungsgesetz.
2. 4480 portions of bread = 750 kgs leaving space for a further load.
3. By comparison, a four-horse team transported 765,000 bullets.
4. By comparison, a horse-drawn artillery munitions column transported 837 baskets with 2,511 7.7-cm shells
5. By comparison, a horse-drawn foot artillery munitions column transported 612 15-cm long shells and their cartridge cases.
6. In field-marching order, 40 men seated.
7. The strength of a company was 270 men, of a batallion 1080 men. A rearward vehicle column could transport the personnel of an infantry battalion in field-marching order 30–50 kms per day in two column-loads.

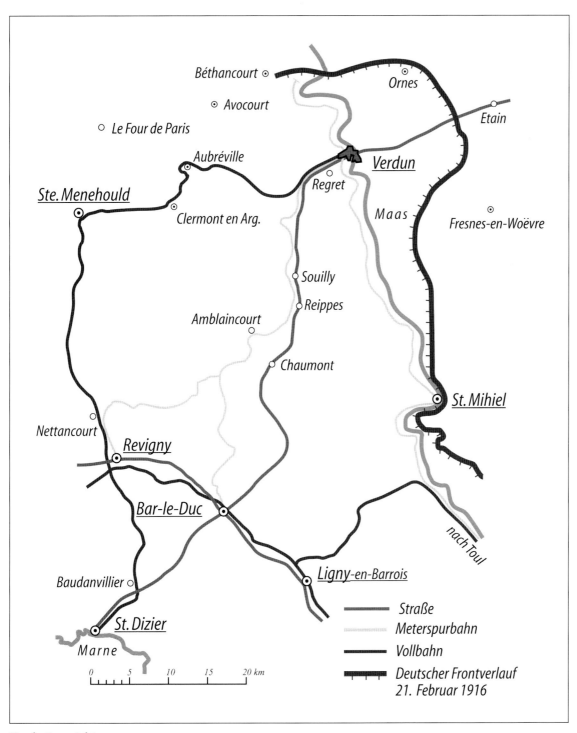

Key, bottom right:

Red line = dual carriageway

Yellow line = small gauge railway (1-metre)

Blue line = highway

Spiked blue line = German front line as at 21 February 1916

Chapter Ten

FROM THE EYE IN THE SKY TO THE FIST OF THE MILITARY LEADERSHIP

The Development of the German Aerial Forces

The development of the aircraft can be compared with that of the lorry – it is the sum of many experiences and inventions – and dreams. The dream of flying, however, is much older than that of moving in a vehicle, as we known from the sages of antiquity. The oldest known sketch of a winged aircraft was made by Leonardo da Vinci in around 1500. Four hundred years later man elevated himself into the skies.

Amongst the aerial pioneers was the German Otto Lilienthal, who in 1893 made a glider flight of 400 metres from a high point. The American O.Chanutes published a book in 1894 *Progress in Flying Machines* describing Lilienthal's experiences which in its turn inspired the inventors Orville and Wilbur Wright to build an aerial craft. After numerous glider flights, around the turn of the century they mounted an engine in a flying apparatus. The brothers enjoyed their first successful flight on 12 December 1903 at Kitty Hawk, North Carolina. From then on, development continued apace. In 1912 the number of aircraft in the world was estimated at barely 2,000 machines, of which 482 were in military service. Leading the field was France, whose armed forces alone had 260 aircraft: at the same time Germany had only 48, for in the Kaiserreich the aircraft was considered unfit for warfare. Much more promising in the military sense because of their far greater load carrying capacity were Graf Zeppelin's airships. From the turn of the century especial emphasis had been laid on the development of motorized airship travel – a false road, as would be proved when war came: according to Jane's, at the end of 1910 the German Army had nine airships and five aircraft; France three airships but 36 aircraft while the British had twice as many aircraft as airships. In October 1913 the German Army had four, then five for the communications troops of the airship batallions.

No great attention was given to the most junior of the German aerial forces, the flying corps. Its exhibitions on the Döberitz exercise grounds in 1911/1912 changed nothing, nor did the so-called "Prinz Heinrich flights". All the same, the Army General Staff was motivated by the reconnaissance results of airships and aircraft at the Kaiser manouevres, and the repeated reports of the progress of military flying in France, to request more support for aviation from the War Ministry. Not until the Army estimates of 1913 did the flying corps had a definite framwork for its further development.

Tactical and Strategic Considerations

In mobile warfare, aircraft had their place in operational reconnaissance: their crews were to report on troop movements below. It was an early experience of the war that they could also render excellent service in artillery spotting and tactical reconnaissance.

In Germany, military aviation belonged within the ambit of the Inspector-General of Military Traffic – not a happy solution and one which speaks for how their value was underestimated. France was not only far ahead of Germany in technology but also in organisation. Cooperation between artillery and observer aircraft was already part of French Army planning shortly before the outbreak of

C-aircraft with camera for aerial photographs and air-cooled MG 08/15 on swivel ring. Photograph taken in 1915.

war. The French were also not far from seeing the aircraft as a "weapon of destruction". Here, however, the operating range of aircraft had set limits (which in turn made the German enthusiasm for airships seem reasonable, since they could venture 400 and more kilometres from base) and neither could those fragile flying machines carry reconnaissance and signals equipment, bombs or weapons.

Typical of the time were the "unified aircraft" such as the Rumpler Taube able to carry a load of 200 kgs and had an operational ceiling of 800 metres. This type of aircraft soon proved unsuitable for military use and was separated out.

The apparently limited tactical and technological possibilities of aircraft caused their relegation to low down in the German organisational structure. It was planned that for the event of a war, every High Command and every active Army Corps would have an aircraft *Abteilung* with six machines each. After mobilization was ordered on 1 August 1914, within five days the five aviation batallions had 34 field- and seven fortress- aircraft *Abteilungen* for a total of 232 aircraft, plus eight rearward aircraft parks and five aircraft reserve *Abteilungen*.

Despite all its shortcomings, the new Arm had good prospects of serving the military leadership as its "flying eye" in the short-lived war of mobility (which everybody expected) since the battlefield could no longer be surveyed by virtue of its extent. Many obstacles had to be overcome, however, partly because the higher Staffs held a false impression of the possibilities of aircraft-supported battlefield observation. Furthermore the lack of training and exercises for aerial observers led to false reports being made, some with serious consequences. Additionally, by when war broke out French troops had been trained to camouflage themselves against aerial spotting while on the march and in rest areas. All the same, German spotter aircraft, favoured by the long period of fine weather in August 1914, were able to submit useful reconnaissance results. At the beginning of September, air reconnaissance was flown towards Paris, and the Supreme High Command received knowledge of the developing French counter-measures.

Air reconnaissance had gaps and with the transition to trench warfare in the West it lost significance. In it place came a geographically limited tactical purpose providing the military leadership with a means of examining the expediency of their own dispositions. Thus air reconnaissance became a part of the search for the means to penetrate the enemy defences

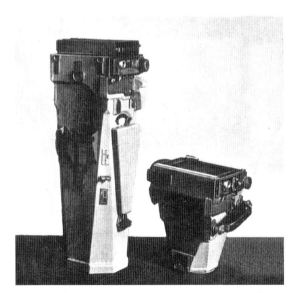

Cameras for aerial photography with 50- and 25-cm focal length.

(bottom right) German aerial photograph taken in May 1916 at 3,200 metres altitude. It documetns the setting up of a heavy British naval gun along the stretch of railway line north-east of Poperinghe in Flanders.

and reinstate the war of mobility. Accordingly the extent and diversity of the task assigned to German aerial forces increased. Now the spectrum no longer embraced merely surveying enemy defensive positions and assembly areas, locating enemy artillery and pinpointing his reserves, but also complementing or replacing the tethered balloons used hitherto for directing German artillery fire.

This new branch of the German armed forces was not prepared for the task. The still inexperienced corps of aviators had problems of a peculiar type to resolve initially. The Flying Corps Inspectorate at Berlin-Schöneberg was far from the Front and therefore hardly in a position to lead the 41 aviation *Abteilungen* in the field. Many technical difficulties remained to be resolved, primarily repairs to and reconditioning of aircraft and the personnel reserve. The aircraft industry was still in its early stages and less prepared for the challenge of wartime requirements than the automobile industry had been. Supplies were only to be had by those who came looking for them. Therefore aviators of the flying corps drove motor cars the length and breadth of Germany looking for spare parts.

Complete aircraft were manufactured and delivered in batches of between six and twelve machines so that especially at the end of 1914 high losses were not being made good. In Germany there was a lack of materials and specialist workers, who had been called up for military service. Only gradually, and by linking the centres of the aircraft industry with the Royal Prussian War Ministry, did it become possible to make progress in this direction, and now orders were submitted for aircraft in series of one hundred and more.

Also in 1915 there were improvements in quality following the development in series of more efficient engines. Aircraft were now arriving to the field-aviation *Abteilungen* which – though still being conceived as a uniform design and supplied by various manufacturers – were powered by 160- to 220-hp engines enabling them to reach altitudes of between 3000 and 5000 metres. They could also carry aerial survey cameras, the radio transmitters available from December 1914, on-board

weapons and bombs. The observer now had a seat behind the pilot and air survey cameras were built into the fuselage.

From Reconnaissance Aircraft to Bomber

Directing artillery fire from observer aircraft was based initially on a primitive and not even uniform manual observe-and-report procedure with coloured ammunition fired from flare pistols. Only with the introduction of aircraft radios and the setting up of special artillery-aircraft units was the work of artillery direction in trench warfare made easier, and created the outline for an increasing division of labour between air and ground. All the belligerents followed the same path. The operations in the air over the sectors of front were limited by time and geography, increasing the probability of meetings with enemy aircraft. Aerial dogfights became common. German aviators were armed with pistols, carbines and aerial self-loading guns, good for threatening gestures but ineffective in aerial battles. It was the French, followed by the British, who took the first steps. In October 1914 they armed their propellor aircraft with a pivoting machine-gun able to fire forward and so inflicted heavy losses on the Germans. For the first time in the history of warfare one side had superiority in the air.

The tension did not ease on the German side until defensive successes followed the introduction of the single-engine double-seater "C-Type" with the observer behind the

Stylized representation of an aerial battle. It shows three C-aircraft of Staffel 28/KG V over the Somme at the beginning of November 1916.

French bomber aircraft Voisin 5 from the year 1915. 350 of these machines were built. They could carry a bombload of 60 kgs and were armed with one machine-gun or a 37-mm cannon. No.5 here was forced to land by German fliers.

pilot manning a machine-gun which could fire astern and to either side. The German *Kampfflugzeuge* ("battle aircraft"), known more correctly as *Jagdflugzeuge* ("fighter aircraft") and identified by the capital letter "D" appeared on the scene with a fixed machine-gun firing forwards and synchronized with the propellor. Hitherto this had not proved satisfactory: the new mechanism was invented by Gerhard Fokker, born in the Dutch East Indies and active as an aircraft manufacturer in Germany.[1] This development and the removal of the second crew member gave the new single-decker Fokker E.III superior speed,

Fokker D.I of Lt.Gontermann. The triplane arrived at the Front in August 1917 and impressed with its manoeuvrability. Take-off weight was 585 kgs, it was fitted with a 110-hp engine and had a speed of 165 kms/hr at 4,000 metres altitude. Armament was two synchronized 7.92-mm machine-guns. Gontermann claimed 39 air victories (21 aircraft and 18 tethered balloons). He died while testing the Fokker triplane Dr.I No.115/117.

manoevrability and rate of climb. This machine changed aerial warfare and for several months in the second half of the war provided Germany with absolute supremacy in the air. This was the era of Oswald Boelcke and Max Immelmann.

The so-called "plague of Fokkers" came to its end when the French and British introduced their own fighters armed with synchronized machine-guns. The Germans responded with E-aircraft armed with one, two or occasionally three machine-guns. C-aircraft received in addition to an observer's traversable machine-gun on a circular mounting a second fixed forward-firing gun. Work was also proceeding on the basis of a patent by Reinhold Becker of Krefeld, ready by the end of the war.

The creation of another group of battle aircraft was in the wind at this time – the bomber. Dropping bombs was not new. The Army used rigid Zeppelin airships and had run trials with them long before the outbreak of war. In action, however, it was soon obvious how difficult and dangerous were bombing raids using Zeppelins. At the beginning of 1917 the raids were restricted, and finally halted in the summer of that year. An alternative long-range weapon had already shown itself in November 1914. That month Supreme Army Command ordered the setting up of a special squadron with 36 aircraft (authorized strength) on the Belgian coast at Ostend. The German literature recognises this unit as the first bomber squadron. It was given the cover name "Pigeon Post Section Ostend". Created to bomb targets in England taking off from the Belgian coast, it did not represent a real threat. In the first place no aircraft existed which were capable of carrying a worthwhile bombload to attack the British Isles, and secondly the bombs developed by the Artillery Testing Commission in peacetime were totally inadequate. Their accuracy and effect left much to be desired, sights and bomb release mechanisms did not yet exist. Assistance was sought from the three scientific sections created from the German Experimental Institute for Aviation (DVL)[2] in 1915 and designated "Prüfanstalt und Werft" (P.u.W: testing institute and repairs hangar). The results of this research appeared at the Front in the spring of 1917 as "P.u.W bombs".

All these activities had commenced as a response to the commencement by the French and British of bombing raids in the late autumn of 1914 against inland targets such as Freiburg im Breisgau, Friedrichshafen and Mannheim.

The making of more efficient large aircraft (*Grossflugzeuge*) and suitable bombs was a further step in the direction of bomber warfare. The military battle on the ground had frozen into indecisive trench warfare with high losses. In order to keep this going, huge quantities of ammunition, food, building materials, weapons and equipment were needed which – as with the transport required to bring it all forward – were frequently warehoused beyond the range of heavy artillery flat trajectory fire. Bomber aircraft were suitable for attacking these targets, functioning as an extension of the arm of the artillery. Supreme Army Command also demanded the destruction of the enemy's industrial installations in his inland regions. That in turn had led to the concept of the G-aircraft with great range and increasingly heavier bombloads. Bomb weights inceased to 50, 100 and more kilograms.

Contemporary representation of a Zeppelin over London. 17 airships were lost in attacks against England: five were shot down over London and crashed in flames. Other targets of Zeppelin attacks in the West were Paris and Liège, in the East Mlava, in the South-east Bucharest. During the war a total of 26 Army and 53 Navy airships became total losses. German industry built 88 airships during the war.

Above the battlefield, fighter-bombers grew in significance with machine-gun fire and dropping hand- or mortar-bombs – increasingly replaced by small-calibre splinter bombs. The Allies used them at the Somme in 1916, aiming directly at infantry and artillery positions. Besides the material damage caused this had a depressive effect on morale.

The most commonly employed type by the Germans was the C-aircraft, in contrast to the fighters and bombers considered a "maid of all work". Despite the increasing number of tethered balloons for artillery spotting in the summer of 1915, the double-seater was indispensable as before for reconnaissance and fire direction. Its effectiveness depended on good training and the cooperation of all involved. Days with heavy artillery fire from both sides within a restricted area presented even the most experienced crews with major problems because it would then be almost impossible to determine which battery was shooting and the effect its fire was having. The airmen then went over to low-level reconnaissance by eye. The development of better protected infantry machines – J-aircraft – was a response to the fighting on the Somme in the summer of 1916 and the enemy fighter-bombers which appeared there. The task of the J-aircraft was to maintain contact with the forward infantry lines as the "monitoring aircraft of the battlefield". Experiences gained were collected and found expression in the 1 January 1917 edition of *Sammelheft der Vorschriften des Stellungskrieges für alle Waffen, Teil 6: Verbindung der Infanterie mit Fliegern und Fesselballonnen*.[3] This stipulated: "It is of great importance during the course of battle for commanders and artillery to be constantly informed of the infantry fighting, the position of the forward infantry lines and to some extent of recognized enemy measures."

Infantry aviators were identified by black-white-red pennants at the extremities of the lower wings. They communicated by means of signal flares, radio, dropped smoke bombs or fired their machine-guns. The infantry for its part responded using morse code by signalling lamps, fired tracer, laid out sheets or used radio. These complicated procedures frequently failed

to work because the infantry in the heat of battle ran the danger of confusing their own aircraft with those of the enemy and so either did not signal or even opened fire.

In preparation for the attack on Verdun early in 1916, Supreme High Command concentrated heavy aerial forces in the region of the Meuse river. Their purpose was comprehensive aerial photography of the French positions without any gaps and the concealing of their own intentions to attack. For this purpose "interception flying" was introduced which simply meant the equivalent of trench warfare in the air. Thus fettered, this offensive weapon was assigned purely defensive tasks and its value fizzled out. Despite the high cost in materials and personnel, Supreme High Command stuck doggedly to the principle and only abandoned it under the impression of Allied air supremacy and the heavy German setbacks in the aerial war.

In the summer of 1916 the German aerial forces reached a low point similar to the situation at the end of 1914. Changes did not become apparent until 29 August 1916 when Hindenburg and Ludendorff took over the Supreme High Command. Their armaments programme was of decisive significance for the reorganisation and reinforcement of the aerial forces. The expression of their personal recognition of the aerial forces as an independent branch of the armed forces was the creation of the office of a Commanding General of the Aerial Forces on 8 October 1916. In this respect the Kaiser's Cabinet Order stated: "(…) corresponding to the growing importance of the air war, all aerial fighting- and anti-aircraft weaponry of the Army, in the field and at home, are to be combined into one service post." Cavalry-General Ernst von Hoeppner was made chargé d'affaires.

Single-seater Fighters Were to Be Decisive

At first all forces attached to the new service office were directed at removing the deficiencies which had come to light on the Somme. The grouping of the available D- and E-single seaters into fighter wings was begun single-mindedly in August 1916: in the

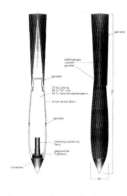

Because the explosive content of the 50 kg-P.u.W. bomb was 50% of its total weight, a pronounced mortar-effect was aimed for. 167,225 of these bombs were used in the war years 1917/1918.

foreground was an increase in numbers, there were to be 36 fighter wings by the spring of 1917. The training of pilots was improved. They received basic training in the general single-seater schools at Grossenhain and Paderborn, then special training in the fighter school at Valenciennes which was not concluded until after the trainee was seconded to the Front. In the battle for supremacy of the air, fighter pilots were to be of decisive significance. After the Fokker monoplane was only able to hold its own to a limited extent against the new designs on the Allied side from the spring of 1916, the aspiring German aircraft industry supplied new fighters, amongst them the Albatros D.II and D.III. With their help the Germans regained air superiority. It lasted almost twelve months until all 37 fighter wings were operating the new aircraft. The Allied answer was not long in coming; improved single-seat fighters like the Spad S.VII and S.XIII, the Sopwith triplane and Sopwith Camel dominated the air above the Front. The struggle for tactical and technological superiority continued: the German fighter wings received machines of the Albatros V and Vs types,

the Siemens-Schuckert D.III and the Fokker D.VIII. It remained their purpose to fight for air superiority and consolidate it. Not until then would German air reconnaissance be effective and enemy reconnaissance impaired. Towards that end the fighting in the air and on the ground had to be better coordinated, an essential component of the new operational concept being a concentration of men and means. At the beginning of July 1917 the fighter *Staffeln* 4, 6, 10 and 11 were combined into Fighter Squadron JG1[4] under Cavalry Captain Manfred von Richthofen, and the concentrated commitment of all available machines above decisive sectors of the Front succeeded in wresting air superiority. Von Hoeppner described it in his memoirs *Deutschlands Krieg in der Luft* (Berlin 1921): "By early assembly of the fighter *Staffeln* and their involvement *en masse* as soon as the enemy attack was recognized, we always succeeded in forcing the enemy back. The fighter force was directed to the focal points of the ground fighting by concise orders(…). " The British and French did not lack for an answer and took the next step towards centralisation by forming aircraft

After the successes of the German fighter pilots with the Albatros D.III in the first half of 1917, in the summer of that year the Albatros aircraft works brought out the Albatros D.V and the Albatros D.Va in November. Take-off weight was 935 kgs: top speed at 1000 metres was 187 kms/hr with the 180-hp engine. Armament was two synchronized machine-guns.

German Aircraft Types

B-Type:	unarmed dual-seater, reconnaissance and trainer.
C-Type:	armed dual-seater, reconnaissance and artillery spotter
CL-Type:	armed dual-seater, infantry and fighter-bomber resp.
D-Type:	single-seat fighter biplane
Dr-Type:	single-seat fighter triplane
E-Type:	single-seat fighter monoplane
G-Type:	armed multi-seat bomber
J-Type:	armed dual-seater, fighter-bomber and liaison
R-Type:	armed multi-seat bomber, giant aircraft

divisions. A long-range air war was planned against Germany for 1919 in which large formations of night bombers were to have been involved.

Undoubtedly the year 1918 represented the highpoint in the development of the air war. The increasing specialization required the design of differing aircraft types, the Germans employed primarily work aircraft (C- and CL types) in which the dividing line between the two types was fluid. The Rumpler C.VII for instance which appeared in the last year of the war was a long-range, high altitude reconnaissance aircraft which defied the narrow type-corset. It was more simple to fit the tactical fighter-bomber (D-aircraft) into a category: these single-seaters were meant for the purpose of achieving air superiority. For the bomber war by day and night the G- and R-aircraft were envisaged.

The Bombing War

The plans conceived by Supreme Army Command to have large bomber aircraft and Zeppelin dirigibles available for a two-pronged bombing war against the Allied hinterland failed initially for the lack of efficient means. The Zeppelin as a long-range bomber proved a washout but accelerated the development of aircraft to replace it. Between 1915 and 1918 the electrical giant AEG delivered the medium-heavy bombers G.I to V which could carry three machine-guns and a 360 kg bombload. Another supplier of G-aircraft was the Gothaer Waggonfabrik whose G.V had a 24-metre wingspan. The larger R-aircraft came from the Zeppelin Works at Staaken. The first prototype of this strategic bomber "VGO I" took off for its maiden flight on 15 April 1915. VGO I with its sisters VGO II and III were attached to the

British aircraft with pilot shot down in an aerial fight over Soissons.

giant-aircraft sub-divisions (RFA) 500 and 501 and taken to quiet sectors of the Eastern Front for trials. On account of setbacks further development was not proceeded with and next came the Zeppelin Staaken R.VI., a true giant with a wingspan of 42 metres, a 2-tonne bombload, four to seven machine-guns and a range of 1000 kilometres.

Parallel to the technical development the structuring and organisation of the bomber formations proceeded, including undoubtedly the Pigeon Post Sections of Ostend and Metz. Supreme Army Command had five bomber squadrons set up, but frequently it was the Army High Commands who decided on their usage. For the long-range air war against England, Supreme Army Command retained only KG 3(Kagohl 3),[5] supported from September 1917 by RFA 501 equipped with the six-engined Zeppelin-Staaken R.VI. KG 3 with 25 Gotha G.IV was concentrated at the end of 1916 on the Flanders Channel coast. It began flights against England in May 1917. After the war, one of the pilots – still with an Albatros – reported on one of the first raids:

The commander of 1.*Staffel*/Bogohl 1, Marshall von Bieberstein (right side) with the complete assortment of P.u.W. bombs: 50 kg, 100 kg, 300 kg, 12.5 kg and 1000 kg. The latter bomb contained 680 kgs explosive and had two anti-spin impact detonators.

The Gothaer Waggonfabrik AG delivered the first bomber aircraft in January 1915 (G.I-IV). In 1917 the Gotha G.V. was ready with better flight characteristics thanks to its two 260-hp Mercedes engines. It had a speed of 140 kms/hr, a range of 840 kms and a bomb payload of 600 kgs. Three to four machine-guns provided it with a strong defence.

This bomber has a payload of 16 P.u.W. bombs: seven 10 kg, four 50 kg, four 100 kg, and one 300 kg; altogether 970 kg of explosive in horizontal racks.

The firm Flugzeugbau Friedrichshafen AG worked from the autumn of 1914 on the development of bomber aircraft. The first powerful bomber was not ready until February 1917 however. It had a bomb payload of one tonne, had an armament of two to four machine-guns and could make 141 kms/hr. In the summer of 1917 the Kagohl 1 made a series of attacks on Dunkirk, and later on Paris. The pictured aircraft came to grief on one of these sorties.

"The aircraft available to us at that time(…) had no great range. Accordingly, for our flight from our airfield at Handzaeme (Flanders) to London we had to await favourable weather.(…)wind from the north-east up to 2000 metres, and above it north-westerly winds. As we had scheduled the flight for that night and there was a full moon we decided to go ahead with it. We reported this to our Abteilung leader who sought approval from the Army Commander of Aviation. Approval was granted but we had to content ourselves with very unsatisfactory maps. Now we made the flight preparations with our Albatros. All equipment not absolutely essential was unshipped, even the machine-gun. Bombs were loaded and the tanks filled with fuel. At midnight we took off in the presence of all comrades of Abteilung 19 at Hanszaeme. In order to use the minimum possible fuel we did not circle but headed straight for Dunkirk. In order to avoid having a rupture of the fuel tank I had the petrol pump disconnected for a while after taking off because it pumped with too much pressure when the tank was full. After leaving the coast at Dunkirk we were at 2000 metres halfway across the English Channel when the engine stopped suddenly. In order to establish the cause I had to look at the instruments. The instruments were unlit. With the aid of a pocket torch I discovered that the pressure had fallen. I shouted to Franz, "Pump!" After a few strokes of the hand-pressure pump supplied for the purpose the engine restarted and ran regularly.

So as not to have to land on enemy territory for lack of fuel, we had decided to use only half the fuel in the main tank for the flight there, and the other half plus the reserve tank for the return flight. Because of the poor maps our direction finding was not very good despite the full moon. Several times we thought about turning back because we could not find London. Finally it lay below us. The north-western part of the city was clouded over but the south-eastern part very clear. We made a sinuous, broad descent to drop our bombs. We had no bomb release apparatus aboard, the bombs were carried below the observer's seat. My observer threw these overboard individually. His movements as he did this felt very heavy. We observed the bombs explode.

Until we dropped the first bomb we had seen no flak or searchlights. Now the flak began to fire from the outskirts and the city centre and at the same time searchlights came on everywhere. The flak shooting was very poor, and neither did the searchlights find us. We got free of the anti-aircraft defences unseen and headed for home.

We were about 50 kilometres from London and at 3500 metres altitude over the south-east coast of England. It was very squally. Suddenly we saw a light at about the same height, but we could not

make out where it was coming from. When we were about to investigate, the light disappeared to the right and now in the moonlight we saw the outline of a British aircraft which must have set off after us in pursuit but had not been able to find us. Since we had no machine-gun there was nothing we could do. The unusually squally weather was therefore responsible for having got us into the propellor wind of the British aeroplane.

Over the Channel we could already see the "fireworks" at the Front and now began a long glide down towards Handzaeme. The relatively short flying time had been achieved by using the favourable wind. On the airfield our ground staff received us and congratulated us on our successful flight. As they established, what remained of the fuel would have been enough for another ten minutes in the air. The first flight by a German aircraft to London was a success."

The main blow was struck against London on 13 June 1917: 22 aircraft took part, 594 persons on the ground were injured of whom 162 died. The attacks lasted several hours and affected the nerves of the Londoners. In order to strengthen the anti-aircraft defences, the military commanders were obliged to withdraw men from the Front, but their increasing successes forced the Germans to abandon daylight raids. The transition to night raids, in which giant aircraft took part from September, caused the Germans some problems, amongst them a lack of night aiming devices, the hurried re-training of crews for night flying and the lighting up of the home airfields for the return. Additionally the payloads were greater, the 1000 kg P.u.W. bomb at the beginning of 1918 being the culmination. Captain Arthur Schoeller, commander of R 27 in RFA 501 reported on one night raid on London in which he participated:

"On 27 March 1918 feverish activity reigned in the newly established aerodrome of the Giant Aircraft Abteilung RFA 501.(…) The Abteilung commander, Captain von Bentivegni, ordered all R-aircraft to take off at 2200 hrs for a bombing raid against England with London as the target.

The six great biplanes rolled out to the T-shaped concrete airstrip and assembled on the cross-stripe. Amongst them was R 27 which had been entrusted to my command. The machines now had to be readied for the night attack. For this purpose every R-aircraft had forty ground crew available. The flight crew consisted of two pilots, one observer officer, two mechanics, one fuel mechanic, one radio operator and one machine-gunner. The R-commander was the highest ranking man aboard, generally the No.1 pilot or observer. Monitored by the commander each crew member now made his preparations for the night attack. The radio operator checked his radio-telegraphy unit for reception and transmitting, the mechanics the two 260-hp engines in two gondolas between the top and bottom wings, the fuel engineer topped up the ten benzine tanks each of 245 litres capacity as required and the gunner readied his four machine guns. Thus it took plenty of time before the giant aircraft, whose 44 metres wingspan, 28 metres length and 6 metres height and extended window-clad nose made such an imposing impression, was ready to bomb-up. The weight empty was about 8200 kgs: 4,500 kgs more of useful weight could be loaded including crew, fuel and the bombload. The bombs weighing individually from 50 kgs to 1000 kgs were hung in the fuselage between the wings in long cases in retaining supports, concealed above the trapdoors and released electrically.

The aircraft lifted off from the ground heavily under its enormous weight, finally it was comfortable in mid air, made a wide partial circuit around the aerodrome and then headed along the course to the North Sea coast laid on the chart. Inside the fuselage was subdued lighting at the map stand, in the radio booth and the instrument panel where the compass and the other indispensable navigational instruments showed us the way.

We were now over England, but where? There was a total blackout in force, it seemed as though we were flying over dead country. We knew from the searchlights that the enemy had heard us, therefore we could ask for a radio fix. The radio operator sent the agreed signal which was picked up by two of our coastal stations in Belgium in service for our night flight. Within a few minutes we were given our position as at the moment our signal was sent. We were south-east of London our target, accompanied by far-reaching searchlights, and now turned for the Thames to bomb the port installations there. Would we recognize them in the limited visibility which the low cloud cover allowed and in the almost complete blackout in which the land below us lay? Ahead of us the English aerodromes were coming alive, their runway lights flaming up. The enemy anti-aircraft fired, our machine-gun replied, even firing on the searchlights. We steered for a particularly well lit aerodrome, and Lt Kamps dropped four bombs, the impact of the explosions could be seen distinctly(...)

Now through a break in the cloud cover we recognized the grey ribbon of the Thames. It disappeared again quickly. We followed along it and at the next glimpse Lt Kamps in the nose of the machine standing at the bomb-release gear pressed the keys one after another which allowed the bombs free fall to the ground. Not far from us we saw a part of the balloon barrage surrounding the periphery of London in the east and south.

We turned away, homewards, following the course of the Thames with its anti-aircraft batteries, which soon had us in their sights. The cloud cover became thinner the closer we came to the coast. As a result the searchlights soon caught us, and the explosive puffs of the anti-aircraft shells came very close. A shell splinter penetrated an upper wing outer cover without causing other damage. The flaming brass projectiles passed so near at hand it seemed we could touch them. Below us we saw the exhaust flame of a pursuing machine, but this would not be a danger to us. Thus we reached the open sea at Margate and headed for Ostend, whose known signals would lead us homewards."

On the flight back R 27 was forced to make an emergency landing behind the Flanders coast. A few days later the crew took over giant aircraft R 28 from the aircraft hangar of the Schütte-Lanz Works near Berlin.

The increase in night bombing raids raised the number of aerial battles. It was especially dangerous if enemy fighters lurked above the lit-up aerodromes for returning bombers. Night bombers, contrary to their real purpose, had to support the ground troops. This happened for example during the fighting in Flanders. On these operations the bombers were accompanied by fighters.

The involvement of the bomber squadrons in the fighting in Flanders showed that the six *Staffeln* and the comprehensive ground organisation were too unwieldy. With the exception of bomber squadron KG 3, in March 1918 they were reorganised into Bomb Squadrons[6] (Bogohl) each with three *Staffeln*, their total raised to eight.

The aerial forces played a substantial part in the preparation for the German spring offensive of 1918. Part of this work was aerial photography of all enemy positions. By the gradual involvement of the mass of German aircraft over the attack sectors their absence would be noticed elsewhere and it became the task of the remaining aircraft to simulate normality while the presence of over 100 aerial groups over the attack sectors required careful disguise. The German fliers won total superiority in the air during the opening days of the Michael Offensive: to maintain it in heavy aerial fighting over the long term was not possible. The bombers succeeded in destroying many railway lines and depots but could not interrupt the deliveries of supplies made by many lorry columns. German fighter *Staffeln*, already equipped with the superior Fokker D.VII, excelled in the defence against enemy bombers, but in the summer of 1918 the mass of the German Army was forced on the defensive together with its aerial force.

By the war's end German bomber aircraft had dropped over one million bombs of a total weight of 27,400 tonnes (including 710 bombs of 1000 kgs). Besides London, targets were also Paris, Dunkirk and the manufacturing industry in the Nancy basin.

The following statistics help to highlight the rise of the German Army aviators during the First World War: In August 1914 Germany had 232 aircraft in the field. By the end of the war in late autumn 1918 there were over 5,000 aircraft at the Front which required 7,000 tonnes of benzine monthly. 3,207 pilots and observers were killed, 4,296 wounded. The Commanding-General of the Aerial Forces reported 7,425 successful aerial battles. In order to meet the spare parts requirement for a small elite, approximately 80,000 men were employed in Germany. At the end, 125,000 male and female workers were employed in 72 aircraft and 45 aircraft engine factories. The constant to and fro in the struggle for air supremacy therefore depended on many people and factors, but primarily it was the technological progress in aircraft design which provided the respective opponents with aircraft having superior flight qualities and weapons which made decisive differences. It was a competition – there were victors only for a few weeks, at best for several months.

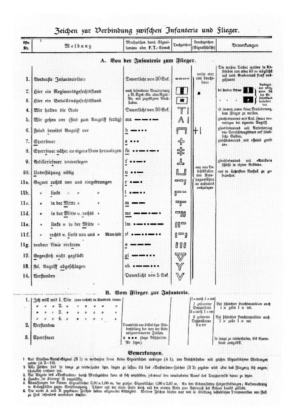

Signals for Liaison between Infantry and Aircraft

Notes

1. The mechanism allowed the machine-gun to fire through the circling aircraft propellor without hitting the propellor blades.
2. DVL = Deutsche Versuchsanstalt für Luftfahrt.
3. English equivalent = "Collected Issue of the Trench Warfare Regulations for All Branches of Service, Part 6: Cooperation of the Infantry with Aircraft and Tethered Balloons".
4. The word *Staffel (*plural *Staffeln)* in German military aviation is a term of convenience to describe a group of aircraft. In this particular case four *Staffeln* went to make a *Geschwader,* "squadron" but there was no hard and fast rule as to the size of either.
5. KG = Kampfgeschwader, bomber squadron.
6. Bombengeschwader.

On 17 September 1917 RFA (= Riesenflugzeug *Abteilung*) 501 flew the first 52 air raids on London. Zeppelin Staaken R VI had a speed of 135 kms/hr, a service ceiling of 4320 metres and could remain in the air for seven hours. Take off weight was 11.824 tonnes.

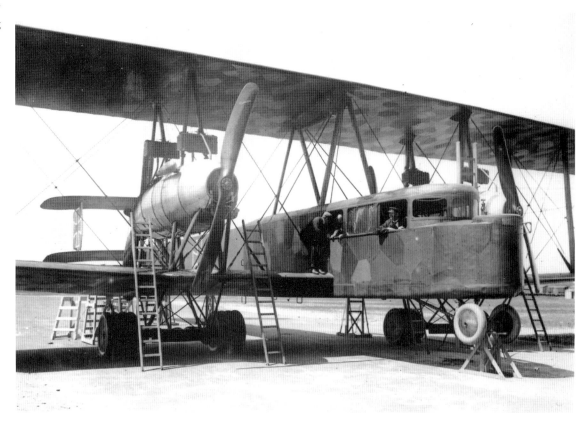

The giant aircraft R VI could carry a bombload of 2 tonnes and had four to seven MGs for defence. It was one of the biggest and most dangerous bombers of the First World War. They dropped 2,772 bombs totalling 196 tonnes on London.

The best known British bomber of the First World War was the Handley-Page 0/100, followed by the 0/400. Both could carry a bomb payload of 700 kgs and had a speed of 157 kms/hr. This photograph was taken on 4 April 1918 and shows the bombing-up with eleven 50 kg explosive bombs.

The single-seater Fokker D.VII fighter arrived at the Front from April 1918 and was attached to fighter squadron JG 1 under Baron Manfred von Richthofen. The aircraft was robust, fast and reasonably manoeuvrable. It weighed 877 kgs, had a speed of 189 kms/hr and a service ceiling of 6,000 metres. From the technical point of view it was the last attempt by the Germans to retain air superiority. Belgium and the Netherlands used the machine often after the First World War.

BIBLIOGRAPHY

Official sources

Anleitung für den Bau minierter Unterstände (Stollen) mit Schurzholz und Wellblechrahmen. o.O. o.J.

Der schwere Minenwerfer alter Art (s.M.W.a.A.). Anhang zum Vorentwurf. Neudruck Mai 1917

Bedienungs-Anleitung für den gl. l. M.W. H.L. o.O. o.J.

Bedienungsanleitung für den leichten Minenwerfer. Rheinische Metallwaren und Maschinenfabrik Düsseldorf o.J.

Bedienungsanleitung für den leichten Minenwerfer n.A. im Flachbahnschuss vom 15. Januar 1918

Betonierungs-Anleitung für das Feld (B.ANl.f.F.) vom 21. Juli 1917, Berlin 1917

Der leichte Minenwerfer (l.M.W.). Vorentwurf, Berlin 1918

Dienstunterricht des deutschen Pioniers, Berlin 1915.

D.V. Nr. 1019 Wirkung der Fußartilleriegeschosse vom 9. August 1914, Berlin 1914.

Exerzier-Reglement für die Infanterie (Ex.R.f.d.I.) vom 29. Mai 1906, Berlin 1906.

Exerzier-Reglement für die Infanterie (Ex.R.f.d.I.) vom 29. Mai 1906.

Neuabdruck mit Einfügung der bis August 1909 ergangenen Änderungen, Berlin 1909.

Exerzier-Reglement für die Infanterie. IV. Teil: Zusatzbestimmungen für die Ausbildung der Maschinengewehr-Kompagnien und Festungs-Maschinengewehr-Formationen vom 26. Oktober 1911, Berlin 1911.

Exerzier-Reglement für die Verkehrstruppen (Ex.R.f.d.V.T.) vom 16. März 1912, Berlin 1912.

Feldbefestigungs-Vorschrift (F.V.), Berlin1893.

Feld-Pionierdienst aller Waffen. Entwurf vom 12. Dezember 1911, Berlin 1911.

Immanuel, Friedrich: Lehnerts Handbuch für den Truppenführer. Für Feldgebrauch, Felddienst, Herbstübungen, Übungsritte, Kriegsspiel, taktische Arbeiten, Unterricht, Vorbereitung zu Prüfungen, Berlin 1915.

Sammelheft der Vorschriften für den Stellungskrieg für alle Waffen, Berlin 1916/1917
– Teil 1a: Allgemeines über Stellungsbau vom 13. November 1916
– Teil 1b: Einzelheiten über Stellungsbau vom 15. Dezember 1916
– Teil 2: Minenkrieg vom 19. April 1916
– Teil 3: Nahkampfmittel vom 1. Januar 1917
– Teil 4: Leuchtmittel vom 31. Mai 1916
– Teil 6: Verbindung der Infanterie mit Fliegern und Fesselballonen vom 1. Januar 1917
– Teil 7: Die Minenwerfer vom 16. November 1916

Lehnert's Handbuch für den Truppenführer, Berlin 1908.

Lehnert's Handbuch für den Truppenführer, Berlin 1915.

Merkblatt für die Tankabwehr vom 7. September 1918.

Michahelles und Ganzer: Nahkampfaufgaben für Kompanien, Züge, Gruppen, Posten, Patrouillen und M.G., Berlin 1918.

Vorschrift für die Ausbildung der Infanterie am leichten Minenwerfer vom 18. November 1916.

Literature

Angelucci, Enzo / Matricardi, Pado: Flugzeuge. Von den Anfängen bis zum 1. Weltkrieg, Wiesbaden 1976.

Azzmi, Luca: Minenwerfen. Lanciamin austriaci da trincea della Grande Guerra. Chiari 2006.

Baur, H....: Deutsche Eisenbahnen im Weltkrieg 1914-1918, Stuttgart 1927.

Benary, Albert (Hrsg.): Das Ehrenbuch der Deutschen Feldartillerie, Berlin o.J.

Berkner, Kurt: Tanks im Angriff, Berlin, Leipzig, Wien o.J.

Borchert, M.: Der Kampf gegen Tanks. Dargestellt an den Ereignissen der Doppelschlacht bei Cambrai, Berlin 1931.

Clarke, Dale / Delf, Brian: British Artillery 1914-1918, Oxford 2005.

Dix, Arthur: Volkswirtschaftliche Kriegsvorsorge. In: Vierteljahreshefte für Truppenführung und Heereskunde, Drittes Heft 1913, Berlin 1913, S. 441-452.

Eisgruber, Hans: So schossen wir nach Paris, Berlin 1934.

Feeser, Friedrichfranz: Artillerie im Feldkriege, Berlin 1930.

Fletcher, David: Landships – British tanks in the First World War, London 1984.

Fletcher, David: War cars – British armoured cars in the First World War, London 1987.

Franke, Herrmann: Handbuch der neuzeitlichen Wehrwissenschaften, Dritter Band, 2. Die Luftwaffe, Berlin 1939.

Geschichte des Lehr-Infanterie-Regiments und seiner Stammformationen, Zeulenroda 1936.

Gey, Karl / Teichmann, H.: Einführung in die Lehre vom Schuss (Ballistik), Leipzig, Berlin 1934.

Grevelhörster, Ludger: Der Erste Weltkrieg und das Ende des Kaiserreiches, Münster 2004.

Griehl, Manfred: Deutsche Flugzeugbewaffnung bis 1945. Stuttgart 2008.

Groehler, Olaf: Geschichte des Luftkrieges, Berlin (Ost) 1981.

Guy, Francois: Les canons de la victoire 1914-1918, Teil 2: L'Artillerie lurde a Grands Puissance, Paris 2008.

Guy, Francois: Les canons de la victoire 1914-1918, Teil 3: L'Artillerie de tranchée, Paris 2010.

Hahn, Fritz: Die Waffen der Luftstreitkräfte, Berlin 1935.

Hamann, Brigitte: Der Erste Weltkrieg, Wahrheit und Lügen in Bildern und Texten, München 2009.

Hanslian, Rudolf: Der chemische Krieg. I. Militärischer Teil, Berlin 1937.

Hanslian, Rudolf / Bergendorff, Fr.: Der chemische Krieg. II. Teil, Gasangriff, Gasabwehr und Raucherzeugung, Berlin 1925.

Heigl, Fritz: Taschenbuch der Tanks, München 1926.

Heigl, Fritz: Taschenbuch der Tanks. Ergänzungsband, München 1927.

Heigl, Fritz: Taschenbuch der Tanks. Ausgabe 1930, München 1930.

Heigl's Taschenbuch der Tanks. Teil I: Wesen der Panzerkraftfahrzeuge, Panzererkennungsdienst A-F, München 1935.

Heigl's Taschenbuch der Tanks. Teil II: Panzererkennungsdienst G-Z. Panzerzüge und Panzerdraisinen, München 1935.

Heigl's Taschenbuch der Tanks. Teil III: Der Panzerkampf, München 1938.

Heinrici, Paul (Hrsg.): Das Ehrenbuch der Deutschen Pioniere, Berlin 1931.

Jost, Walter / Felger, Friedrich: Was wir vom Weltkrieg nicht wissen, Leipzig 1938.

Jünger, Ernst (Hrsg.) Luftfahrt ist not! Leipzig und Nürnberg o.J.

Kilian, Hans: Totentanz auf dem Hartmannsweiler Kopf 1914-1917, Neckargemünd 1971.

Kraschel, Günter / Stützer, Helmut: Die deutschen Militärflugzeuge 1910-1918, Augsburg 1994.

Kronprinz Rupprecht: Die Tankschlacht und die Angriffsschlacht bei Cambrai. A.O.K. 2, April 1918.

Leonhardt, Walter: Wehrchemie. II. Teil: Der chemische Krieg Luftschutz und Gasschutz, Frankfurt a.M. 1938.

Linnekohl, H.: Vom Einzelschuß zur Feuerwalze. Der Wettlauf zwischen Technik und Taktik im Ersten Weltkrieg. Bonn 1986.

Lezius, Martin: Ruhmeshalle unserer alten Armee Teil I und II, Fürstenwalde/Spree o.J.

Meyer, Julius: Der Gaskampf und die chemischen Kampfstoffe, Leipzig 1925.

Müller, Eduard: Der englische Panzerangriff bei Cambrai am 20.11.1917 und seine Lehren für die Gegenwart. In: Militärwissenschaftliche Rundschau Heft 3/1939, Berlin 1939, S. 389 ff.

Muther, Alfred: Das Gerät der leichten Artillerie. I. Teil: Feldgeschütze, Berlin 1925.

Muther, Alfred: Das Gerät der leichten Artillerie. II. Teil: Infanteriegeschütze, Tankabwehr und Tankbestückung, Berlin 1932.

Muther, Alfred: Das Gerät der leichten Artillerie. IV. Teil: Flugabwehrwaffen, Berlin 1929.

Neumann, Georg Paul: Die deutschen Luftstreitkräfte im Weltkriege, Berlin 1920.

Ortner, M. Christian: Die österreichisch-ungarische Artillerie von 1867 bis 1918, Wien 2007.

Otto, Helmut / Schmiedel, Karl: Der Erste Weltkrieg, Berlin (Ost) 1976.

Przemysław, Jaskółowski: Działa okopowe C. IK. Armii 1914-1918, Przemysl 2008.

Riebicke, Otto: Unsere Pioniere im Weltkriege, Berlin 1925.

Riebicke, Otto: Was brauchte der Weltkrieg? Tatsachen und Zahlen aus dem deutschen Ringen 1914/18, Berlin o.J.

Schirmer, Hermann: Das Gerät der schweren Artillerie, Berlin 1937.

Schliephake, Hanfried: Flugzeugbewaffnung. Stuttgart 1977.

Schmid, Bastian: Deutsche Naturwissenschaft, Technik und Erfindung im Weltkriege, München, Leipzig 1919.

Schuh, Horst: Peter Falkenstern und das BOGOHL 1. Teile 1 und 2. In: Luftwaffen-Revue Nr. 2 und 3/2008, Rothenburg o.d.T. 2008.

Schwab, Otto: Ingenieur und Soldat, Nidda o.J.

Schwarte, Max (Hrsg.): Der Weltkampf um Ehre und Recht, 1.-10. Teil, Leipzig 1927-1933.

Schwarte, Max: Die Technik im Weltkriege, Berlin 1920.

Sering, Max: Die deutsche Kriegswirtschaft im Bereich der Heeresverwaltung 1914-1918, Berlin und Leipzig 1922.

Stöhr, Ralf /Kießlich-Köcher, Harald: Chemie des Todes, Berlin (Ost) 1987.

Thiede, Günter: Die »reine« Wissenschaft und der Gaskrieg, 1914-1918. Dokumente zur Militärgeschichte, o.O. o.J.

Vanderveen, B. H.: The Observers Army vehicles Directory, London 1974.

Vauvillier, Francois: Les canons de la victoire 1914-1918, Teil 1: L'Artillerie de Champagne, Paris 2006.

Volkart, W...: Die Gasschlacht in Flandern im Herbst 1917. In: Wehrwissenschaftliche Rundschau, Beiheft 7, Berlin, Frankfurt a.M. 1957.

von Bülow, Kurd: Wehrgeologie, Leipzig 1938.

von Claer: Meine Tätigkeit als Chef des Ingenieur- und Pionierkorps und General-Inspekteur der Festungen sowie als General vom Ingenieur- und Pionierkorps im Großen Hauptquartier. In: Vierteljahreshefte für Pionier, Heft 4/1937, Berlin 1937, S. 198 ff.

von Eberhardt, Walter: Unsere Luftstreitkräfte 1914-18, Berlin 1930.

von Hoeppner, Ernst: Deutschlands Krieg in der Luft, Leipzig 1921 und 1936.

von Ludendorff, Erich: Meine Kriegerinnerungen 1914-1918, Berlin 1921.

von Leeb, ..: Die Abwehr. II. Teil: Die Abwehr im Weltkriege. In: Militärwissenschaftliche Rundschau Heft 2/1937, Berlin 1937, S. 154 ff.

von Schell, A....: Kampf gegen Panzerwagen, Oldenburg, Berlin o.J.

Weiß: Ueber moderne Schlachtbefestigung. Vortrag, gehalten in der Militärischen Gesellschaft zu Berlin am 8. März 1899, Berlin 1899.

Der Weltkrieg 1914 bis 1918, Bd. 1-12, Berlin 1925-1939.

Weyrauch, R.: Waffen- und Munitionswesen. Die deutsche Kriegswirtschaft im Bereich der Heeresverwaltung, Band III, Berlin und Leipzig 1922.

Zimmermann, P.: Technik für Rüstung und Krieg. In: Mitteilungen aus dem Institut für Mechanik. Nr. 1/88, Neubiberg 1988.